F A N T A S Y
O R I G A M I

Duy Nguyen

Sterling Publishing Co., Inc.
New York

Library of Congress Cataloging-in-Publication Data

Nguyen, Duy, 1960–
    Fantasy Origami / Duy Nguyen.
      p. cm.
    Includes index.
    ISBN 0-8069-8007-9
    1. Origami. I. Title.

    TT870 .N486 2001
    736.982—dc21

                       2001040081

10 9 8 7 6 5 4 3 2 1

First paperback edition published in 2002 by
Sterling Publishing Company, Inc.
387 Park Avenue South, New York, N.Y. 10016
© 2001 by Duy Nguyen
Distributed in Canada by Sterling Publishing
℅ Canadian Manda Group, One Atlantic Avenue, Suite 105
Toronto, Ontario, Canada M6K 3E7
Distributed in Great Britain and Europe by Chris Lloyd at Orca
Book Services, Stanley House, Fleets Lane, Poole BH15 3AJ, England
Distributed in Australia by Capricorn Link (Australia) Pty. Ltd.
P.O. Box 704, Windsor, NSW 2756 Australia

Sterling ISBN 0-8069-8007-9 Hardcover
         ISBN 1-4027-0117-9 Paperback

Contents

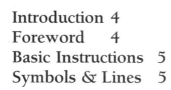

Introduction

"Origami," the simple art of paper folding, originated in Japan and was passed down by generations of Japanese who taught their children the basics, and the joy, of creating fantasy worlds from paper. With several or more folds, simple square pieces of paper become beautiful objects: animals, flowers, or even people.

Seeing these transformations, it is easy for new origami hobbyists to gain an enthusiasm that leads them to quickly improve their creative ability and artistic skills.

Selected for this book are a number of interesting figures created using these simple folding techniques. Each one includes step-by-step diagrams with short, clear directions that will make origami technique easy to understand and learn. I wish you hours, days, and years of paper-folding joy.

Foreword

Base folds are common starting points in creating origami. Since these basic forms are not very interesting to most readers, I have kept them to a minimum. This book contains only three simple base folds. Once they are learned, they become springboards to the creation of more complex, and fun-to-do, forms and figures.

The small size of the paper regularly used in origami can sometimes create a problem for beginners, due to the lack of folding skills. The origami projects here, however, are designed to be worked easily and quickly with regularly sized origami squares as well as to produce satisfyingly attractive and interesting origami creations.

Although not usual in classic origami, some of the figures here call for cutting the paper. I also recommend gluing multi-piece forms during assembly for added stability. In addition, I hope you will give some thought to the nature of each object being created. Origami of animals and people should have "movement" and be given natural finishing touches: painted detail work, posed, placed in a setting, etc. I call that "giving life" to my imitation of nature through the art of origami.

Basic Instructions

Paper: The best paper to use for origami will be very thin, keep a crease well, and fold flat. It can be plain white paper, solid-color paper, or wrapping paper with a design only on one side. Regular typing paper may be too heavy to allow the many tight folds needed for some figures. Be aware, too, that some kinds of paper may stretch slightly, either in length or in width, and this may cause a problem in paperfolding. Packets of paper especially for use in origami are available from craft and hobby shops.

Unless otherwise indicated, the usual paper used in creating these forms is square, 15 by 15 centimeters or approximately 6 by 6 inches. Some forms may call for half a square, i.e., 3 by 6 inches or, cut diagonally, a triangle. A few origami forms require a more rectangular (legal) size or a longer piece of paper. For those who are learning and have a problem getting their fingers to work tight folds, larger sizes of paper can be used. Actually, any size paper squares can be used—slightly larger figures are easier to make than overly small ones.

Glue: Use a good, easy-flowing but not loose paper glue, but use it sparingly. You don't want to soak the paper. A toothpick makes a good applicator. Allow the glued form time to dry. Avoid using stick glue, as the application pressure needed (especially if the stick has become dry) can damage your figure.

Technique: Fold with care. Position the paper, especially at corners, precisely and see that edges line up before creasing a fold. Once you are sure of the fold, use a fingernail to make a clean, flat crease. Don't get discouraged with your first efforts. In time, what your mind can create, your fingers can fashion.

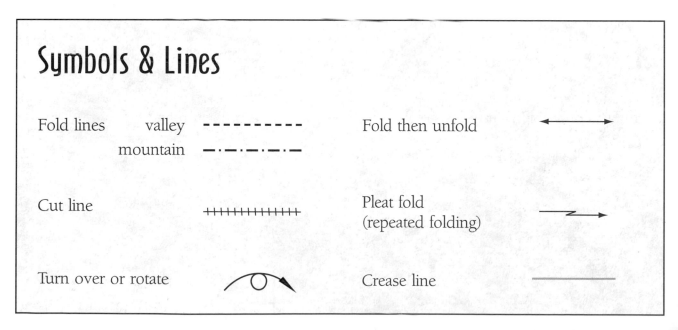

Symbols & Lines

Fold lines valley	Fold then unfold	
mountain		
Cut line	Pleat fold (repeated folding)	
Turn over or rotate	Crease line	

Basic Folds

Kite Fold

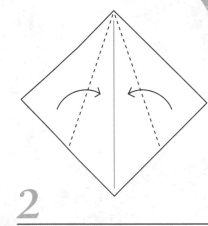

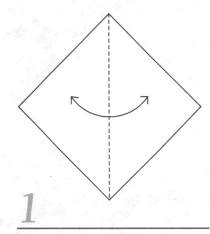

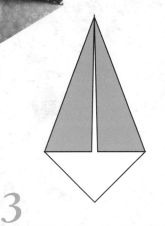

1
Fold and unfold a square diagonally, making a center crease.

2
Fold both sides in to the center crease.

3
This is a kite form.

Valley Fold - - - - - - - - - - - - - - - - -

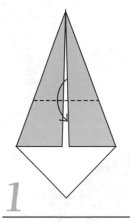

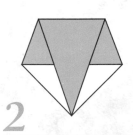

1
Here, using the kite, fold form toward you (forward), making a "valley."

2
This fold forward is a valley fold.

Mountain Fold - · - · - · - · - · - · -

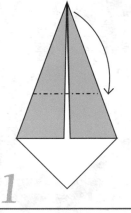

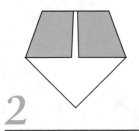

1
Here, using the kite, fold form away from you (backwards), making a "mountain."

2
This fold backwards is a mountain fold.

Inside Reverse Fold

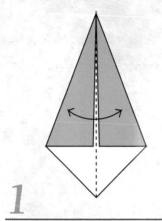

1

Starting here with a kite, valley fold kite closed.

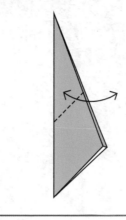

2

Valley fold as marked to crease, then unfold.

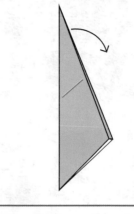

3

Pull tip in direction of arrow.

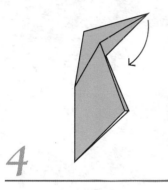

4

Appearance before completion.

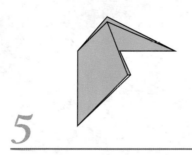

5

You've made an inside reverse fold.

Outside Reverse Fold

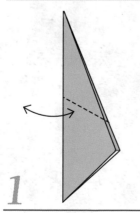

1

Using closed kite, valley fold, unfold.

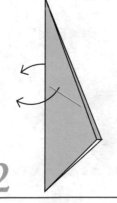

2

Fold inside out, as shown by arrows.

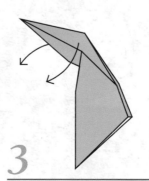

3

Appearance before completion.

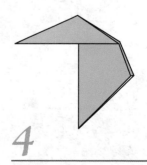

4

You've made an outside reverse fold.

Basic Folds

Pleat Fold

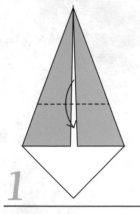

1

Here, using the kite, valley fold.

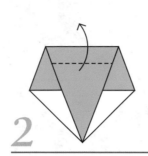

2

Valley fold back again.

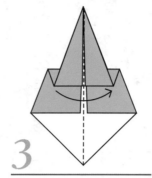

3

This is a pleat. Valley fold in half.

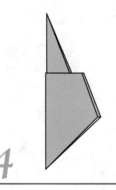

4

You've made a pleat fold.

Pleat Fold Reverse

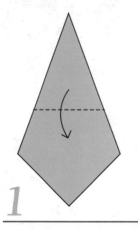

1

Here, using the kite form backwards, valley fold.

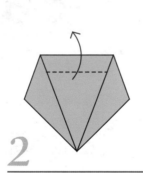

2

Valley fold back again for pleat.

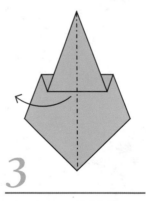

3

Mountain fold form in half.

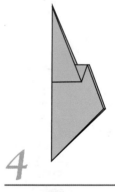

4

This is a pleat fold reverse.

Squash Fold I

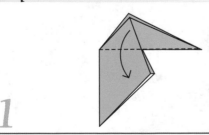

1

Using inside reverse, valley fold one side.

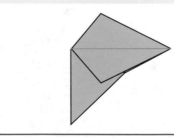

2

This is a squash fold I.

Squash Fold II

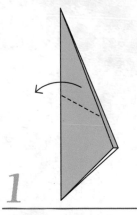

1

Using closed kite form, valley fold.

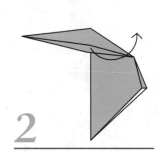

2

Open in direction of the arrow.

3

Appearance before completion.

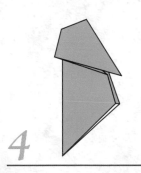

4

You've made a squash fold II.

Inside Crimp Fold

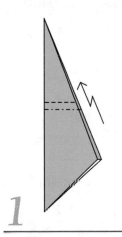

1

Here using closed kite form, pleat fold.

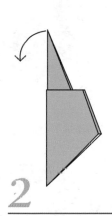

2

Pull tip in direction of the arrow.

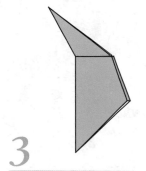

3

This is an inside crimp fold.

Outside Crimp Fold

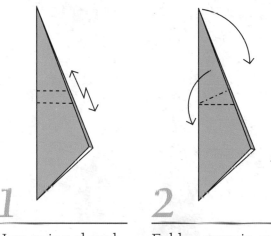

1

Here using closed kite form, pleat fold and unfold.

2

Fold mountain and valley as shown, both sides.

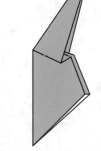

3

This is an outside crimp fold.

Base Folds

Base folds are basic forms that do not in themselves produce origami, but serve as a basis, or jumping-off point, for a number of creative origami figures, some quite complex. Like beginning other crafts, learning to fold these base folds is not the most exciting part of origami. They are, however, easy to do, and will help you with your technique. They also quickly become rote, so much so that you can do many using different-colored papers while you are watching television or your mind is elsewhere. With completed base folds handy, if you want to quickly work up a form or are suddenly inspired with an idea for an original, unique figure, you can select an appropriate base fold and swiftly bring a new creation to life.

Base Fold I

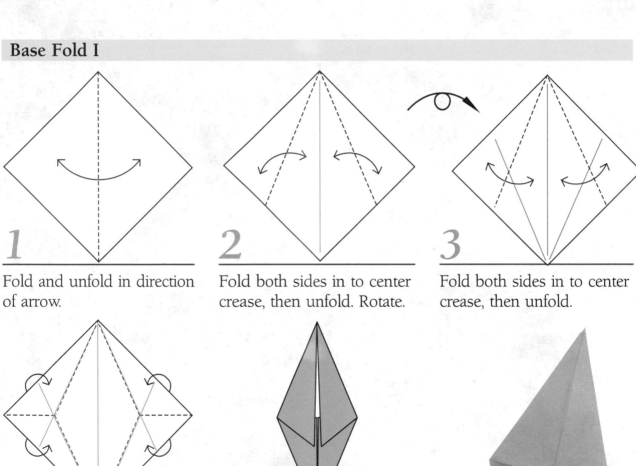

1 Fold and unfold in direction of arrow.

2 Fold both sides in to center crease, then unfold. Rotate.

3 Fold both sides in to center crease, then unfold.

4 Pinch corners of square together and fold inward.

5 Completed Base Fold I.

Base Fold II

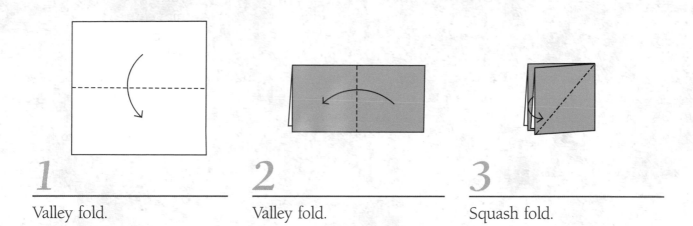

1
Valley fold.

2
Valley fold.

3
Squash fold.

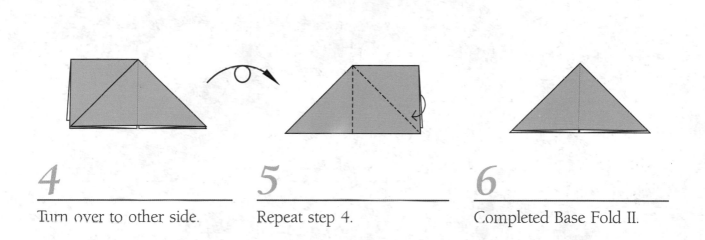

4
Turn over to other side.

5
Repeat step 4.

6
Completed Base Fold II.

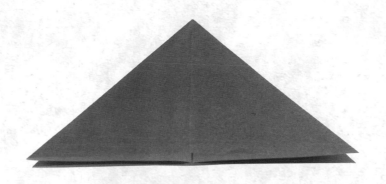

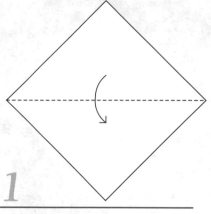

1
Valley fold.

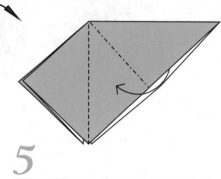

2
Valley fold.

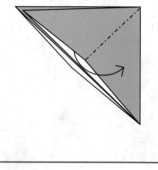

3
Squash fold.

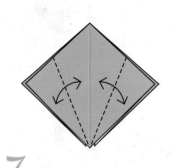

4
Turn over.

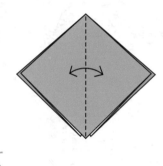

5
Squash fold.

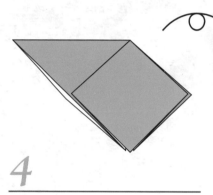

6
Valley fold, unfold.

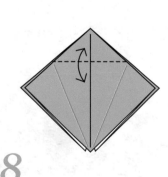

7
Valley folds, unfold.

8
Valley fold, unfold.

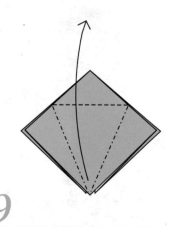

9
Pull in direction of arrow, folding inward at sides.

10

Appearance before completion of fold.

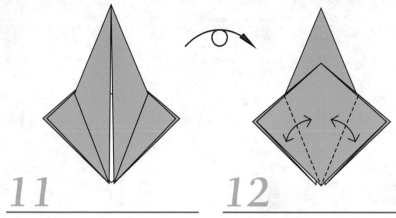
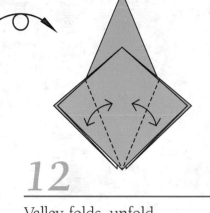

11

Fold completed. Turn over.

12

Valley folds, unfold.

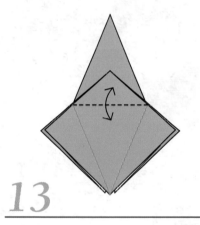

13

Valley fold, unfold.

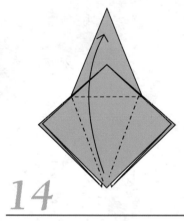

14

Repeat, again pulling in direction of arrow.

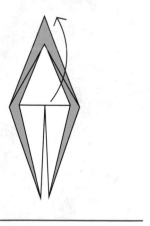

15

Appearance before completion.

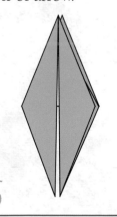

16

Completed Base Fold III.

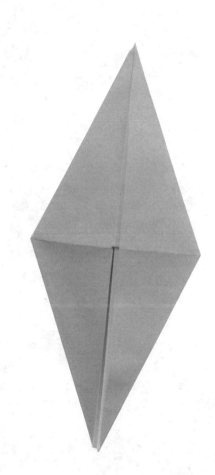

Rattlesnake

1

Start with long strip of paper (e.g., 1 by 17 inches), then valley fold along the dashed line.

2

Valley fold.

3

Mountain fold.

4

Continuing at "head" end, see close-ups.

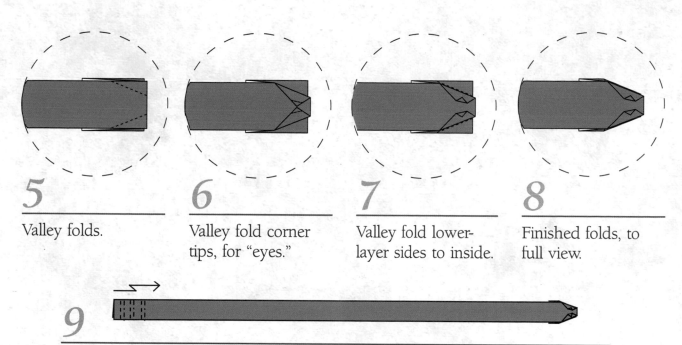

5
Valley folds.

6
Valley fold corner tips, for "eyes."

7
Valley fold lower-layer sides to inside.

8
Finished folds, to full view.

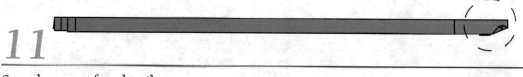

9
Pleat fold "tail" 3 times as indicated.

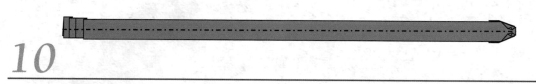

10
Mountain fold along dashed line.

11
See close-up for details.

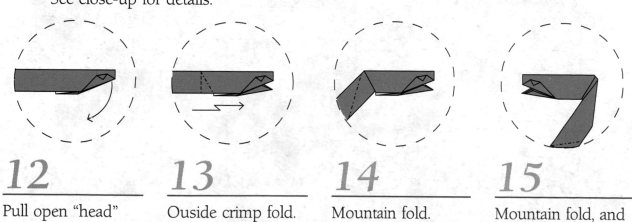

12
Pull open "head" end.

13
Ouside crimp fold.

14
Mountain fold.

15
Mountain fold, and return to full view.

Rattlesnake

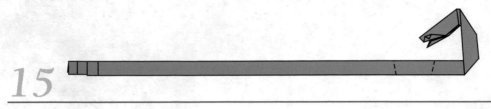

15

To coil body, valley fold in sets of two.

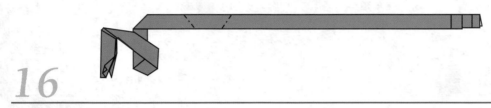

16

For ease in folding, turn snake form and do set of mountain folds instead.

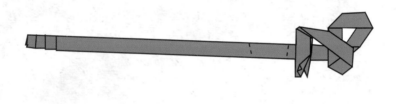

17

Continue valley folds and/or mountain folds down length of snake's "body."

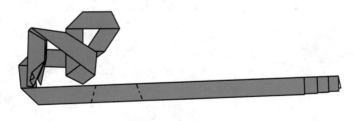

18

Continue coiling folds. Reverse a fold (valley/mountain) to break coil for a more natural motion.

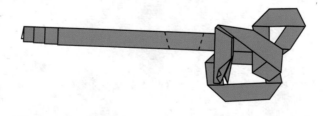

19

Approaching "tail," make folds closer together, add variety to folds.

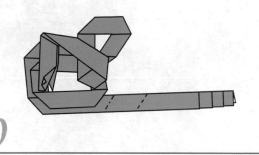

20

Mountain then valley for variety.

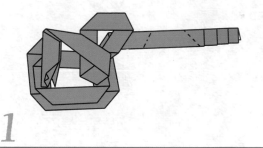

21

Again, mountain then valley fold.

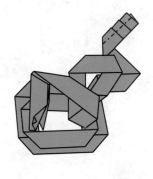

22

Mountain fold "tail" front and back.

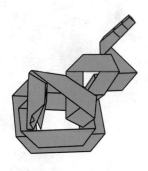

23

Adjust creased folds to give snake natural "body" movement.

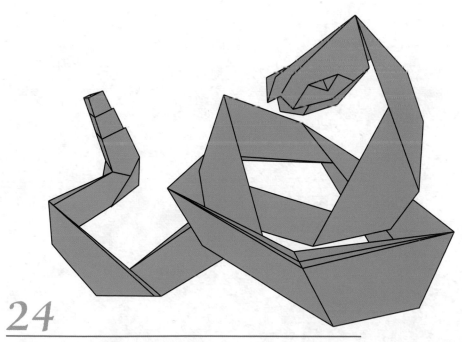

24

Completed Rattlesnake.

Rhinoceros

Part 1

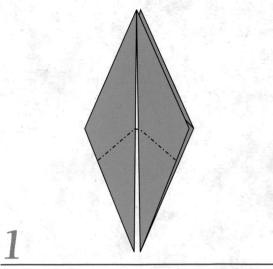

1

Start with Base Fold III, inside reverse folds.

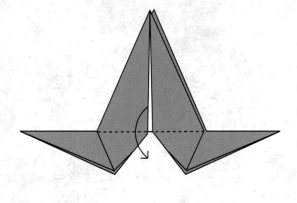

2

Valley fold.

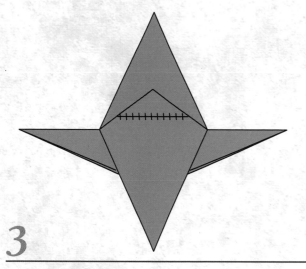

3

Cut off corner as indicated.

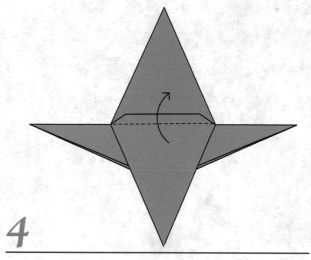

4

Valley fold.

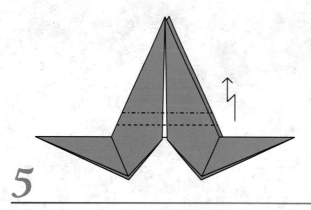

5

Pleat fold both layers together.

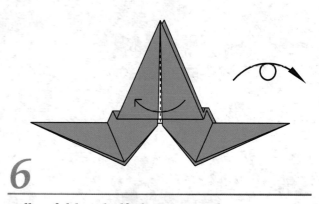

6

Valley fold in half, then rotate form.

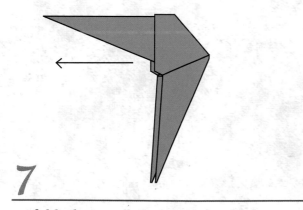

7

Unfold pleat. Pull in direction of arrow.

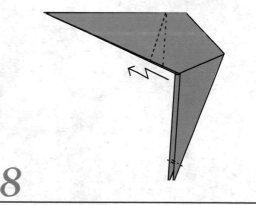

8

Pleat fold at top, inside reverse folds at bottom.

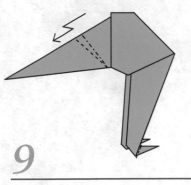

9

Pleat fold at top, inside reverse folds for front "feet."

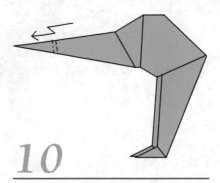

10

Pleat fold top layer only.

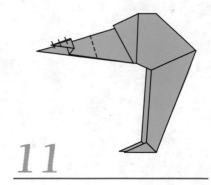

11

Cut apart as shown, then valley fold top layer.

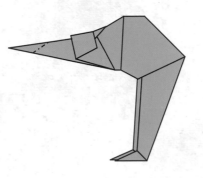

12

Inside reverse fold, then see close-ups.

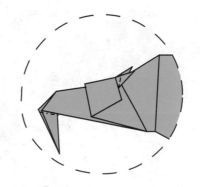

13

Inside reverse fold to shape "horn," squash folds for "ears."

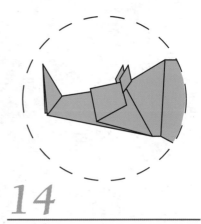

14

Completed head detail of rhinoceros.

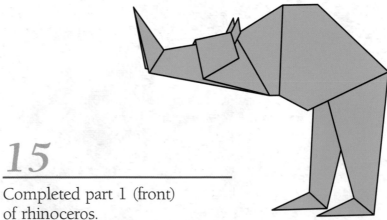

15

Completed part 1 (front) of rhinoceros.

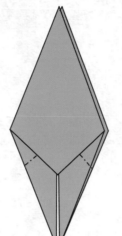

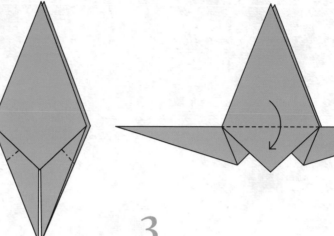

1

Start with Base Fold III, valley fold each side.

2

Inside reverse.

3

Valley fold.

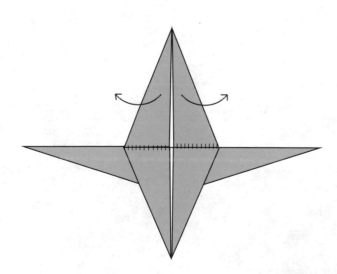

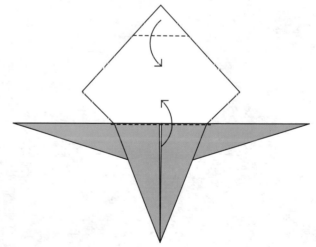

4

Cut as shown, then unfold in direction of arrows.

5

Valley folds.

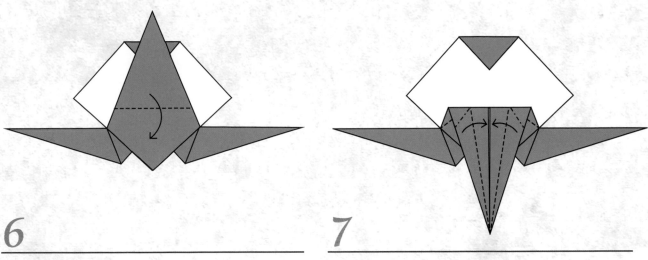

6

Valley fold.

7

Valley folds, then squash folds as indicated.

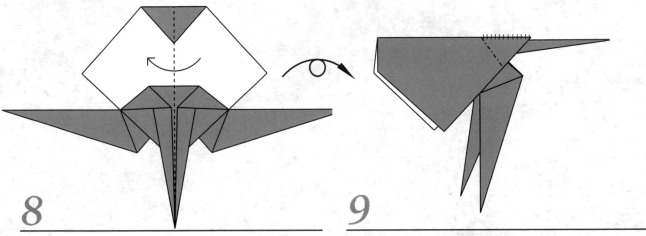

8

Valley fold in half, then rotate form.

9

Cut as shown, then mountain fold front and back.

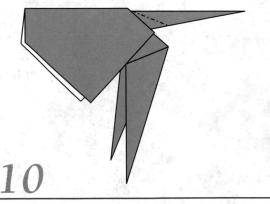

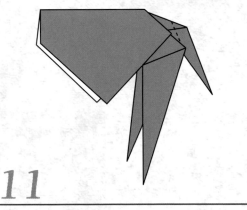

10

Inside reverse fold.

11

Valley fold front and back.

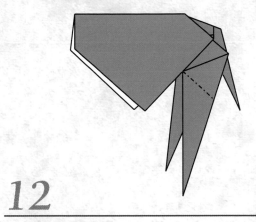

12

Inside reverse folds.

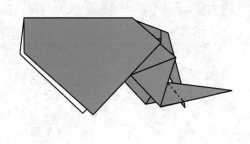

13

Inside reverse fold "legs."

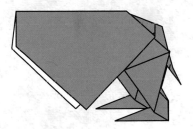

14

Inside reverse fold "tail."

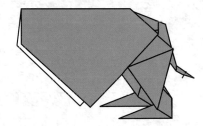

15

Outside reverse fold for "tail" tip.

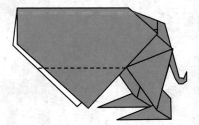

16

Valley fold layers together. Glue to secure.

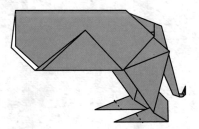

17

Inside reverse folds on "feet."

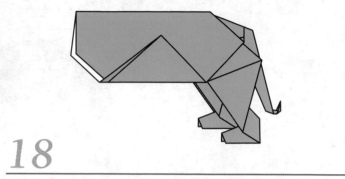

18

Completed part 2 (rear) of rhinoceros.

To Assemble

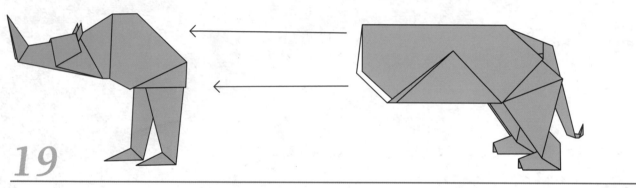

19

Attach rhinoceros parts 1 and 2 as shown; apply glue to hold.

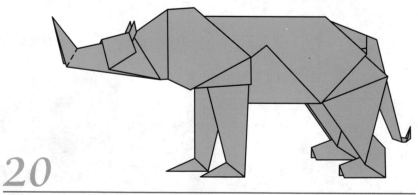

20

Completed Rhinoceros.

Killer Whale

Part 1

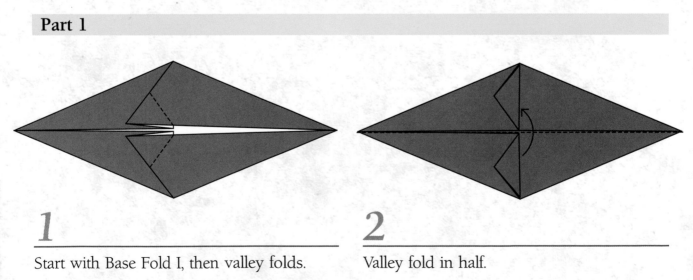

1

Start with Base Fold I, then valley folds.

2

Valley fold in half.

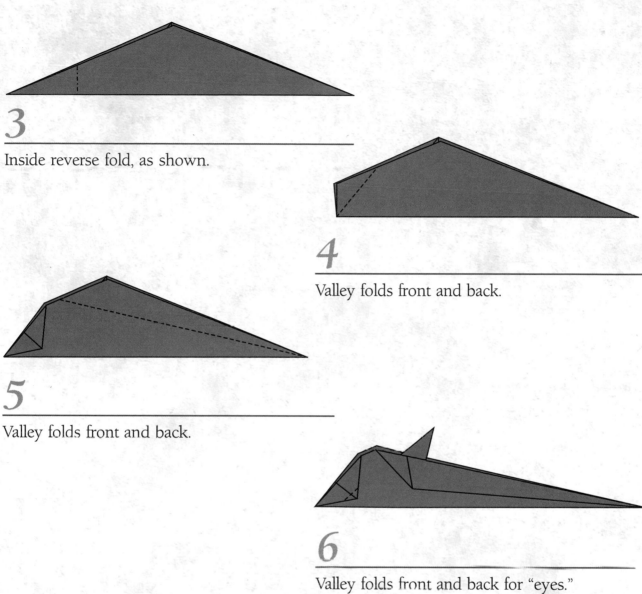

3

Inside reverse fold, as shown.

4

Valley folds front and back.

5

Valley folds front and back.

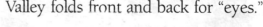

6

Valley folds front and back for "eyes."

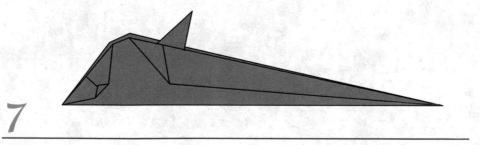

7

Completed part 1 (top) of killer whale.

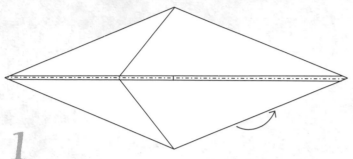

1

Start with Base Fold I, then mountain fold in half.

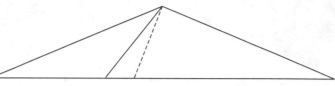

2

Valley folds both sides.

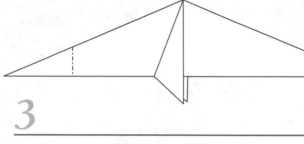

3

Inside reverse fold.

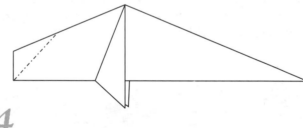

4

Mountain folds front and back.

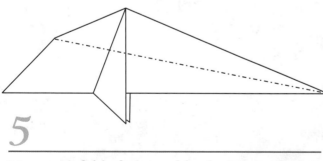

5

Mountain folds front and back.

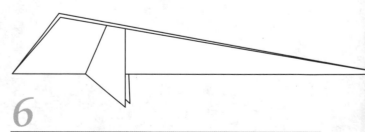

6

Completed part 2 (bottom) of killer whale.

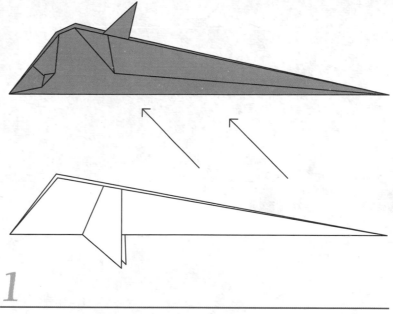

1

Put parts 1 and 2 together, as shown, and glue front body part to hold.

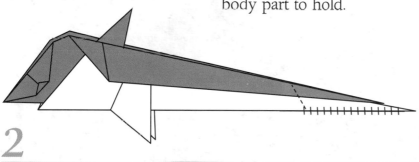

2

Cut through layers as indicated, lightly valley fold "tail fin" layers front and back to separate.

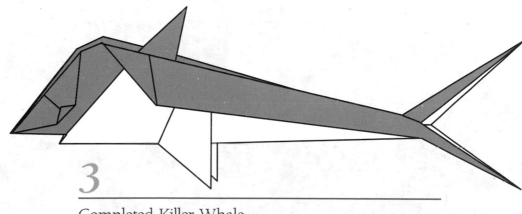

3

Completed Killer Whale.

Killer Whale.

Swordfish

Part 1

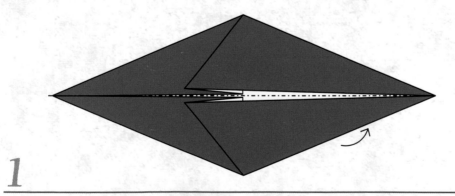

1

Start with Base Fold I, then mountain fold in half.

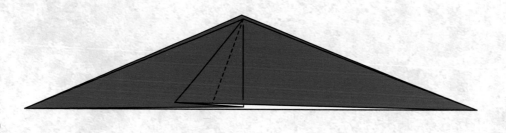

2

Valley folds front and back.

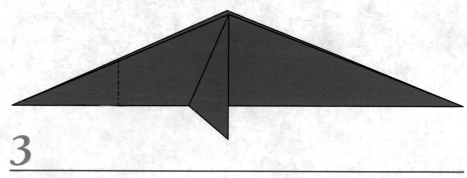

3

Inside reverse fold.

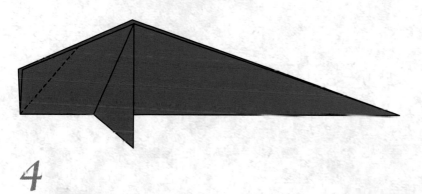

4

Valley folds front and back.

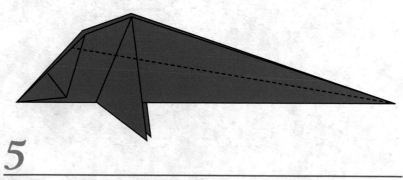

5

Valley folds front and back.

Swordfish

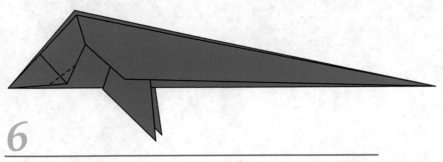

6

Valley folds, for "eyes."

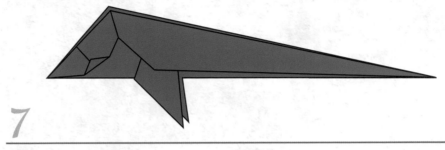

7

Completed part 1 (rear) of swordfish.

Part 2

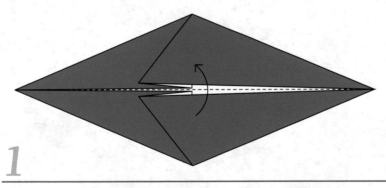

1

Start with Base Fold I, then valley fold in half.

2

Make cut through layers as indicated.

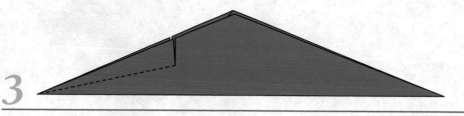

3

Valley folds to each side.

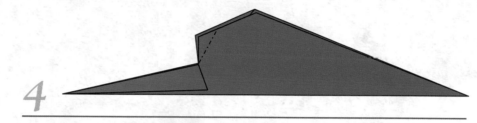

4

Mountain folds inward, both front and back.

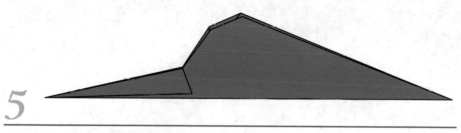

5

Completed part 2 (front) of swordfish.

To Assemble

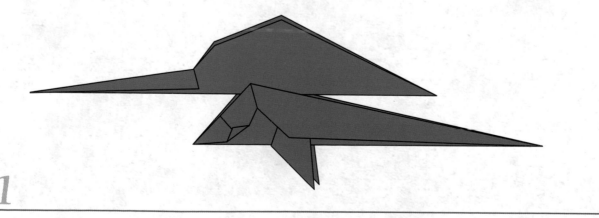

1

Attach parts 1 and 2 together as shown; lightly glue to hold.

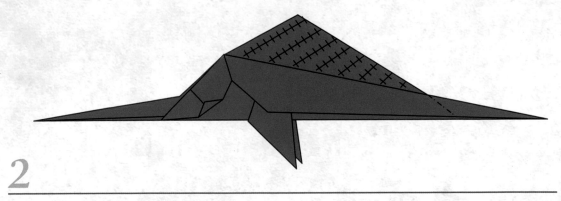

2

Make "topfin" cuts both sides as shown. Lightly, inside reverse fold top "tailfin."

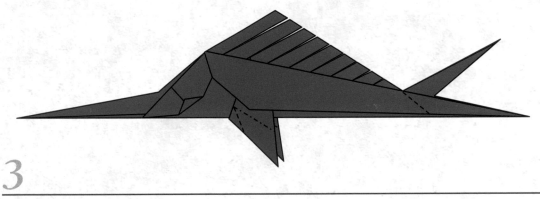

3

In same way, outside reverse fold lower "tailfin." Squash fold both "side fins."

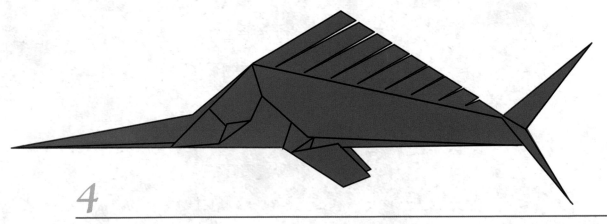

4

Completed Swordfish.

Pegasus

Part 1

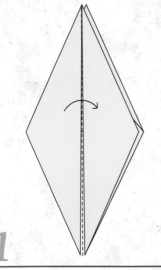

1

Start with Base Fold III and valley fold front and back.

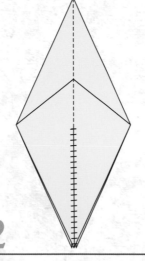

2

Cut through layers, valley fold front and back again.

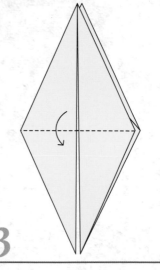

3

Valley fold top layer.

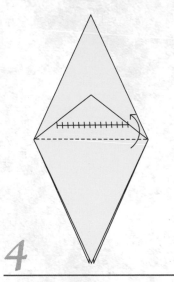

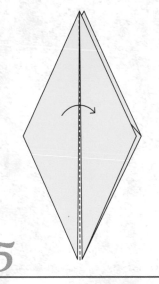

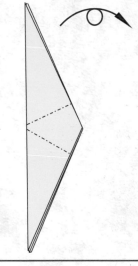

4

Cut off corner, as shown, then valley fold layer back.

5

Valley fold form in half.

6

Mountain fold front and back layers; inside reverse fold. Rotate.

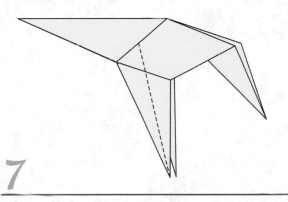

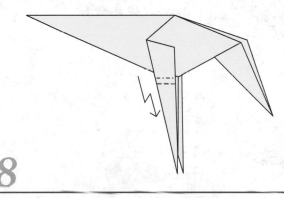

7

Valley folds front and back.

8

Pleat folds front and back.

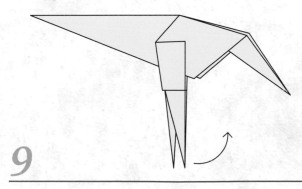

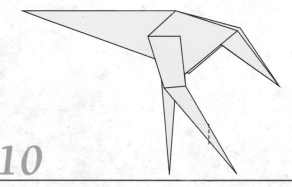

9

Pull front "leg" outward and in direction of arrow, squash into position.

10

Outside reverse fold.

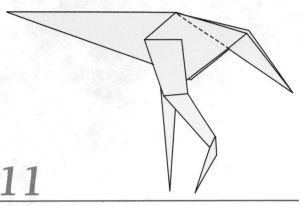

11

Valley fold.

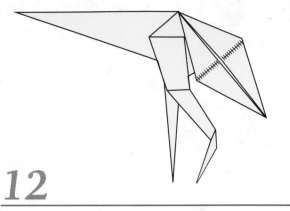

12

Make cuts in layer as indicated.

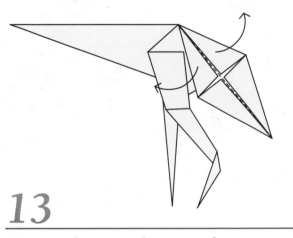

13

Open cut layers in direction of arrows. Valley fold in half.

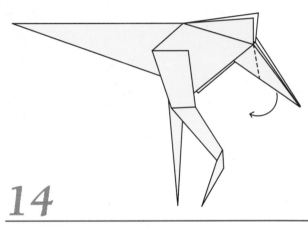

14

Valley fold to crease, then outside reverse fold lower layer only.

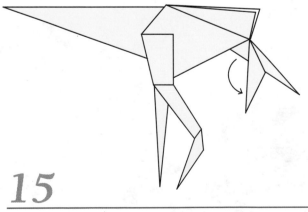

15

Pull paper out from inside of reversed layer and flatten to form "head."

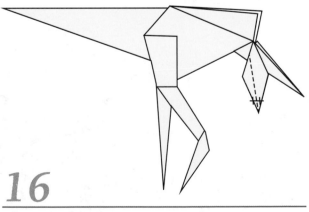

16

Valley fold and cut tip. See close-ups on next page for "head" detail.

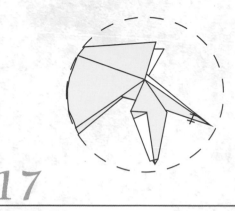

17

Cut off other tip.

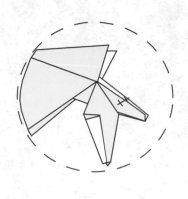

18

Partially cut through both sides as shown.

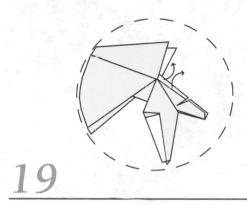

19

Open upper folds in direction of arrows, and outside reverse fold tip to form "mask."

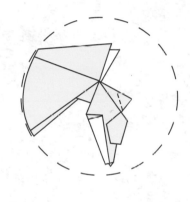

20

Valley fold both sides.

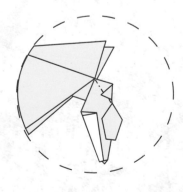

21

Mountain fold both "ears" into head section.

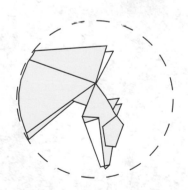

22

Completed "head," to full view.

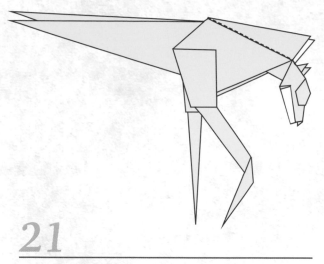

21

Valley fold "mane" to one side.

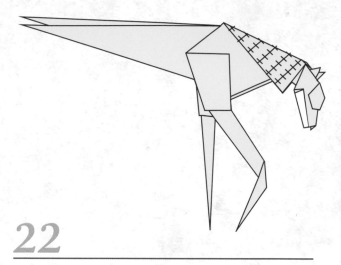

22

Make cuts through layers as indicated.

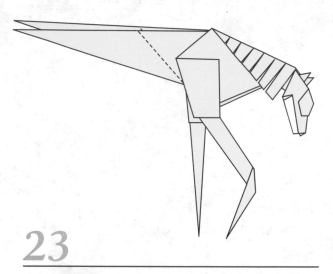

23

Valley fold "wings" front and back.

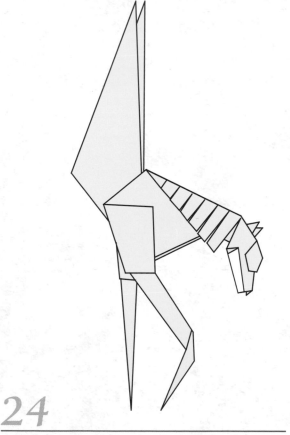

24

Completed part 1 (front) of Pegasus.

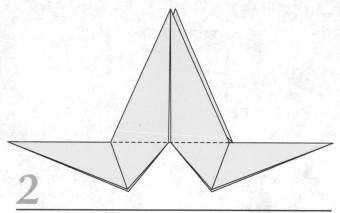

2

Valley folds.

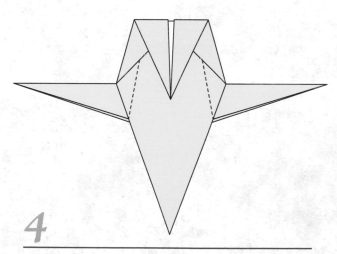

1

Start with Base Fold III, then inside reverse folds.

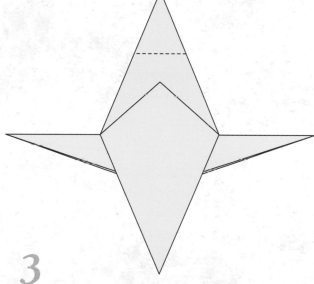

3

Valley fold.

4

Valley folds.

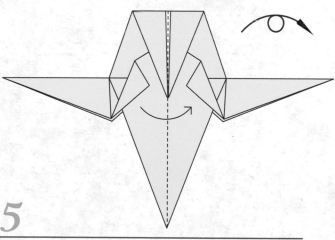

5

Valley fold in half and rotate.

Pegasus

41

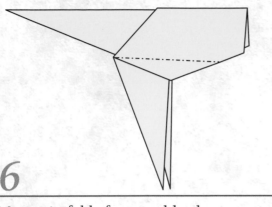

6

Mountain folds front and back.

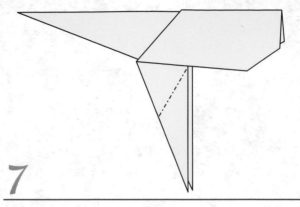

7

Inside reverse folds front and back.

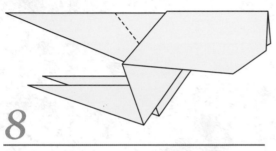

8

Outside reverse fold.

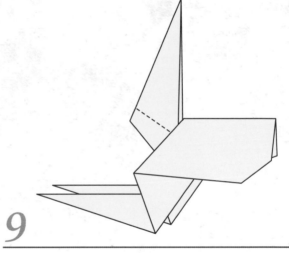

9

Outside reverse fold.

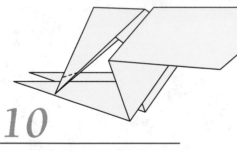

10

Outside reverse fold, to finish "tail."

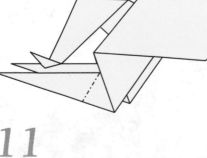

11

Inside reverse folds front and back.

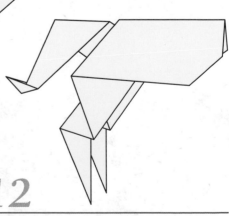

12

Completed part 2 (rear) of Pegasus.

To Assemble

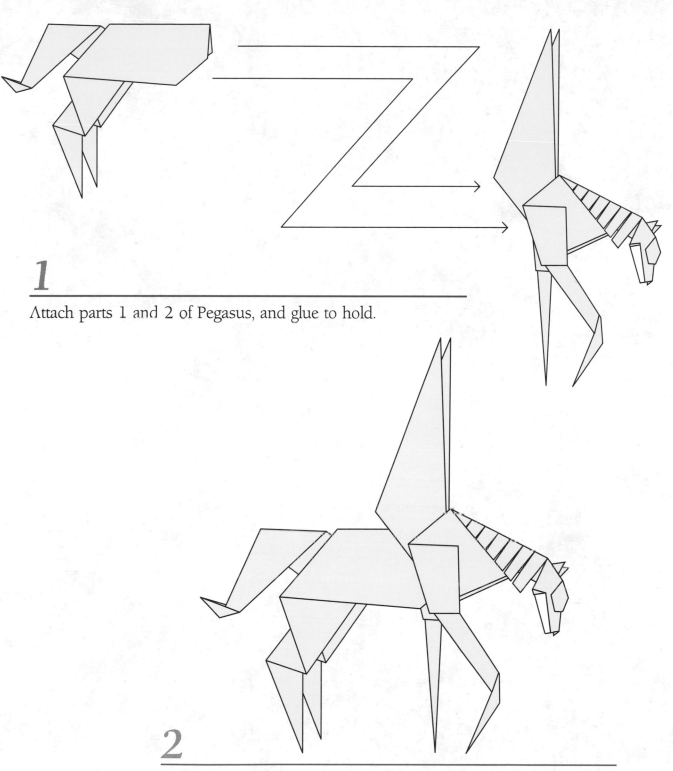

1

Attach parts 1 and 2 of Pegasus, and glue to hold.

2

Completed Pegasus.

Sand Crab

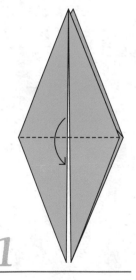

1

Start with Base Fold III, valley fold.

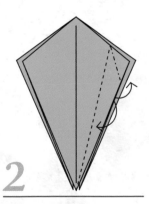

2

Squash fold in the direction of arrows.

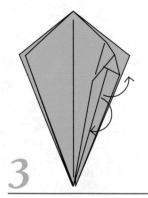

3

Appearance before completion.

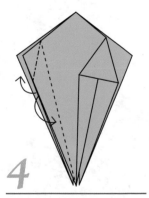

4

Squash fold other side.

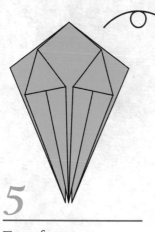

5

Turn form over.

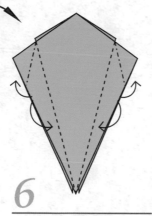

6

Repeat squash folds.

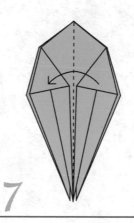

7

Valley fold. Repeat behind.

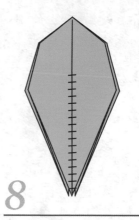

8

Cut as shown.

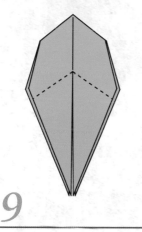

9

Valley folds.

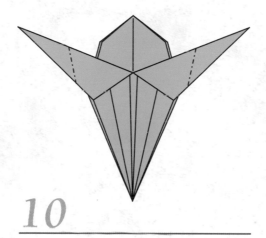

10

Inside reverse folds.

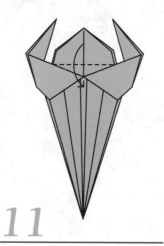

11

Valley fold.

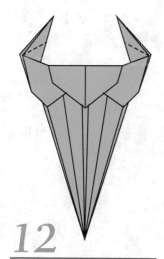

12

Outside reverse folds.

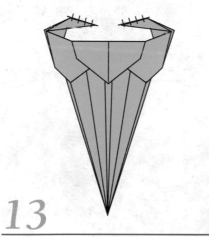

13

Cuts as shown, for "pincers."

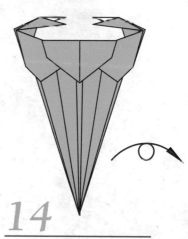

14

Turn over.

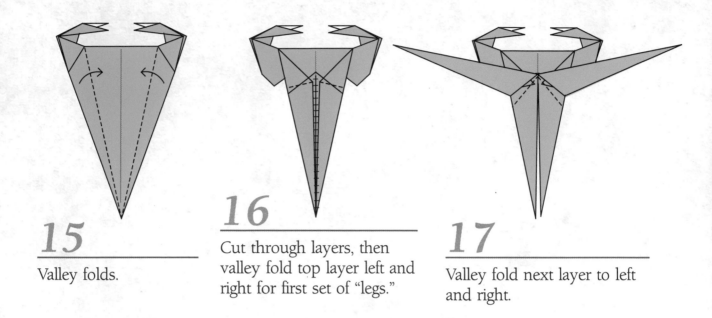

15

Valley folds.

16

Cut through layers, then valley fold top layer left and right for first set of "legs."

17

Valley fold next layer to left and right.

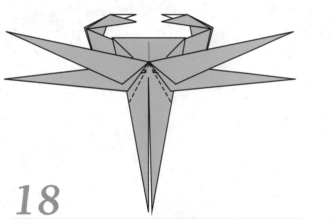

18

Valley folds again to left and right.

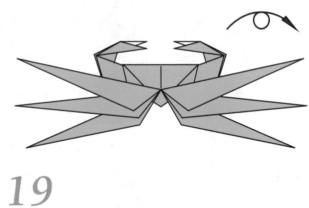

19

Turn form over.

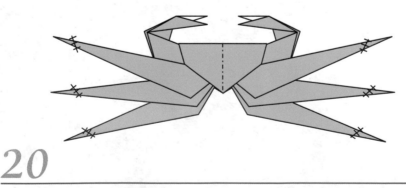

20

Make cuts, trimming "feet" as indicated. Mountain fold in half.

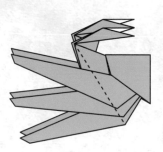

21

Valley folds.

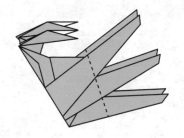

22

Valley folds.

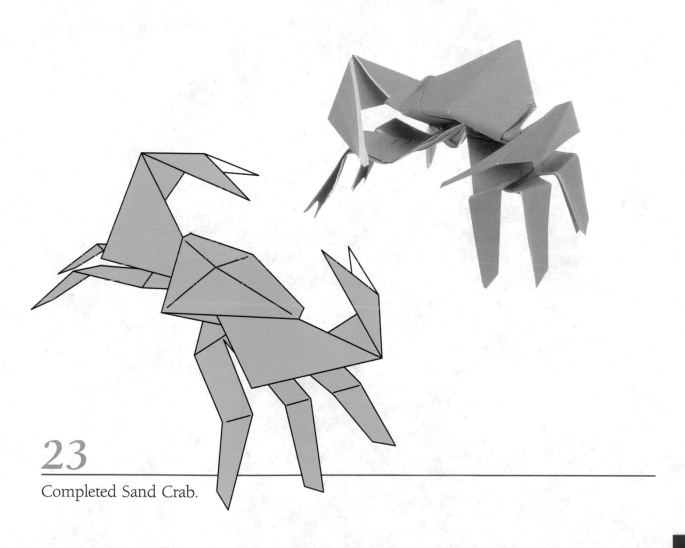

23

Completed Sand Crab.

Oriental Dragon

Part 1

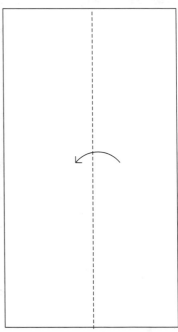

1

Start with legal-sized sheet and valley fold it in half lengthwise. Rotate.

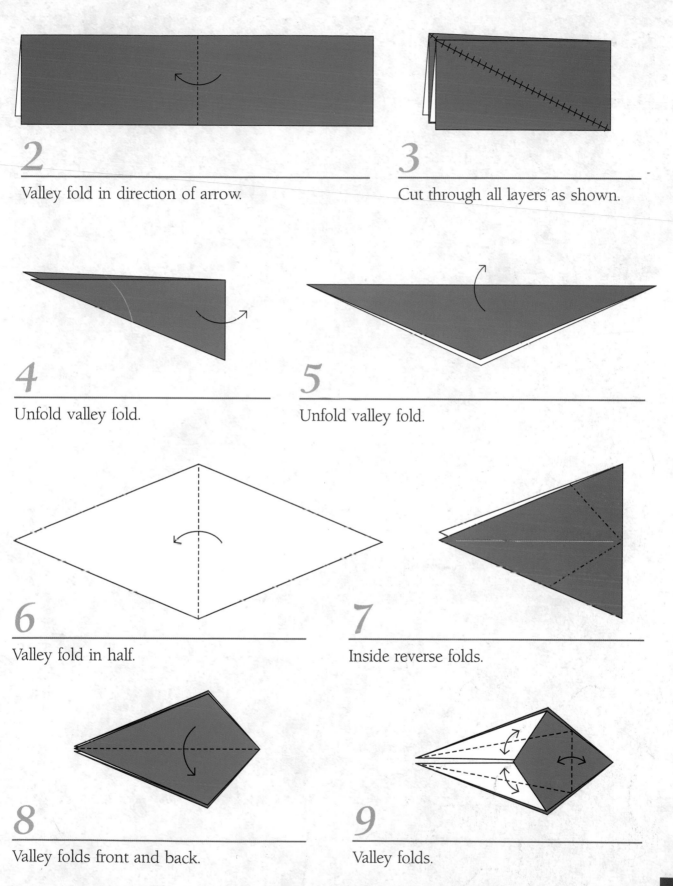

2
Valley fold in direction of arrow.

3
Cut through all layers as shown.

4
Unfold valley fold.

5
Unfold valley fold.

6
Valley fold in half.

7
Inside reverse folds.

8
Valley folds front and back.

9
Valley folds.

Oriental Dragon

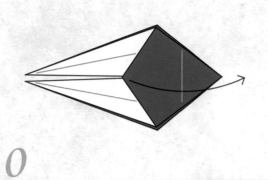

10

Valley fold in creases, in direction of arrow.

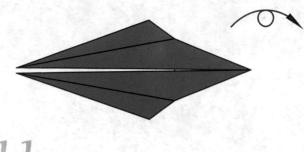

11

Turn form over.

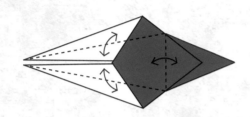

12

Valley folds.

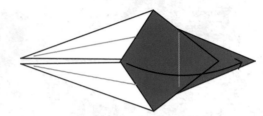

13

Repeat step **10**.

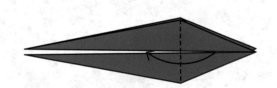

14

Valley fold.

15

Turn form over.

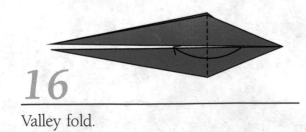

16

Valley fold.

17

Valley fold in half. Repeat behind.

18

Cut, then valley fold.

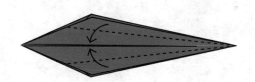

19

Valley folds. Look closer, now, at detail.

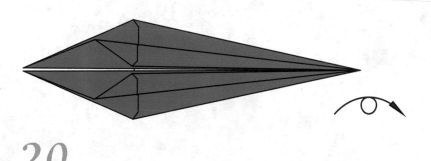

20

Turn over.

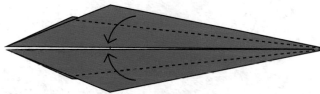

21

Valley folds.

22

Cuts as indicated (only top layer).

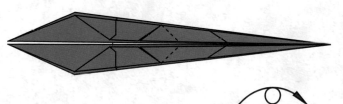

23

Valley folds. Turn over.

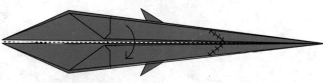

24

Cuts as shown, then valley fold in half.

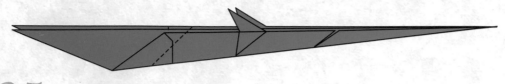

25

Outside reverse fold.

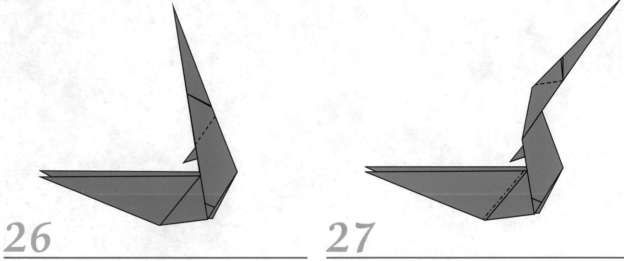

26

Outside reverse fold.

27

Inside reverse folds.

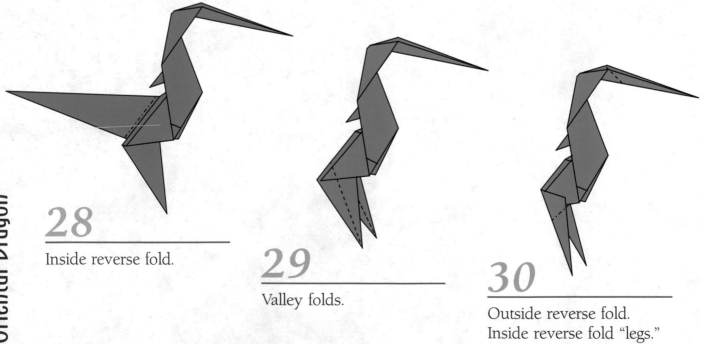

28

Inside reverse fold.

29

Valley folds.

30

Outside reverse fold.
Inside reverse fold "legs."

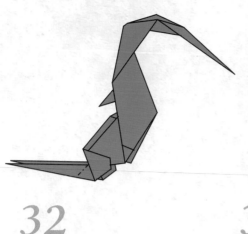

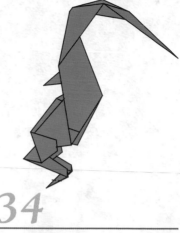

32
Inside reverse folds.

33
Inside reverse folds.

34
Outside reverse folds.

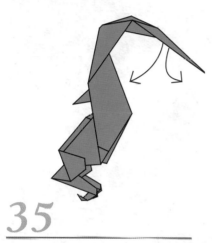
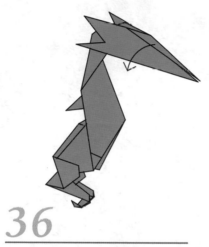

35
From inside the lower fold, pull some paper outward.

36
Pull some paper from inside the top layer, too.

37
Make cuts front and back; outside reverse fold upward.

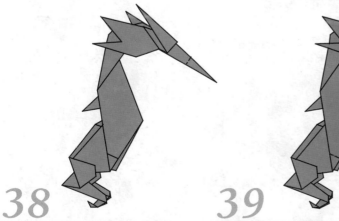

38
Inside reverse fold.

39
Inside reverse for "mouth."

40
Inside reverse tip.

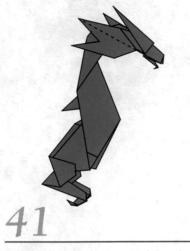

41

Valley folds front and back.

42

Valley folds front and back.

43

Pull open both sides.

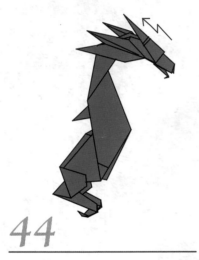

44

Pleat fold.

45

Cut as shown, spread apart.

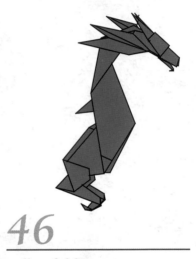

46

Valley fold tips.

47

Completed part 1 (front)
of Oriental dragon.

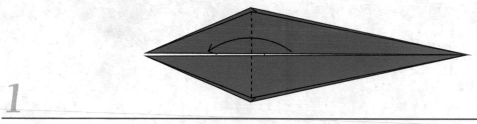

1

To reach this starting point, turn to part 1 and complete steps **1** through **20**; then valley fold.

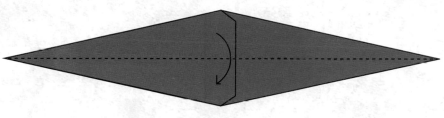

21

Valley fold in half.

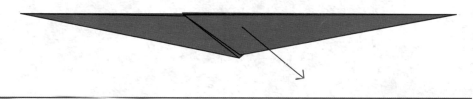

22

Press open in direction of arrow.

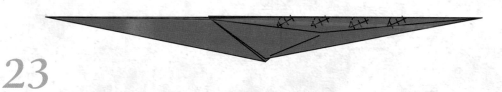

23

Make cuts to middle layer as shown, then outside reverse folds.

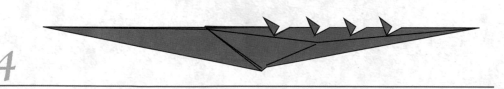

24

Release layer back to original state.

25

Valley fold, then repeat cut and outside reverse fold step.

26

Valley fold.

27

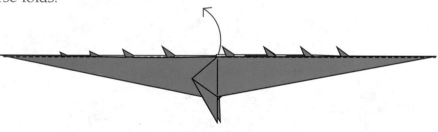

Inside reverse folds.

28

Valley fold back layer in direction of arrow.

29

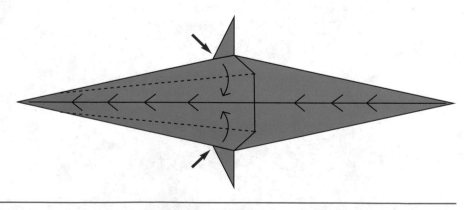

Valley fold sides to center, also at points shown.

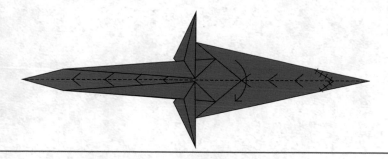

30

Cut as shown, then valley fold in half.

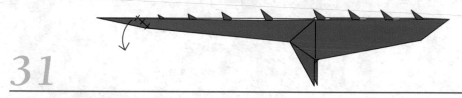

31

Cuts on both sides, top layer only, then valley fold open.

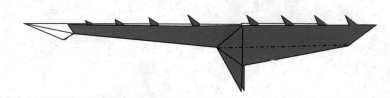

32

Mountain folds both sides.

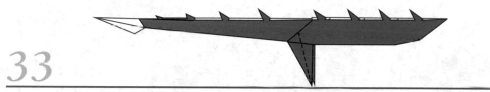

33

Valley folds both sides.

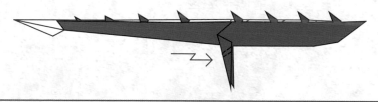

34

Pleat folds both sides.

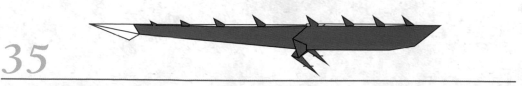

35

Outside reverse folds, for "feet."

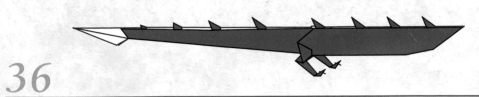

36

Inside reverse folds, for "toe tips."

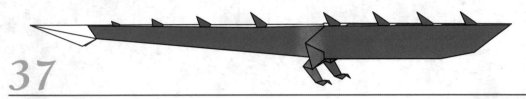

37

Completed part 2 (rear) of Oriental dragon.

To Assemble

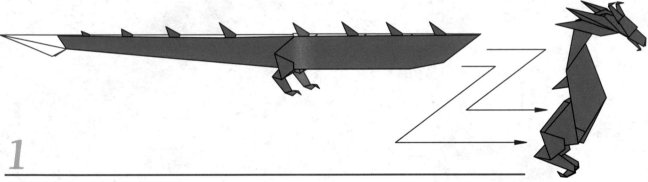

1

Join parts 1 and 2 as indicated, and glue.

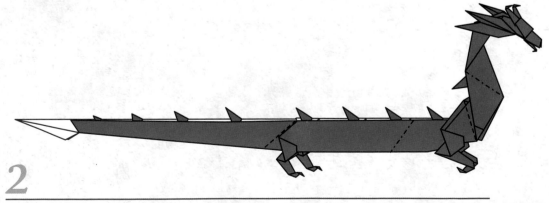

2

Mountain fold, then valley fold.

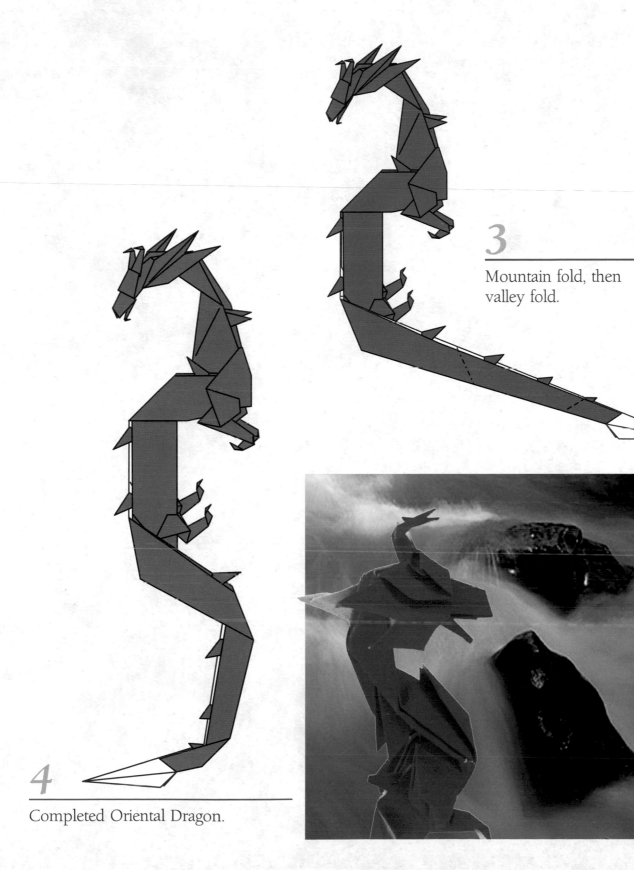

3

Mountain fold, then valley fold.

4

Completed Oriental Dragon.

Flying Fox

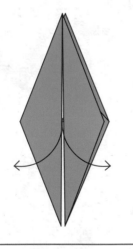

1

Start with Base Fold III; pull open in direction of arrows.

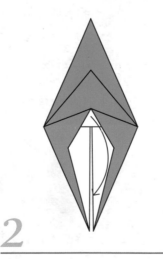

2

Squash fold as shown.

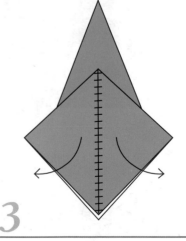

3

Cut, then unfold.

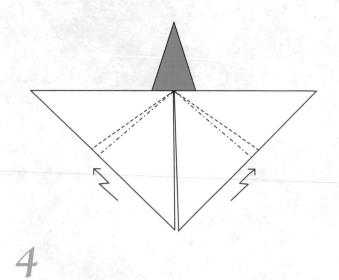

4

Pleat folds on both sides.

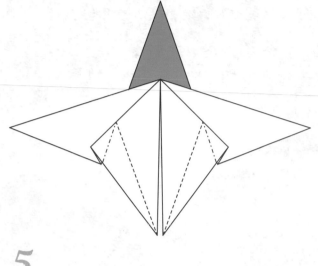

5

Squash folds.

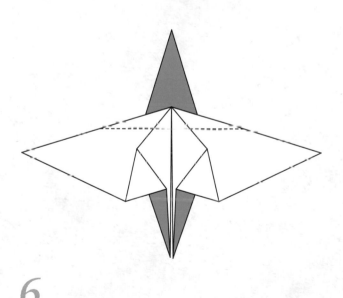

6

Valley fold.

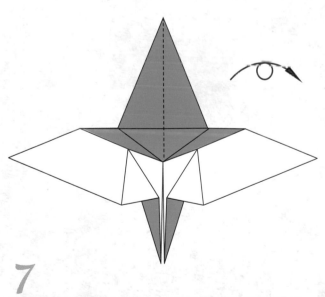

7

Valley fold in half, then rotate form.

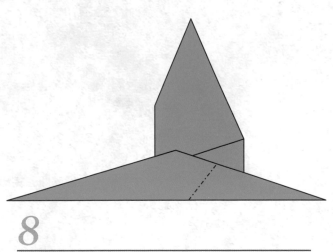

8

Inside reverse folds.

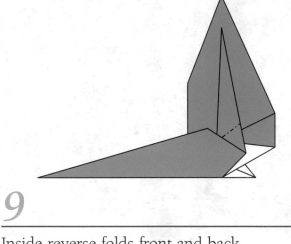

9

Inside reverse folds front and back.

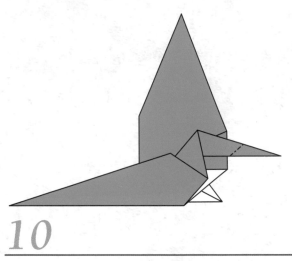

10

Again, inside reverse folds.

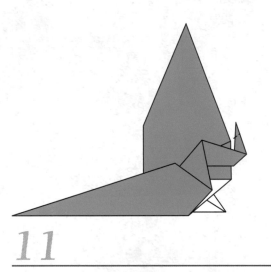

11

Now outside reverse folds.

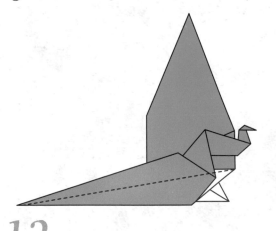

12

Valley folds front and back.

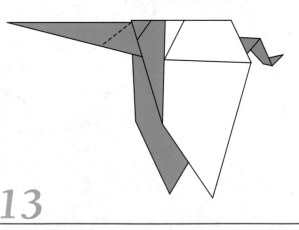

13

Outside reverse fold.

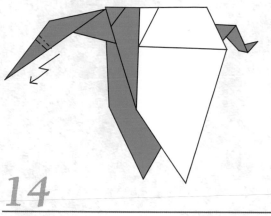

14

Pleat fold.

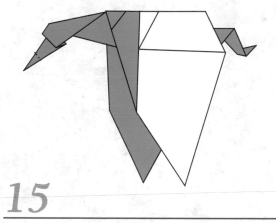

15

Inside reverse fold.

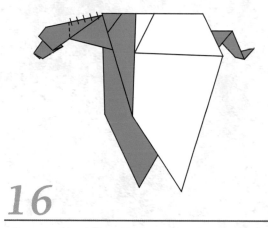

16

Cuts as shown, then valley folds for "ears."

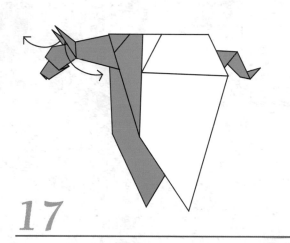

17

Squash fold "ears" to open.

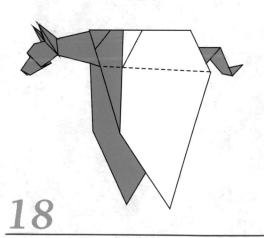

18

Valley fold "wings" front and back.

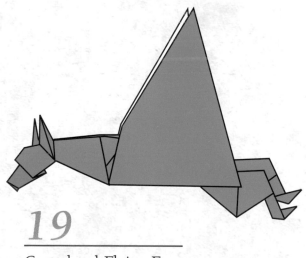

19

Completed Flying Fox.

Wild Duck

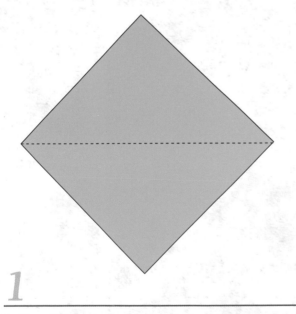

1
Valley fold square in half, diagonally.

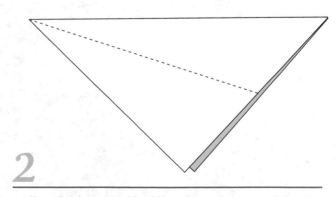

2
Valley folds to half of baseline, front and back.

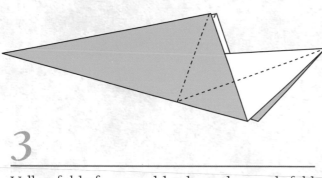

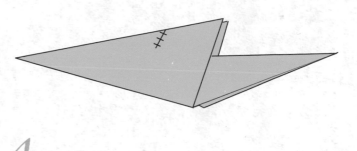

3

Valley folds front and back, and squash fold as you go.

4

Cuts as shown.

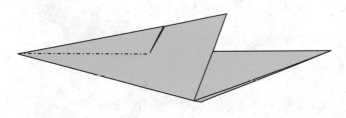

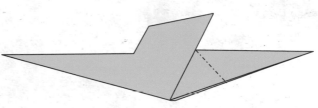

5

Now mountain folds.

6

Inside reverse fold.

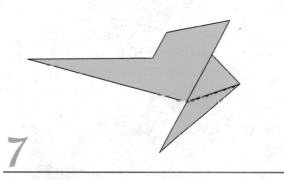

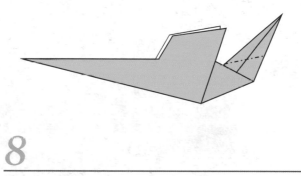

7

Another inside reverse fold.

8

Inside reverse fold again.

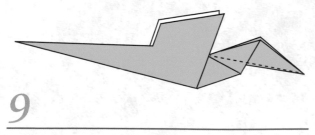

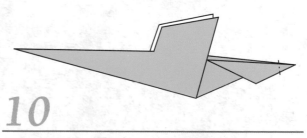

9

Valley folds, front and back.

10

Mountain fold, to form "tail" end.

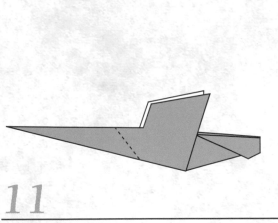

11

Outside reverse fold.

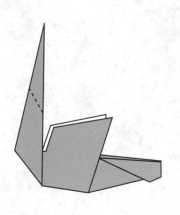

12

Outside reverse fold.

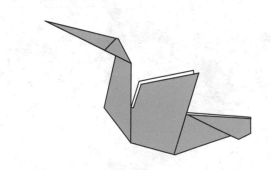

13

Outside reverse fold.

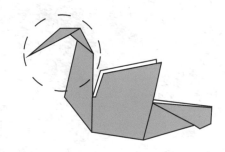

14

Completed fold, see close-ups for head detail.

15

Pull to sides and flatten.

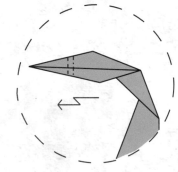

16

Pleat fold.

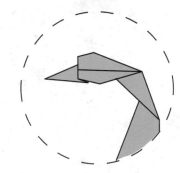

17

Return to full view.

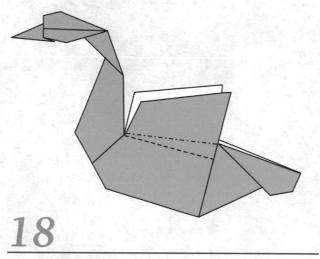

18

Pleat fold "wings" front and back.

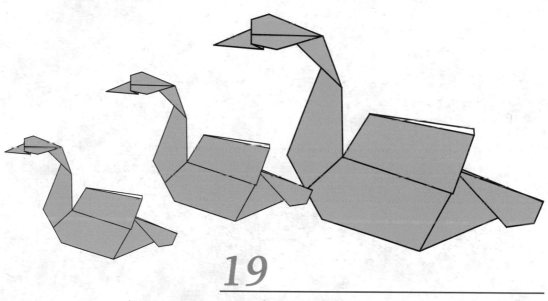

19

Completed Wild Duck.

Flamingo

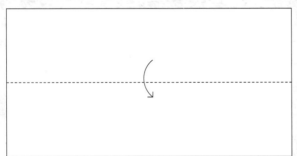

1 Start with legal-sized sheet; valley fold in half.

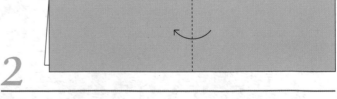

2 Valley fold in direction of arrow.

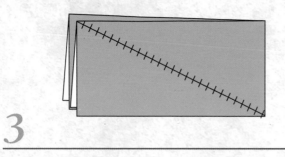

3

Make cut as shown, through all layers.

4

Unfold.

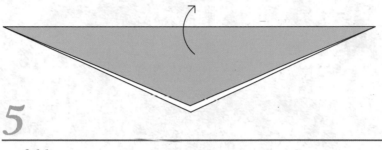

5

Unfold.

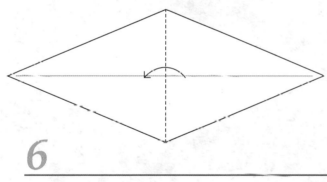

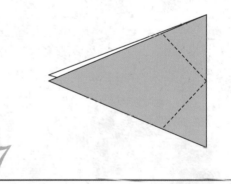

6

Valley fold in half.

7

Inside reverse folds.

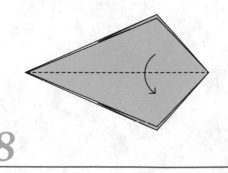

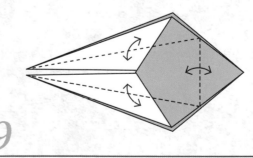

8

Valley folds front and back.

9

Folds then unfolds.

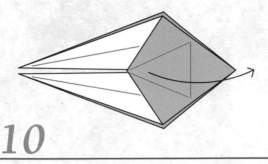

10

Pull in direction of arrow, folding in creases.

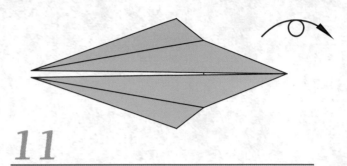

11

Turn over.

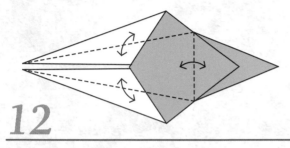

12

Repeat steps **9** to **11**.

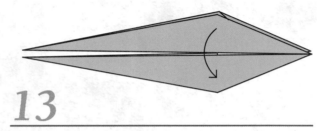

13

Valley folds, front and back.

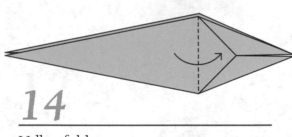

14

Valley folds.

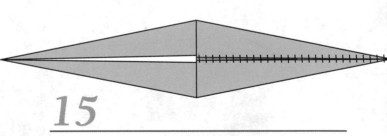

15

Cut as shown.

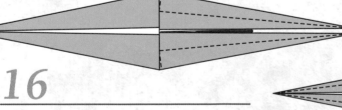

16

Valley folds with squash folds.

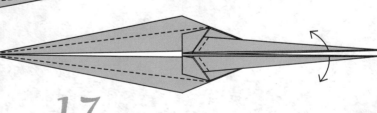

17

Valley folds inward; outside reverse folds in direction of arrows.

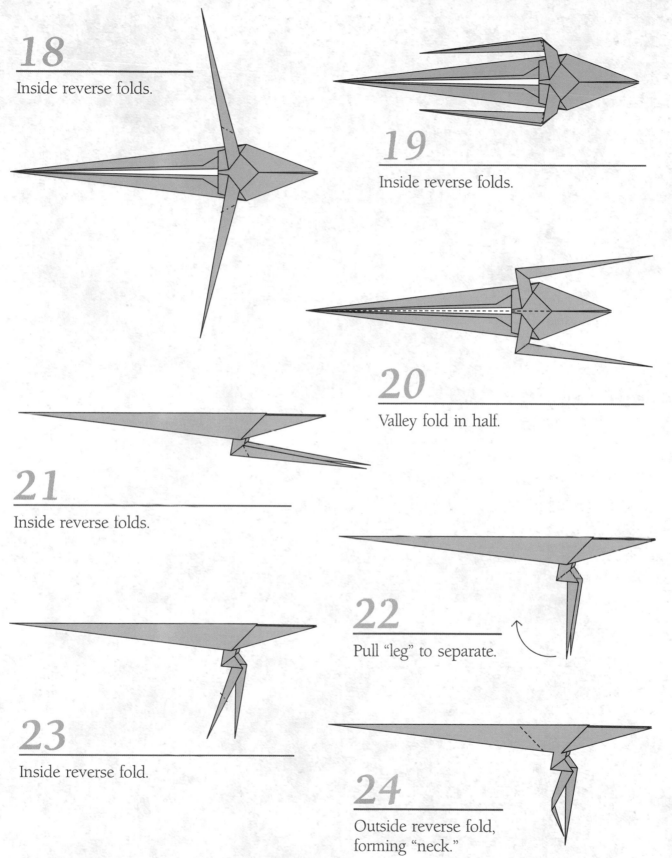

18
Inside reverse folds.

19
Inside reverse folds.

20
Valley fold in half.

21
Inside reverse folds.

22
Pull "leg" to separate.

23
Inside reverse fold.

24
Outside reverse fold,
forming "neck."

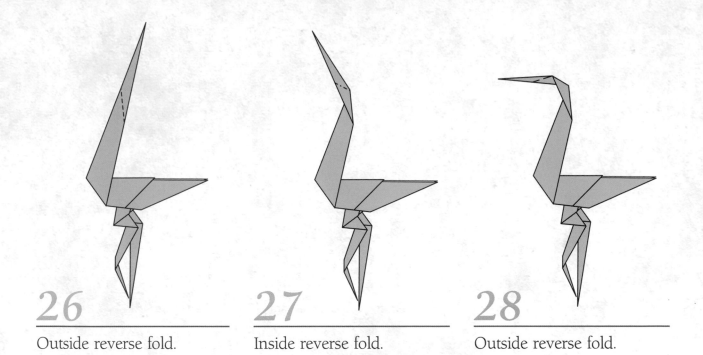

26

Outside reverse fold.

27

Inside reverse fold.

28

Outside reverse fold.

29

Pull paper out to sides and flatten to form "head."

30

Pleat fold for "beak."

31

Inside reverse fold.

32

Completed Flamingo…and friends.

Greyhound

Part 1

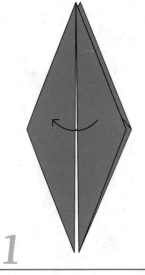

1

Start with Base Fold III, valley fold.

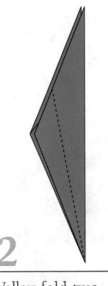

2

Valley fold two layers, both sides.

3

Inside reverse fold.

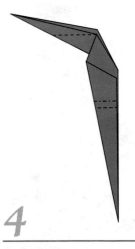

4

Pleat folds, then outside reverse fold.

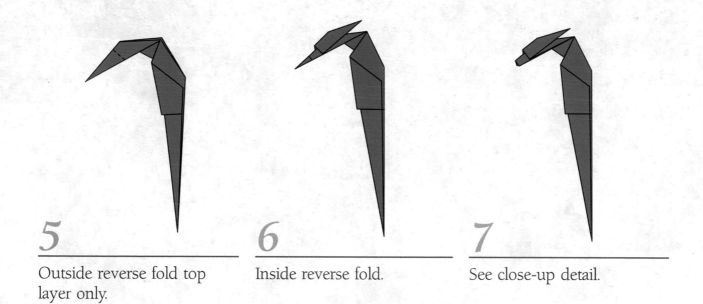

5

Outside reverse fold top layer only.

6

Inside reverse fold.

7

See close-up detail.

8

Pleat fold.

9

Cut to separate "ears," as shown.

10

Squash fold "ears."

11

Completed detail, to full view.

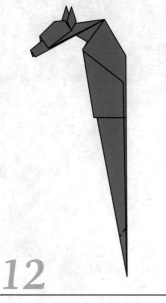

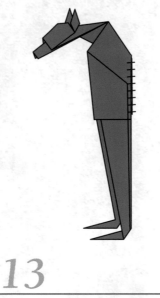

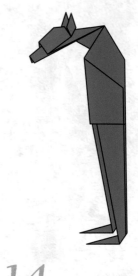

12

Inside reverse folds, for front "paws."

13

Cuts as shown.

14

Completed part 1 (front) of greyhound.

Part 2

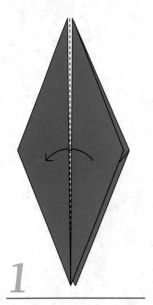

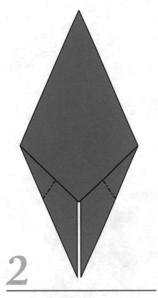

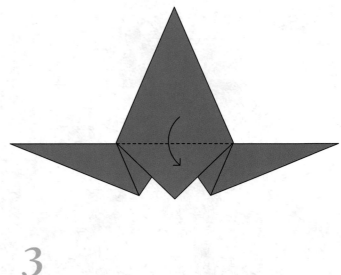

1

Start with Base Fold III, valley fold and repeat behind.

2

Inside reverse folds.

3

Valley fold.

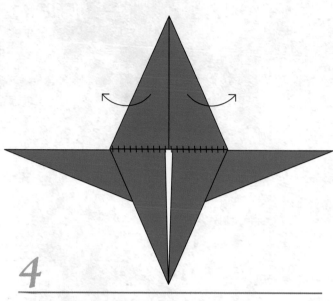

4

Cuts as shown, then valley fold.

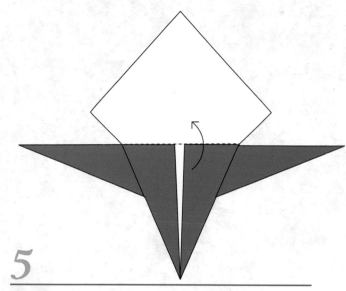

5

Valley fold.

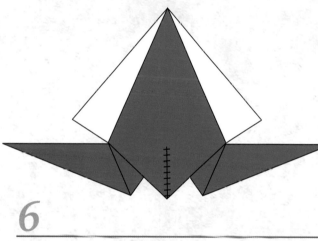

6

Cuts as indicated.

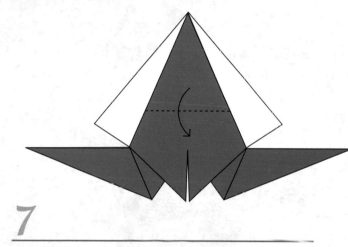

7

Valley fold.

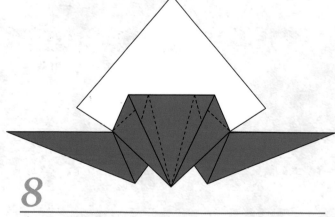

8

Squash folds.

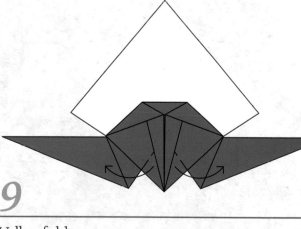

9

Valley folds.

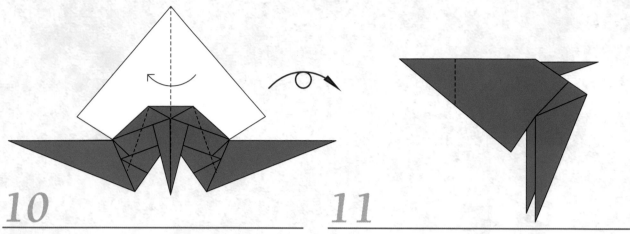

10

Valley folds. Then valley in half and rotate.

11

Valley fold.

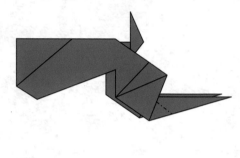

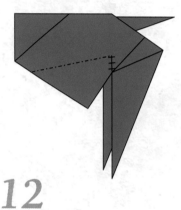

12

Make cut as shown and mountain fold. Repeat behind.

13

Inside reverse fold "legs." Outside reverse "tail."

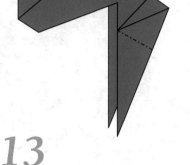

14

Inside reverse folds again.

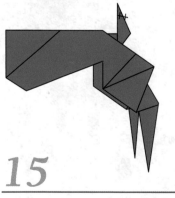

15

Cut to form "tail."

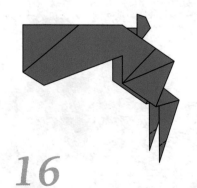

16

Outside reverse folds to form back "paws."

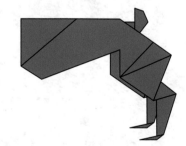

17

Completed part 2 (rear) of greyhound.

To Assemble

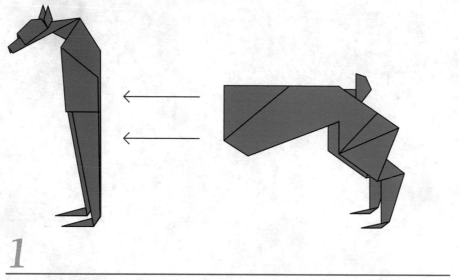

1

Join parts 1 and 2 together per arrows, and glue to secure.

2

Completed Greyhound.

Phoenix

Part 1

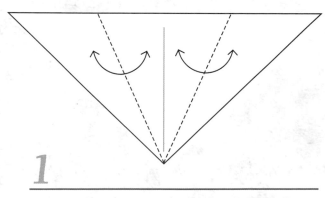

1

Start with a square sheet cut diagonally; valley folds and crease, then unfold.

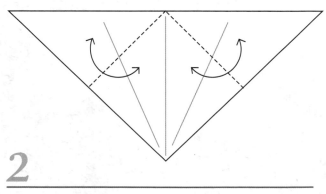

2

Valley folds again and crease, then unfold.

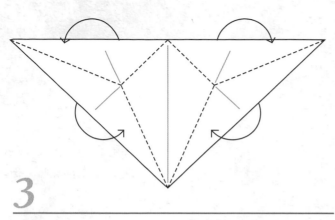

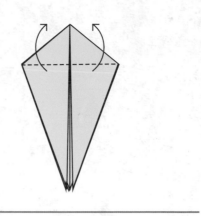

3

Pinch corners together, folding inward along dashed lines.

4

Valley folds.

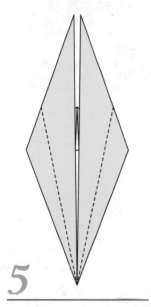

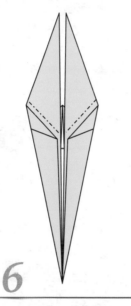

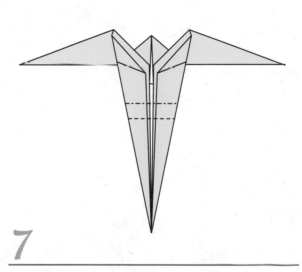

5

Valley folds.

6

Mountain folds.

7

Pleat fold.

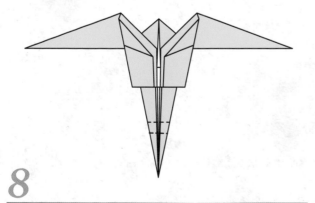

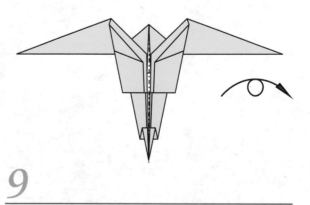

8

Pleat fold.

9

Mountain fold in half, and rotate form.

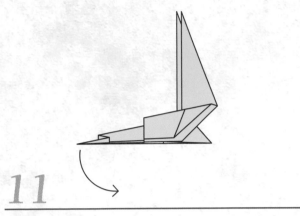

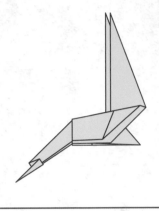

11

Pull point downward and crimp to position "head."

12

Part 1 (front) of phoenix, ready for head detail (part 3).

Part 2

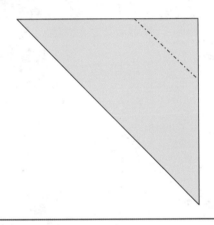

1

Valley fold.

2

Inside reverse fold.

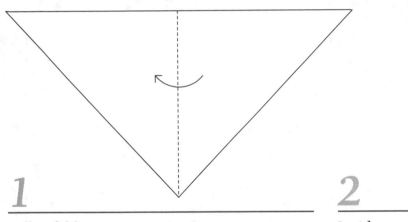

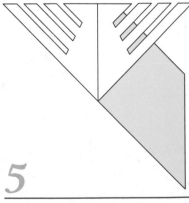

3

Make double cuts for width as shown.

4

Valley fold the first layer.

5

Completed part 2 (back) of phoenix.

Part 3

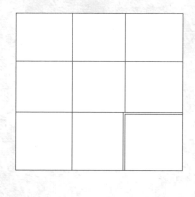

1

Cut 1/9th square of origami paper, and make Base Fold I.

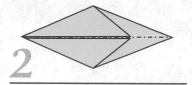

2

Mountain fold in half.

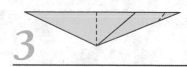

3

Squash fold both sides, outside reverse fold tip.

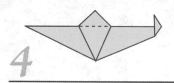

4

Valley fold both sides.

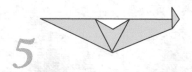

5

Completed part 3 ("head" section) of phoenix.

To Assemble

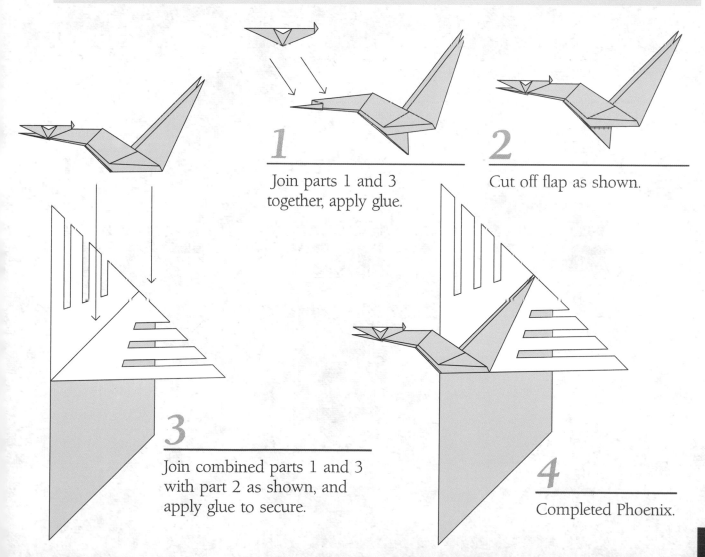

1

Join parts 1 and 3 together, apply glue.

2

Cut off flap as shown.

3

Join combined parts 1 and 3 with part 2 as shown, and apply glue to secure.

4

Completed Phoenix.

Bucking Bronco

Part 1

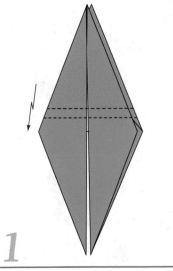

1

Start with Base Fold III.
Pleat fold layers together.

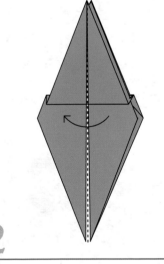

2

Unfold pleat and valley fold
in half.

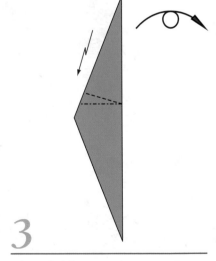

3

Pleat fold in creases, and
rotate form.

Bucking Bronco

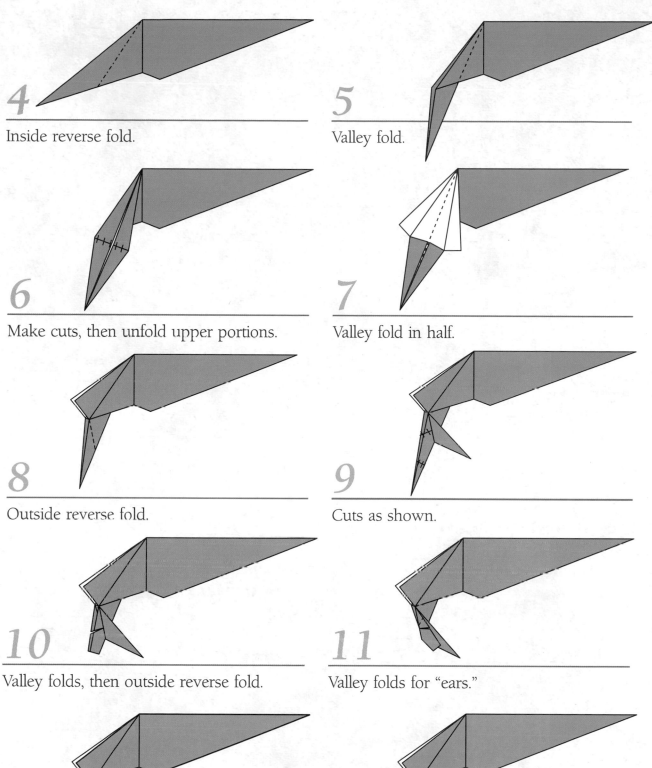

4

Inside reverse fold.

5

Valley fold.

6

Make cuts, then unfold upper portions.

7

Valley fold in half.

8

Outside reverse fold.

9

Cuts as shown.

10

Valley folds, then outside reverse fold.

11

Valley folds for "ears."

12

Pull some paper outward, both sides.

13

Valley folds.

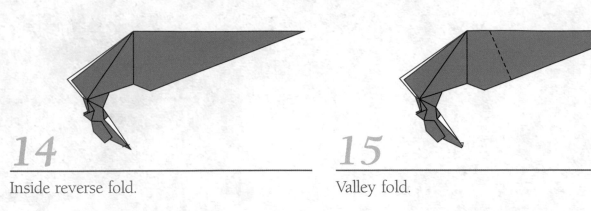

14

Inside reverse fold.

15

Valley fold.

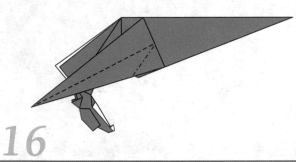

16

Valley fold and squash fold.

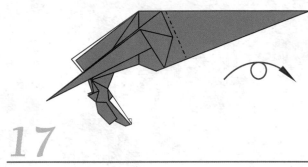

17

Mountain fold and turn over.

18

Valley fold and squash fold.

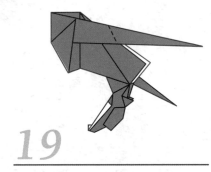

19

Outside reverse fold.

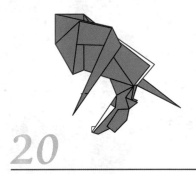

20

Inside reverse fold.

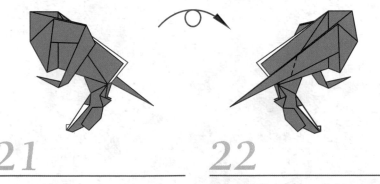

21

Turn over.

22

Outside reverse fold.

23

Inside reverse fold.

24

See next steps for close-up detail.

25

Reversefold "ears" into "head" fold.

26

Back to long view.

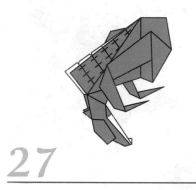

27

Cuts on "mane" as shown.

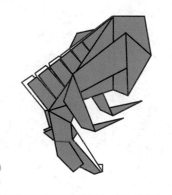

28

Completed part 1 (front) of bucking bronco.

Part 2

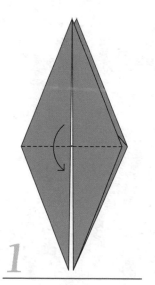

1

Start with Base Fold III, then valley fold.

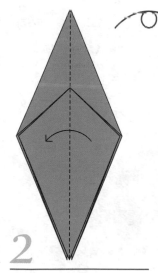

2

Valley fold in half, and rotate.

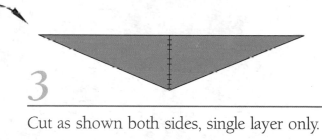

3

Cut as shown both sides, single layer only.

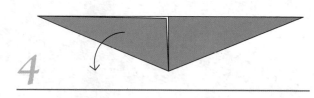

4

Unfold both sides in direction of arrow.

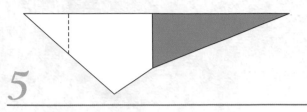

5

Outside reverse fold.

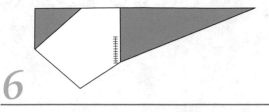

6

Cuts as shown through all layers.

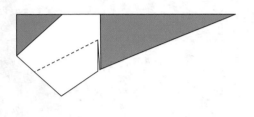

7

Valley fold both sides.

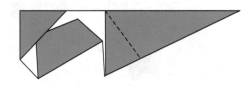

8

Valley fold each side to start "legs."

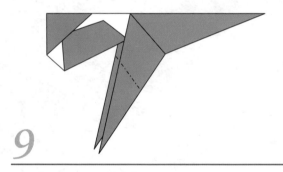

9

Inside reverse folds.

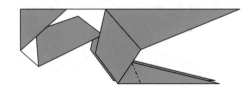

10

Inside reverse folds.

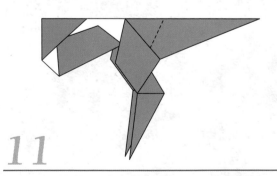

11

Outside reverse fold to start "tail."

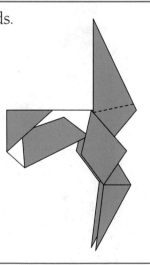

12

Outside reverse fold.

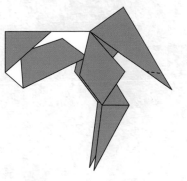

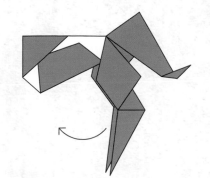

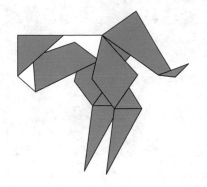

13
Outside reverse fold tip of "tail."

14
Pull "leg" forward and squash fold it into place.

15
Completed part 2 (rear) of bucking bronco.

ber arrows,

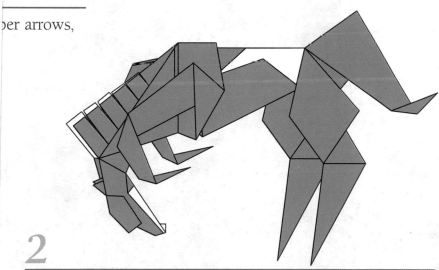

2
Completed Bucking Bronco.

Rodeo Cowboy

Part 1

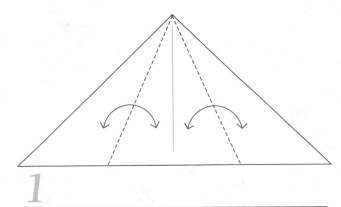

1 Start with a square sheet cut diagonally; valley folds to crease, then unfold.

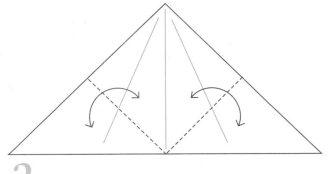

2 Valley folds again to crease, then unfold.

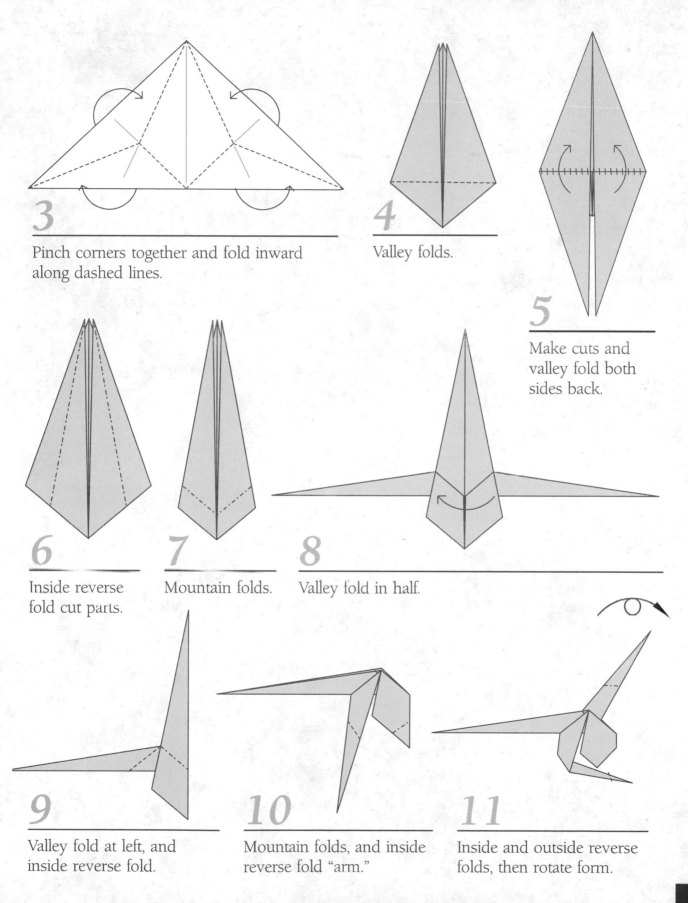

3

Pinch corners together and fold inward along dashed lines.

4

Valley folds.

5

Make cuts and valley fold both sides back.

6

Inside reverse fold cut parts.

7

Mountain folds.

8

Valley fold in half.

9

Valley fold at left, and inside reverse fold.

10

Mountain folds, and inside reverse fold "arm."

11

Inside and outside reverse folds, then rotate form.

Rodeo Cowboy

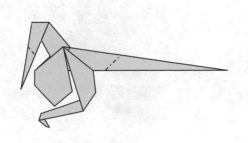

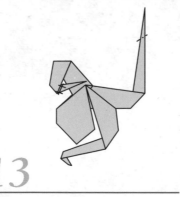

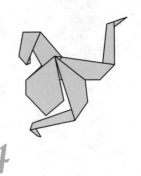

12

Mountain then inside reverse fold.

13

Cut, and inside reverse fold.

14

Completed part 1 of rodeo cowboy.

Part 2

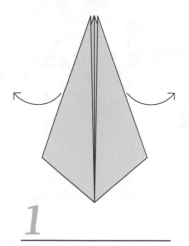

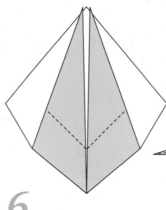

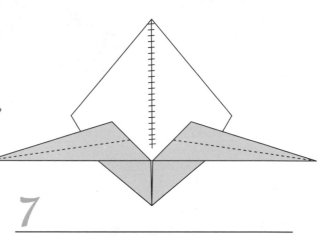

1

To start, repeat part 1 steps **1** through **5**, then valley fold cuts apart as shown.

6

Valley folds.

7

Make cuts and valley folds.

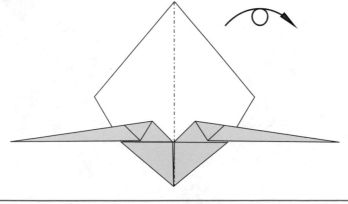

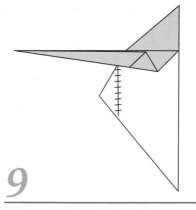

8

Mountain fold in half, and rotate form.

9

Make cuts as shown.

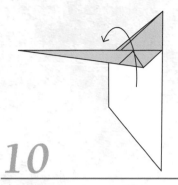
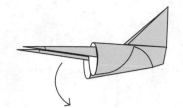
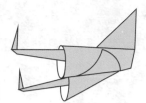

10
Wrap flaps into tubular shape "pant legs," then glue.

11
Inside reverse folds, then pull "leg" as indicated.

12
Completed part 2 of rodeo cowboy.

To Attach

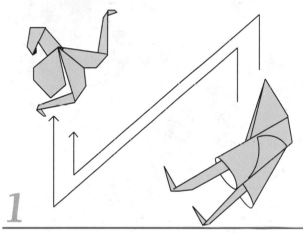

1
Join both parts together.

2
Completed cowboy, ready for hat.

Part 3 (cowboy hat)

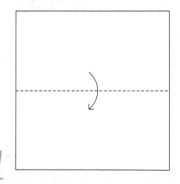
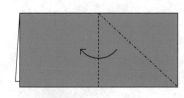
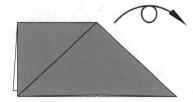

1
Start with small (2½ in.) square sheet; valley fold.

2
Squash fold.

3
Turn to other side.

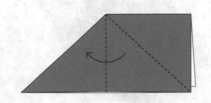

4

Squash fold.

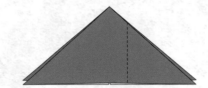

5

Valley fold to crease.

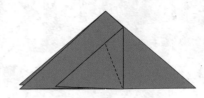

6

Valley fold to crease.

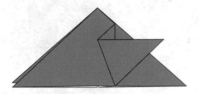

7

Undo folds.

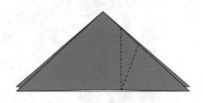

8

Pleat fold.

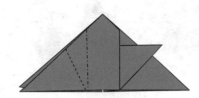

9

Repeat steps **5** to **8** on opposite end.

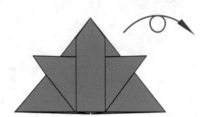

10

Turn to other side.

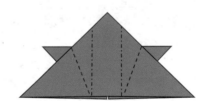

11

Repeat same steps, **5** to **8**, on each end this side.

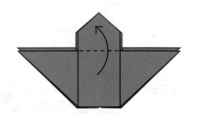

12

Valley fold, both sides.

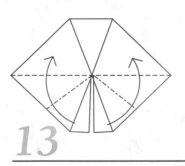

13

Pleat fold sides, front and back, squashing underfolds.

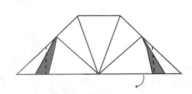

14

Unfold, then valley, bringing corners together, and glue

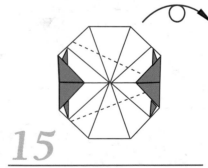

15

Valley folds to add shape to "brim." Rotate.

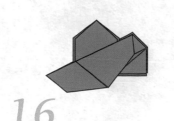
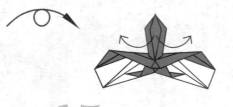
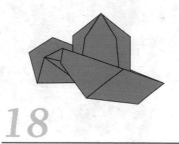

16
View of shaped "hat."
Rotate to front.

17
Open out, loosen, folds as shown.

18
Completed cowboy hat.

To Assemble

1
Place hat on cowboy, place cowboy on bronco's back.

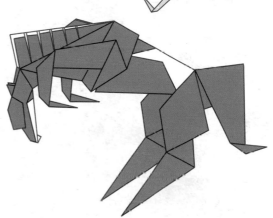

2
Completed Rodeo Cowboy on Bucking Bronco.

Index

W9-CPE-349

Contents

Gentle 1

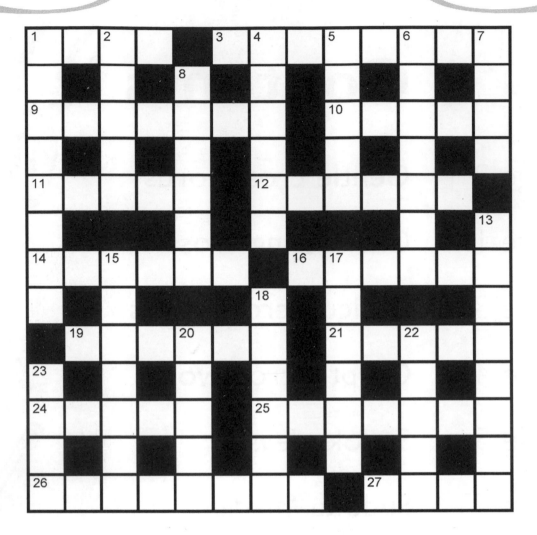

Across

1 Equine creature (4)
3 Wizard (8)
9 Ginger-haired individual (3-4)
10 Flat boats (5)
11 Perfect (5)
12 Rectangular (6)
14 Practical (6)
16 Single-room accommodation (6)
19 False (6)
21 Inuk dwelling (5)
24 Female living quarters (5)
25 Japanese art of paper folding (7)
26 Alone (8)
27 Eccentric (4)

Down

1 Almond-based paste (8)
2 Large spoon (5)
4 Likely, in gambling parlance (4-2)
5 Christmas song (5)
6 Pays back (7)
7 Hurry (4)
8 Style of red wine (6)
13 Cruel act (8)
15 Finger-like plant part (7)
17 Potion (6)
18 Consume (6)
20 Send payment (5)
22 Camel-like South American animal (5)
23 Units of electrical resistance (4)

Gentle 2

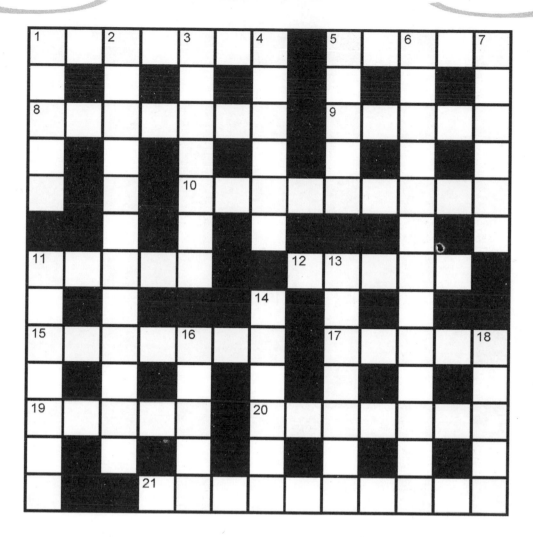

Across

1 Trip, expedition (7)
5 Truths (5)
8 Short work of fiction (7)
9 Abundant (5)
10 Mentally uncomfortable, troubled (3,2,4)
11 Hirsute (5)
12 Employing, exploiting (5)
15 Wander aimlessly (7)
17 Gag involuntarily (5)
19 Trip, empty (5)
20 High class drinking establishment (4,3)
21 Derogatory term for office workers (10)

Down

1 Military government (5)
2 Stuffy, airless (12)
3 Cancel, neutralize (7)
4 Annual (6)
5 Banquet (5)
6 Most prestigious place to eat on a ship (8,5)
7 Scandinavian country (6)
11 German city through which the Elbe runs (7)
13 Psychiatrists, makes smaller (7)
14 Become older (4,2)
16 Avoid (5)
18 Throws hard (5)

Gentle 3

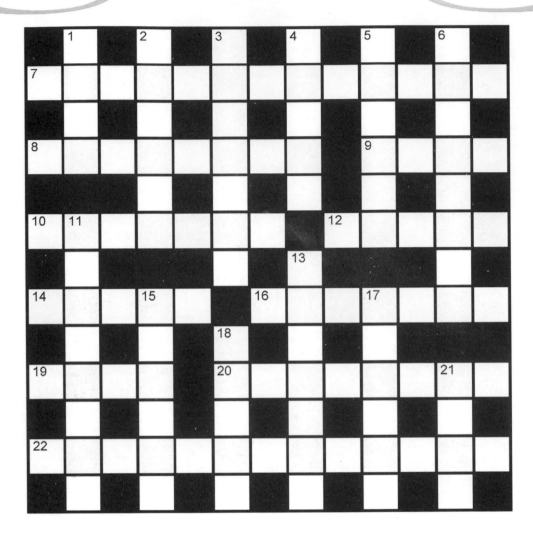

Across

7 Well-known personality (9,4)
8 Drink (8)
9 Annoy (4)
10 Blood-sucking creature (7)
12 Mark ___, author of "Tom Sawyer" (5)
14 Country, territory (5)
16 Riding waves, accessing the Internet (7)
19 Brother of Kane in the Bible (4)
20 Survived longer (8)
22 Retail worker (4-9)

Down

1 White bird (4)
2 Not awake (6)
3 Performance playhouse (7)
4 Change (5)
5 Lloyd-Webber, composer (6)
6 Type of paint (8)
11 German motorway (8)
13 European country with the capital city of Vienna (7)
15 Flowers for which Holland is famous (6)
17 Collapses (6)
18 Rodent, computer accessory (5)
21 Mount___, Sicilian volcano (4)

Gentle 4

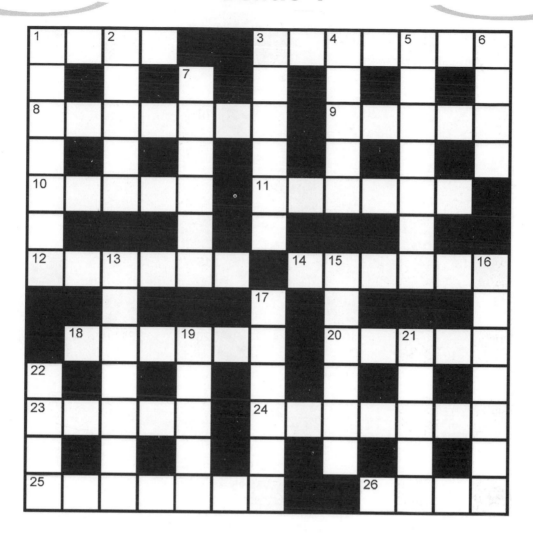

Across

1 Tree, yearn (4)
3 Parcel (7)
8 Commence a boat journey (3,4)
9 Bird of prey (5)
10 Hoarder of money (5)
11 Vacation area (6)
12 American gambling state (6)
14 Small sea fishes (6)
18 Disease caused by a lack of vitamin C (6)
20 Large serving spoon (5)
23 Multi-layered edible bulb (5)
24 Remains, hangs on (7)
25 Clothed (7)
26 Norse god (4)

Down

1 Deliverer of mail (7)
2 Writings, observes (5)
3 Hugely inadequate (6)
4 Strategic board game (5)
5 North African country (7)
6 Garden of the Creation (4)
7 Intense dislike (6)
13 Immunity drug (7)
15 European nation that includes the cities of
   Warsaw and Krakow (6)
16 Cowboy hat (7)
17 Rode a bike (6)
19 Steps of a ladder (5)
21 Feeling of terror (5)
22 Small forest (4)

Gentle 5

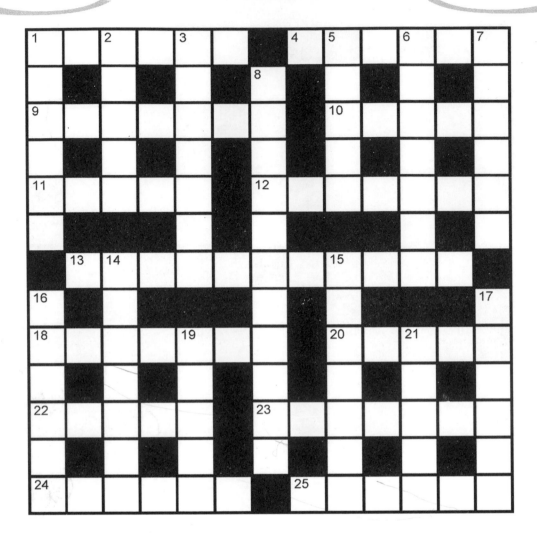

Across

1 What is used to make balloons airborne (3-3)
4 Felt for, looked into (6)
9 North western American city, famous for Nirvana and the grunge music scene (7)
10 Comes close to (5)
11 Language of ancient Rome (5)
12 Someone who breathes out (7)
13 Vessels for fermented grape juice (4,7)
18 Illness (7)
20 Marsupial pocket (5)
22 Executed Italian philosopher, English heavyweight boxer (5)
23 Eight-limbed sea creature (7)
24 Bones connecting the feet to the legs (6)
25 Czech city (6)

Down

1 Minor problem (6)
2 Browned bread, raise drinks to celebrate (5)
3 Extreme (7)
5 Cattle farm (5)
6 Reading system for the blind (7)
7 Want, wish for (6)
8 Lady kidnapped by Paris in Greek mythology (5,2,4)
14 Poor fortune (3,4)
15 Someone who gives advice on likely winners at the racetrack (7)
16 Surname of Rocky in the hit films (6)
17 Pure, celibate (6)
19 Wear away (5)
21 Remove implements used to hold the washing on the line (5)

Gentle 6

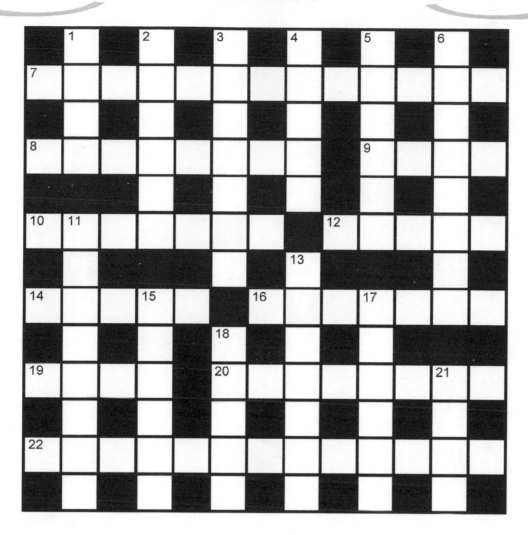

Across

7 Any number from 10 to 99 (6,7)
8 French loaf (8)
9 Shoot a weapon, terminate employment (4)
10 Venetian canal boat (7)
12 Breathe audibly while asleep (5)
14 Japanese fencing art using bamboo swords (5)
16 Nazi secret police (7)
19 Mark left on the skin by an injury (4)
20 Egyptian tombs with four triangular sides (8)
22 According to the proverb, this saves nine (1,6,2,4)

Down

1 Popular fizzy drink (4)
2 Ludicrous (6)
3 Lizard or alligator, for example (7)
4 Poisonous snake (5)
5 Seabird resembling a penguin (6)
6 A product of crying (4-4)
11 Cloudy (8)
13 American city made famous by its car production (7)
15 Knock a train from the track (6)
17 Round red fruit. Or is it a vegetable? (6)
18 The final frontier, according to Captain Kirk (5)
21 Hemispherical roof (4)

Gentle 7

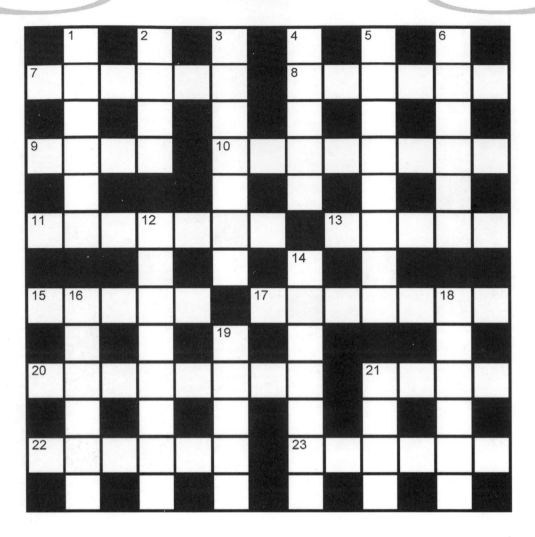

Across

7 Glass or plastic drink container (6)
8 Young cow (6)
9 Cut violently, like a butcher (4)
10 Landlocked South American republic (8)
11 Green gemstone (7)
13 Drink made from fermented apples (5)
15 Treasure container! (5)
17 Set free (7)
20 Crimson (5-3)
21 Cure (4)
22 Population count (6)
23 Beginner (6)

Down

1 Fictional city where Batman lives (6)
2 Dance move (4)
3 Long-distance correspondents (3,4)
4 The land by the sea (5)
5 Extra large—fit for royalty! (4-4)
6 Ten-year period (6)
12 Answer (8)
14 Necklace adornment (7)
16 Protective headwear (6)
18 In short supply (6)
19 A loaf of bread has one, as does planet Earth (5)
21 Bee house (4)

Gentle 8

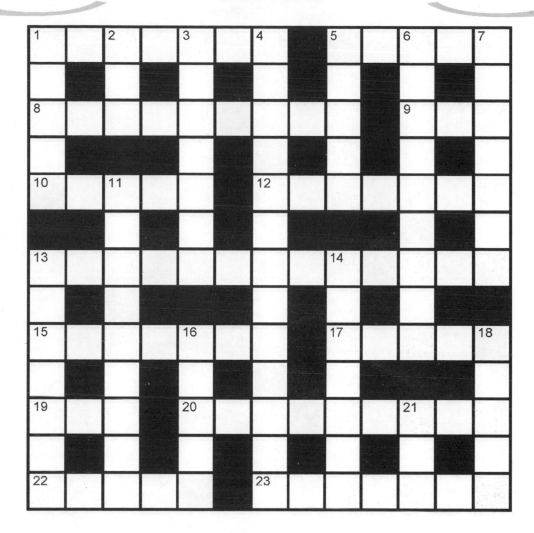

Across

1 Heirs to the throne (7)
5 Wrist clock (5)
8 Interrupted (9)
9 ___ away means to recede (3)
10 Sri ___, name for the country formerly known as Ceylon (5)
12 Overseas postal service (3,4)
13 The force surrounding a moving charged particle (8,5)
15 Small, simple house in the country (7)
17 Raw fish, as eaten in Japan (5)
19 ___ constrictor, large snake (3)
20 Nurserymen (9)
22 Foe (5)
23 Electrical power (7)

Down

1 Accelerator on a bicycle! (5)
2 ___ and buts are excuses (3)
3 Bravery (7)
4 Sailors on a U-boat (9,4)
5 Less narrow (5)
6 Adolescents (9)
7 Limped (7)
11 Bad dream (9)
13 Gruesome (7)
14 Quickest (7)
16 Annoyed (5)
18 Important question (5)
21 Extended time period (3)

Gentle 9

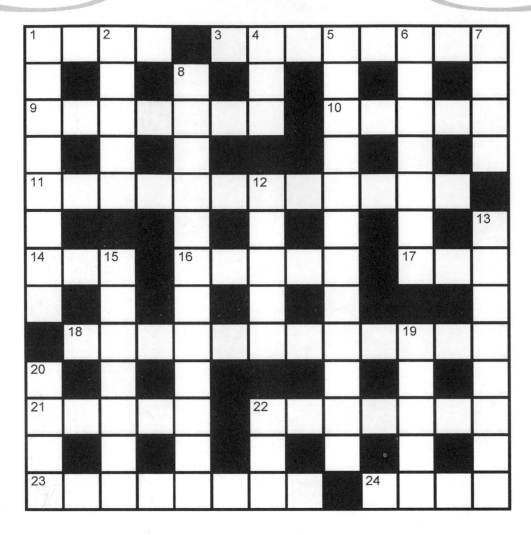

Across

1 Plants used to brew beer (4)
3 Break (8)
9 Pamphlet (7)
10 Suggest (5)
11 A low blow would strike here (5,3,4)
14 A fisherman would use one (3)
16 Toxic substance found in snake poison (5)
17 Sauce added to Chinese food (3)
18 Misunderstanding (7,5)
21 Spanish wine (5)
22 Family resort in Florida (7)
23 High singing voice, as used by
   The Bee Gees (8)
24 Vessel that carries blood back to the heart (4)

Down

1 Dangerously determined (4-4)
2 Jewel found inside an oyster (5)
4 Groove (3)
5 Structure used for mountaineering practice (8,4)
6 Opens out (7)
7 Deserve (4)
8 Traditional belief or maxim (3,5,4)
12 Flexible joint (5)
13 The call used to signal the start of a game
   of bingo (4,4)
15 Upheaval (7)
19 Golfers hit balls on the driving ___ (5)
20 Steffi ___, legendary tennis player (4)
22 Opposite of in (3)

Gentle 10

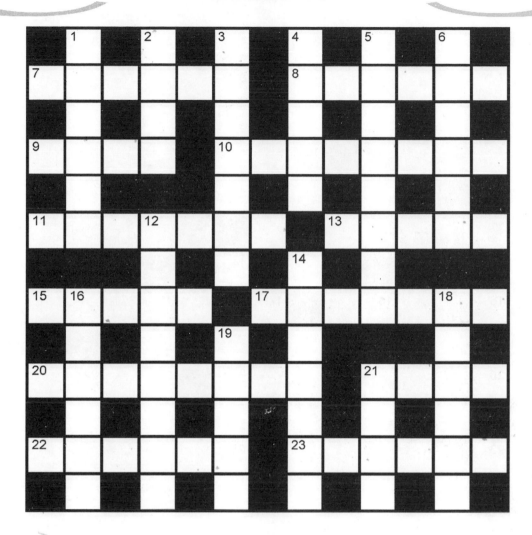

Across

7 Official seal (6)
8 Country in Scandinavia (6)
9 Amongst (4)
10 Body of water in Scotland, famous for its monster! (4,4)
11 Went in (7)
13 Tale (5)
15 Mode of public transport (5)
17 Without moisture (4-3)
20 Canine assistant used by the blind (5,3)
21 Golfing bat (4)
22 Calm (6)
23 Cure (6)

Down

1 Hired killer (3,3)
2 ___ Blyton, author of books for children (4)
3 Ben ___, actor, star of "Meet the Parents" and "Dodgeball" (7)
4 Food eaten between meals (5)
5 Brown-haired (8)
6 Julius ___, once Emperor of Rome (6)
12 "The ___", classic 1981 horror movie (4,4)
14 Fake (7)
16 Wakes up (6)
18 Three-minute segments of a boxing match (6)
19 Stranger (5)
21 Collection of tents (4)

Gentle 11

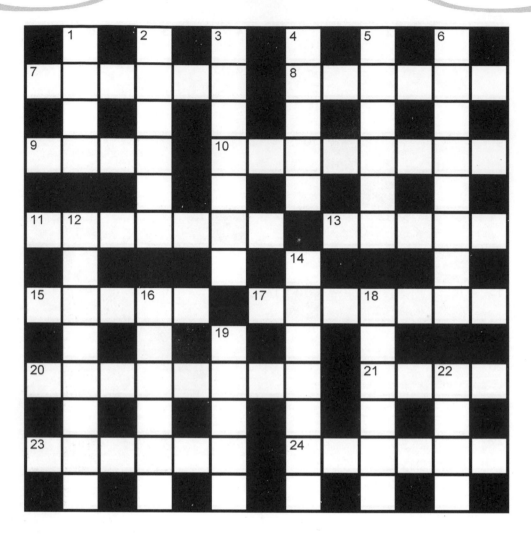

Across

7 Author (6)
8 Mythical creature, as slain by St George (6)
9 Casino game (4)
10 Small onions (8)
11 Plate-shaped disk thrown for enjoyment (7)
13 Short (5)
15 Hue about the not taxed economy (5)
17 Makes more difficult (7)
20 Move people, often in an emergency (8)
21 European mountain range (4)
23 Fisherman (6)
24 Sign up (6)

Down

1 Not false (4)
2 Backless chairs (6)
3 Elvis ___, singer, also known as The King (7)
4 Thoughts (5)
5 Mariner (6)
6 Shoes, for example (8)
12 Salient (8)
14 There were three at the birth of Jesus, according to The Bible (4,3)
16 Wicked laugh (6)
18 Lethal (6)
19 African country, venue of "The Rumble in the Jungle" (5)
22 Opposite of pull (4)

Gentle 12

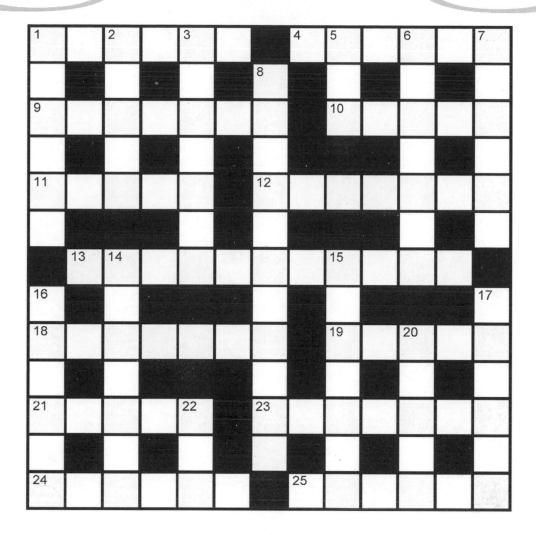

Across

1 Soak up (6)
4 Dead body (6)
9 Waterfall on the border of Canada and USA (7)
10 Panache (5)
11 Own up (5)
12 Texan city—home to NASA (7)
13 Disney movie about a lost fish (7,4)
18 The Bible contains four, written by Matthew, Mark, Luke, and John (7)
19 Stand out (5)
21 Not sleeping (5)
23 Fashionable (2,5)
24 Bank clerk (6)
25 Contaminate (6)

Down

1 Once a year (6)
2 Collective term for bees (5)
3 Cooked in an oven (7)
5 Opposite of on (3)
6 Ghost (7)
7 Wayward (6)
8 Swimming costume (7,4)
14 Load a program onto the hard drive of a computer (7)
15 Leslie ___, star of the "Naked Gun" movies (7)
16 Shocked (6)
17 Customer (6)
20 Bonnie's partner in crime (5)
22 This organ allows us to see (3)

Gentle 13

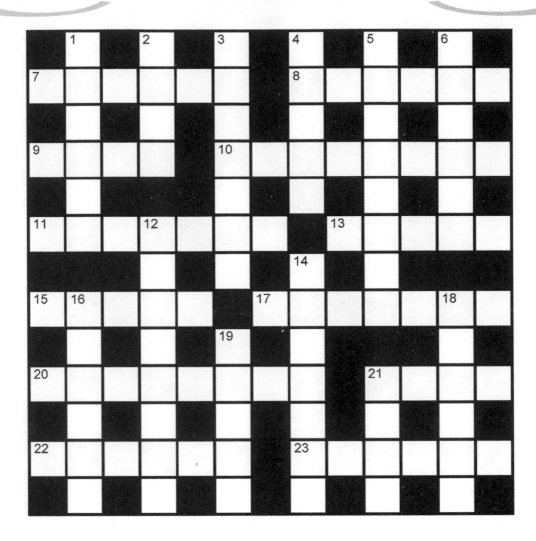

Across

7 This is what makes balloons rise (3-3)
8 Company of entertainers (6)
9 White drink obtained from cows (4)
10 Cartoon cat (8)
11 Set fire to (7)
13 Michael ___, actor, star of "The Cider House Rules" (5)
15 ___ Kravitz, singer of "Are You Gonna Go My Way" (5)
17 Uncontrolled fire (7)
20 This would be a bad golf score (5,3)
21 Whirlpool (4)
22 Device such as a radiator, used to warm a room (6)
23 Afloat and not going anywhere in particular (6)

Down

1 Manufacturer of the 747 aircraft (6)
2 Communal area (4)
3 Pulled unwillingly (7)
4 Neck warmer (5)
5 Supply with water (8)
6 Capital city of the Republic of Ireland (6)
12 Introduce something new (8)
14 In the dock (2,5)
16 Logo (6)
18 Fall asleep, often without meaning to (3,3)
19 Left over, as in a bowling game (5)
21 Makes mistakes (4)

Gentle 14

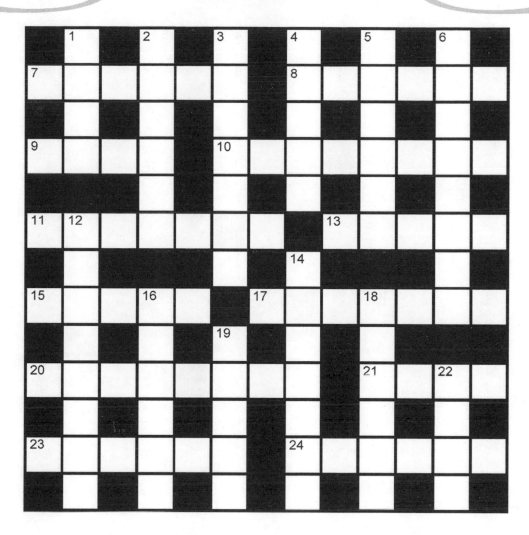

Across

7 Which movie starred Dudley Moore as a drunk millionaire? (6)

8 Who is known as the Caped Crusader? (6)

9 What sort of animal is Bambi? (4)

10 Robert Palmer performed the song "___ To Love" (8)

11 A myopic is short-___ (7)

13 One of the 150 lyrical poems in the Old Testament is known as a ___ (5)

15 White (5)

17 James Bond was created by Ian ___ (7)

20 An immensely skilled rendition can be called a ___ performance (8)

21 Which heavy flightless bird is now extinct? (4)

23 Beautiful view (6)

24 What was an ancient Greek seer known as? (6)

Down

1 Not charged for (4)

2 What is a Christian worship building called? (6)

3 Produced (7)

4 Home (5)

5 ___ and shares are traded on Wall Street (6)

6 Strategy, especially in sport (4,4)

12 Sharon Stone starred in "Basic ___" (8)

14 What common ingredient do wine, beer, and tequila share? (7)

16 Make longer (6)

18 Which futuristic movie starred Mel Gibson? (3,3)

19 Flashlight (5)

22 Toy often played with by girls (4)

Gentle 15

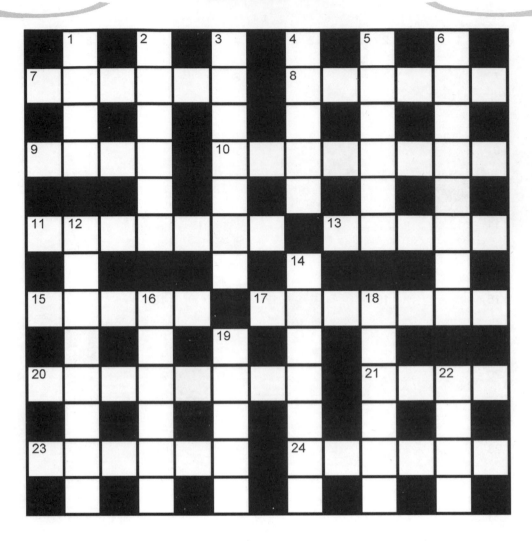

Across

7 Sad in French (6)
8 Contraption or gadget that is useful for a particular job (6)
9 This has to be scratched! (4)
10 Mull over (8)
11 Disease of the central nervous system, also known as lockjaw (7)
13 Lending money at very high interest (5)
15 Hat worn by a bishop (5)
17 Woodworking tool (7)
20 Intrude, especially when referring to private land (8)
21 Agreement (4)
23 Plays the guitar (6)
24 Triangular sail (6)

Down

1 Faster than a walk, slower than a run (4)
2 Breathing disorder (6)
3 Containing iron (7)
4 Low-lying land that is flooded regularly (5)
5 Handsome man of Greek mythology (6)
6 Penitentiary cellblock where inmates await capital punishment (5,3)
12 Move to another country (8)
14 Grapple (7)
16 Save from danger (6)
18 Second in charge (6)
19 Type of lightweight wood (5)
22 Cook (4)

Challenging 1

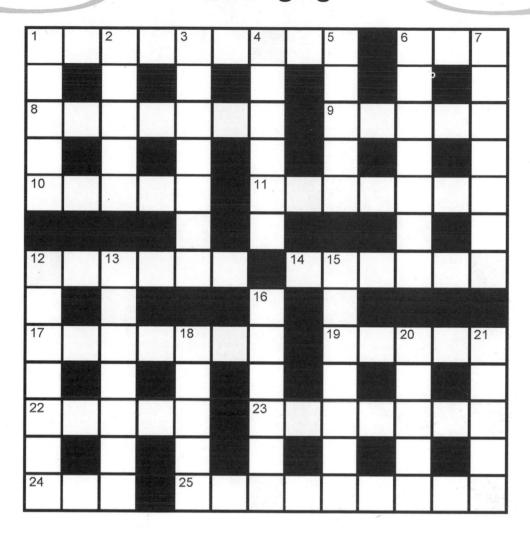

Across

1 Australian water-bird (5,4)
6 Pricing label (3)
8 Ancient Greek city (7)
9 Buddhist theory of fate (5)
10 Wheat used for making pasta (5)
11 Card game using only three queens (3,4)
12 Ringed planet (6)
14 Myth (6)
17 Mozart's middle name (7)
19 Hideous beasts, often giants (5)
22 Female garment (5)
23 Easy-going (7)
24 Falsehood (3)
25 Bedtime songs (9)

Down

1 Mixture (5)
2 Detest (5)
3 Region disputed by India and Pakistan (7)
4 Worldly knowledge (6)
5 Unclothed (5)
6 Paved area, row of houses (7)
7 Your father's father (7)
12 Outrage, disgraceful event (7)
13 High-flying circus act (7)
15 Sexy literature (7)
16 Country, formerly part of Palestine (6)
18 Tripod used by artists (5)
20 Jewish spiritual leader (5)
21 Looks for (5)

Challenging 2

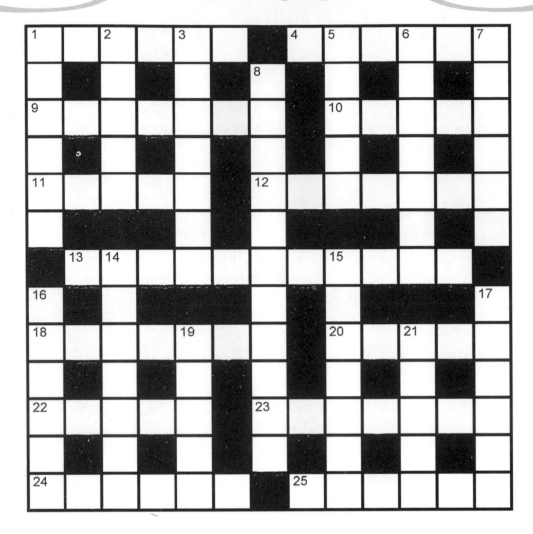

Across

1 Shoulder gun with a long barrel (6)
4 Examination of bodily tissue (6)
9 Highest point of a church building (7)
10 Without these, I could not compile this puzzle (5)
11 Thespian, performer (5)
12 Chinese river (7)
13 West African country with the capital city of Freetown (6,5)
18 Driving force (7)
20 Small snake (5)
22 Reefed island (5)
23 Brave (7)
24 Direction to leave the stage (6)
25 Break free (6)

Down

1 Grape variety producing sweet wine (6)
2 Mixture of snow and rain (5)
3 Male monarch to an empire (7)
5 Hale ___, US Open winning golfer (5)
6 Morally strict individual (7)
7 Aides who always agree with their boss (3,3)
8 December 31 (3,5,3)
14 Burst inward (7)
15 Makes possible (7)
16 Climax (6)
17 Contort, squirm (6)
19 Hooked claw (5)
21 Performance genre (5)

Challenging 3

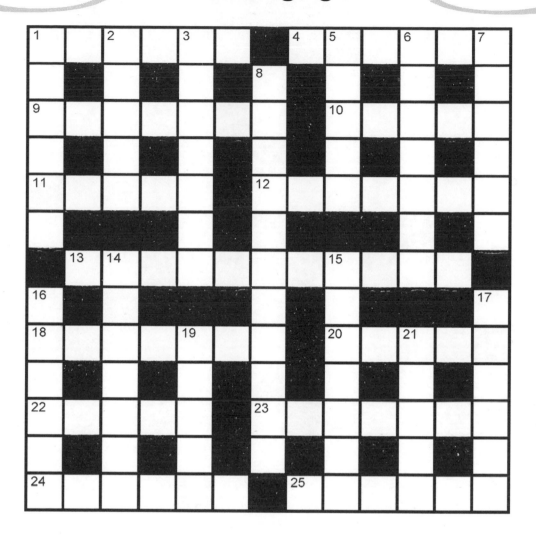

Across

1 Break free (6)
4 Cutter of men's hair (6)
9 Authorisation (7)
10 "The ___", epic poem about Troy (5)
11 Latin-American dance (5)
12 Flier (7)
13 Capital of Argentina (6,5)
18 Loss of memory (7)
20 Ski slope (5)
22 Shipment of goods (5)
23 Army helicopter (7)
24 Ancient Greek city, home of Oedipus (6)
25 Structural supports (6)

Down

1 Hostility (6)
2 Body of accepted rules (5)
3 Vietnam movie starring Charlie Sheen (7)
5 Excuse (5)
6 Easily broken (7)
7 Jockeys (6)
8 Period of European history around the 15th century (11)
14 Frighten (7)
15 Currently published (2,5)
16 Wealthy or overpaid person (3,3)
17 Harmless lizards (6)
19 Hard centre of a fruit (5)
21 Venue for the 1988 Olympic Games (5)

Challenging 4

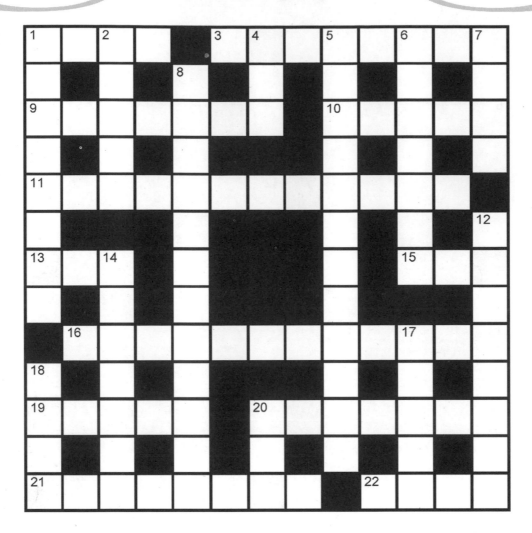

Across

1 Milkless style of chocolate (4)
3 Step down (8)
9 Lawlessness (7)
10 Trunk of the body (5)
11 Geographical area from Mexico to Argentina (5,7)
13 Hard-shelled seed (3)
15 Open water container, often used for bathing (3)
16 Short-handed (12)
19 Shoulder gesture indicating indifference (5)
20 Make ready (7)
21 Supplying a remedy (8)
22 What is owed (4)

Down

1 Final acceptable time (8)
2 Respond (5)
4 Indented shoreline (3)
5 Questioned (12)
6 Peach-like fruit (7)
7 Electronic point of sale (4)
8 Recognized (12)
12 Faithful (8)
14 Outburst of temper (7)
17 Picture housing (5)
18 Emperor (4)
20 Small green vegetable (3)

Challenging 5

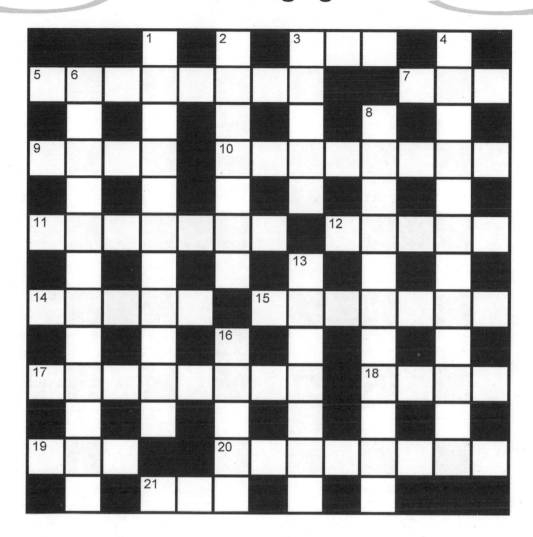

Across
3 Indian tourist resort (3)
5 Military plan (8)
7 Assist (3)
9 Walkway (4)
10 Barging and pushing (8)
11 Champagne and peach cocktail (7)
12 Huge expanse of water (5)
14 Move to music (5)
15 Look for nothing in particular (7)
17 Reason, instil belief (8)
18 Hind (4)
19 Basque separatist group (3)
20 Sealed (8)
21 Unwell (3)

Down
1 Major religion of Italy (11)
2 Capital city of China (7)
3 Romany (5)
4 System of communication where a person uses hands to speak (4,8)
6 They sell vacations (6,6)
8 Platform for the sale of illegal goods (5,6)
13 Music machine (7)
16 Capital city of Afghanistan (5)

Challenging 6

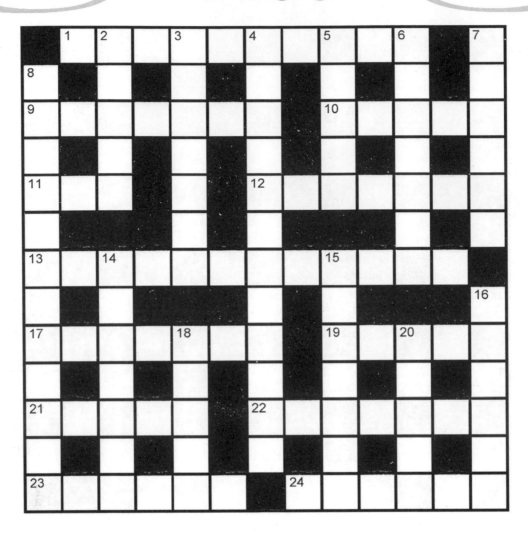

Across

1 Well-spoken (10)
9 Green gemstone (7)
10 Highbrow musical style (5)
11 Tell falsehoods (3)
12 Crowned head of state (7)
13 Bath robe (8,4)
17 Peculiar (7)
19 Ulan ___, capital city of Mongolia (5)
21 Giant, moon of Saturn (5)
22 Gravestone inscription (7)
23 Avoided, stooped (6)
24 Wine container (6)

Down

2 Pass through, usually with a rope (5)
3 Slanted letters (7)
4 Not depleted (12)
5 Decorate, make attractive (5)
6 Arch of forehead hair (7)
7 Indifference (6)
8 Schooled to a high level (4-8)
14 Inconsistent (7)
15 Biblical archangel (7)
16 Parentless child (6)
18 Imperial unit of weight (5)
20 Inflection, pluck a stringed instrument (5)

Challenging 7

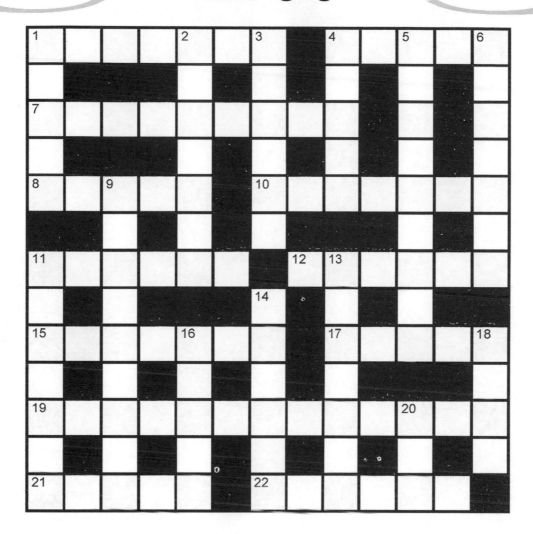

Across
1 Prominent aspect, magazine article (7)
4 Harmonious sounds or singing (5)
7 Unfaithful spouse (9)
8 City in Vietnam (5)
10 Payment to ex-worker (7)
11 Pagan priests (6)
12 Lover of Romeo (6)
15 One of three babies born at the same time (7)
17 Investment return (5)
19 Teachers (13)
21 Soft drinks (5)
22 Capital of the Bahamas (6)

Down
1 Cocky, burst of light (5)
2 Not tested (7)
3 Frozen moon of Jupiter (6)
4 Idiot (5)
5 Clean thoroughly, make infertile (9)
6 Display case, collection of prominent government ministers (7)
9 Fed, nurtured (9)
11 Hates (7)
13 Novel by James Joyce (7)
14 Reproductive part of a plant (6)
16 Observes, glances (5)
18 Memory device for computers (4)
20 Geological time period (3)

Challenging 8

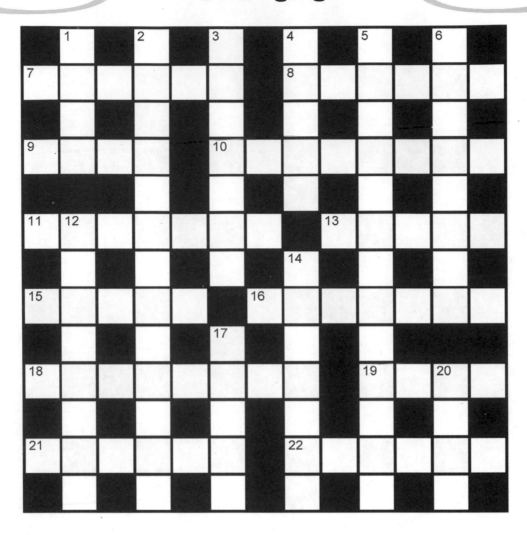

Across

7 Expel from the law profession (6)
8 Impact hole, as found on the moon (6)
9 Fruit used to make perry (4)
10 Strainer (8)
11 False courage (7)
13 Bring together (5)
15 Smudge (5)
16 Capital of Venezuela (7)
18 Conjurer (8)
19 Escape, often of water from a pipe (4)
21 Verse of a poem (6)
22 Looked for (6)

Down

1 Rent (4)
2 Shortened versions (13)
3 Go before (7)
4 Burn with water (5)
5 Film starring Burt Reynolds about a car race across America (10,3)
6 Reduction or loss of mental faculty (8)
12 Leftovers (8)
14 Rein (7)
17 Crucial (5)
20 Arthur ___, first black man to win Wimbledon (4)

Challenging 9

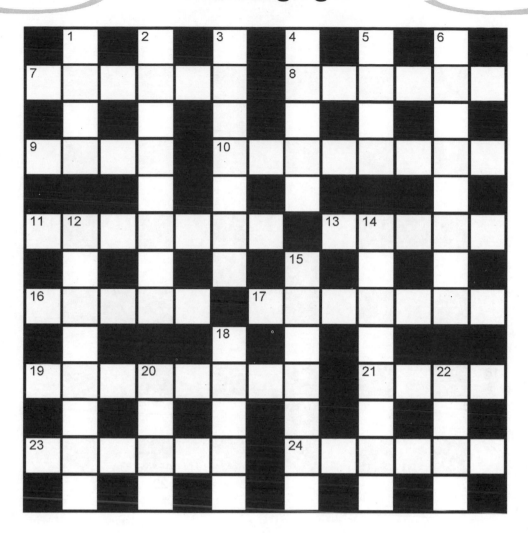

Across

7 Agree (6)

8 Loans out (6)

9 Cheap, cut (4)

10 Drug in tobacco (8)

11 Emptied, devoid of energy (7)

13 Not given food (5)

16 Entertain (5)

17 Digits of the hand (7)

19 Unmarried man (8)

21 Used to not cause offense (4)

23 Walked with purpose (6)

24 Almost (6)

Down

1 Planetary satellite (4)

2 Non-believers, UK spelling (8)

3 Suntanned (7)

4 Bravery, to remove feathers (5)

5 Agreement (4)

6 Arctic animal used by Santa Claus (8)

12 Defensive walls, especially around castles (8)

14 Alcoholic bedtime drink (8)

15 Lively, energetic (7)

18 Stuck down (5)

20 Foot of a horse (4)

22 Young cow (4)

Challenging 10

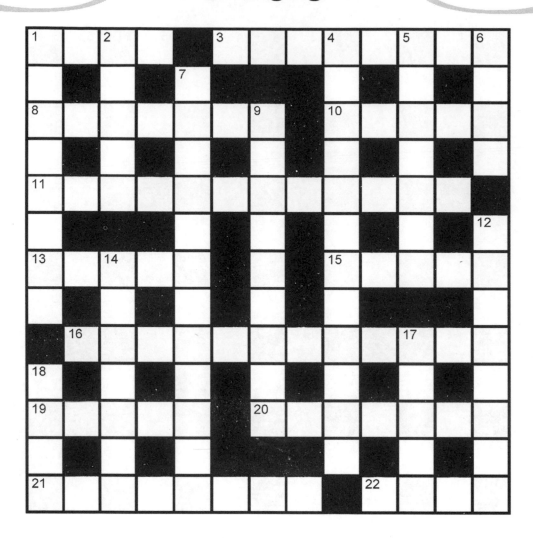

Across

1 Manage (4)
3 Unable to leave (8)
8 Cigarette buyers (7)
10 Work tables (5)
11 The 24 hours with the shortest night of the year (9,3)
13 Tasting like almonds, for example (5)
15 Large artery (5)
16 Prerequisites (12)
19 Joint connecting the foot to the leg (5)
20 Weapon used by archers in medieval times (7)
21 Supporting act (4-4)
22 Tax, charge (4)

Down

1 Hinged window frame (8)
2 Pleased with oneself (5)
4 Article of clothing worn beneath the outer clothing (12)
5 Hopelessness (7)
6 Twilight (4)
7 Pageant winners (6,6)
9 Partially countrified (9)
12 Path or road above the water level (8)
14 Hiked a considerable distance (7)
17 Chivalrous (5)
18 Conflicts (4)

Challenging 11

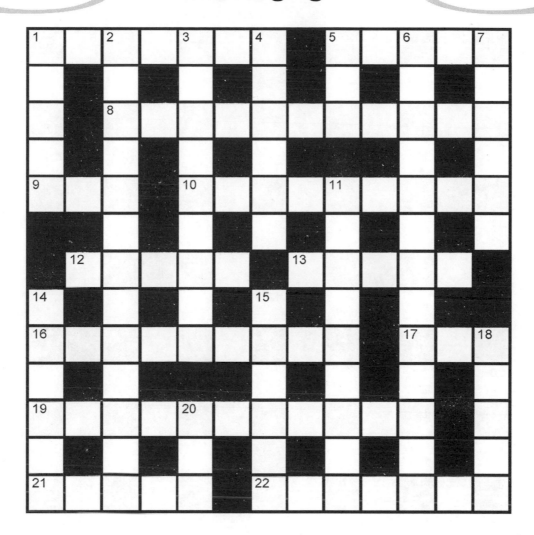

Across

1 Knight of the Round Table (7)
5 African tribe (5)
8 Accusations (11)
9 Species of tree, cigarette by-product (3)
10 Arthritic (9)
12 Natural stream (5)
13 Dog, pester (5)
16 Principal navy vessels (9)
17 Wrongful act (3)
19 Cost, as quoted by the vendor (6,5)
21 Old fashioned (5)
22 Sang with one other person (7)

Down

1 Italian port city (5)
2 Animal-hide coat (7,6)
3 Incredibly amusing (9)
4 Knife used as a weapon (6)
5 Floor covering (3)
6 Brief (5,3,5)
7 Arthropod (6)
11 Strong liquor, usually distilled illegally (9)
14 Scared (6)
15 Torn with force (6)
18 Wanderer (5)
20 Signal to the affirmative using the head (3)

Challenging 12

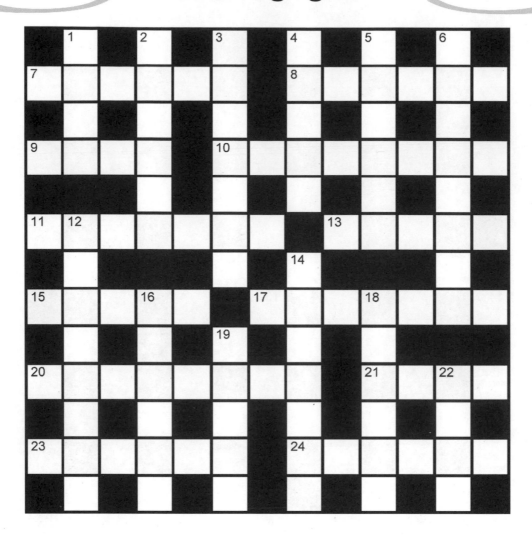

Across

7 Agatha Christie's Belgian detective (6)
8 Capital city of Cuba (6)
9 Spell of cold weather (4)
10 Without end (8)
11 A less busy time (3-4)
13 Precious stone (5)
15 Vital organ protected by the skull (5)
17 Closest planet to the Sun (7)
20 Follower (8)
21 Leaf of a book (4)
23 Imbecile (6)
24 Man who betrayed Julius Caesar (6)

Down

1 Midday (4)
2 Cover gifts, put on lots of clothes (4,2)
3 Morally correct (7)
4 Cooks (5)
5 Retaliate, gain perceived justice (6)
6 Clothing from wool yarn (8)
12 Fitters of horseshoes (8)
14 Echoes (7)
16 Encourage, egg on (6)
18 Isle in the Mediterranean (6)
19 Backbone (5)
22 Adhesive (4)

Challenging 13

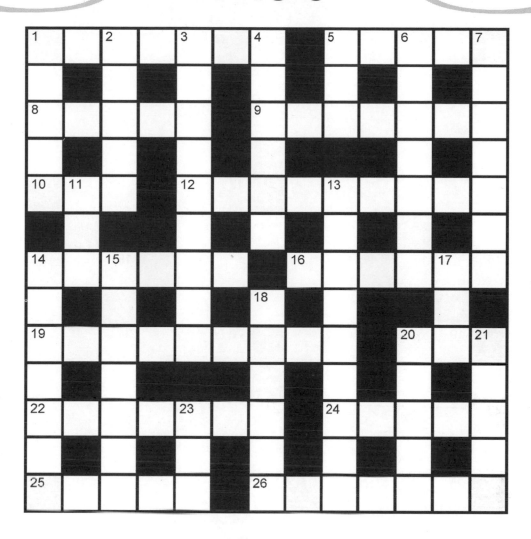

Across

1. Phrase used by bank robbers (5,2)
5. Burn, blister (5)
8. Bigger than medium (5)
9. English city, American president (7)
10. Organ of sight (3)
12. Cuts, slices (9)
14. Voluntary, when referring to work (6)
16. Fatal (6)
19. Tree-mounted animal shelter (9)
20. Hail for a ride (3)
22. On-line information page (7)
24. Charges, usually for use of a road (5)
25. Ambition (5)
26. Lures away (7)

Down

1. Split into two (5)
2. Hospital carer (5)
3. Crustacean (9)
4. Decadent home, usually for royalty (6)
5. Male offspring (3)
6. Terminated (7)
7. Family line, American TV show (7)
11. Japanese currency (3)
13. Voted in again (2-7)
14. Upright (7)
15. Fable, moral story (7)
17. Pasture (3)
18. National leaders, straight-edged measuring tools (6)
20. Abdominal pain, more common for babies (5)
21. Exposes, often to the sun (5)
23. "___ What I Am", hit song for Gloria Gaynor (1,2)

Challenging 14

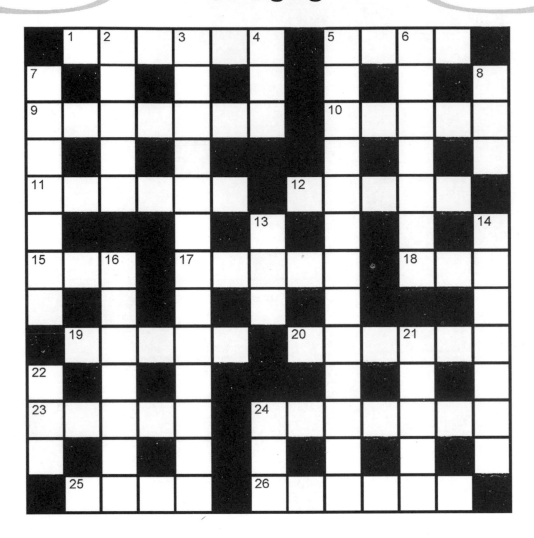

Across

1 Medic (6)
5 Brand of beer drunk by Homer Simpson (4)
9 You might find an ill person on their ___ (4-3)
10 European country containing Rome (5)
11 Concurs (6)
12 Scavenging mammal (5)
15 Throw (3)
17 Film-making award (5)
18 ___ Sayer, singer (3)
19 Keyed musical instrument (5)
20 Phrases, dialects (6)
23 Crown for a woman (5)
24 Chaperones (7)
25 Having no identity (4)
26 Inhabit (6)

Down

2 Happen (5)
3 Cape Town landmark (5,8)
4 Shade loved by bulls! (3)
5 Milk, cheese, butter etc. (5,8)
6 Cloth used to wash the face (7)
7 Attack (7)
8 Cereal grass (3)
13 Perfect serve in tennis (3)
14 Own (7)
16 Great ___ (7)
21 Rowed (5)
22 Eye infection (3)
24 Hearing organ (3)

Challenging 15

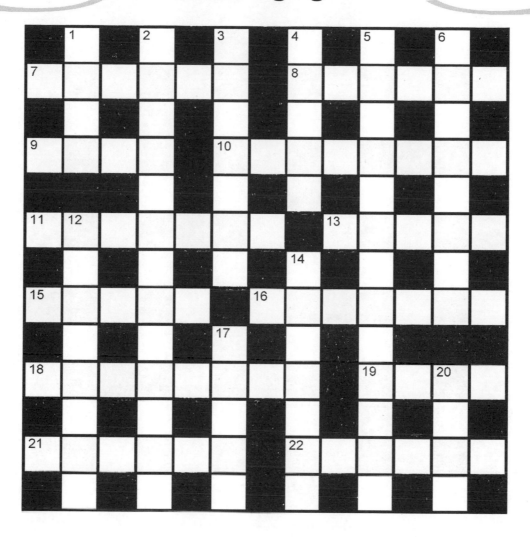

Across

7 London river (6)

8 Despise (6)

9 Sharp point on a cowboy boot (4)

10 Just married (5-3)

11 Problem (7)

13 Tobacco product (5)

15 "___ In Wonderland", book by Lewis Carroll (5)

16 Small falcon (7)

18 Celestial body (8)

19 The longest river in the world (4)

21 Reason (6)

22 ___ Walton, first scientist to split the atom (6)

Down

1 Retail outlet (4)

2 Fire escape, for example (9,4)

3 Tidal wave (7)

4 Circus fool (5)

5 Relaxing genre of music (4,9)

6 Footwear fastener (8)

12 Magic trick (8)

14 Interfered (7)

17 Fictional book (5)

20 Speech impediment (4)

Difficult I

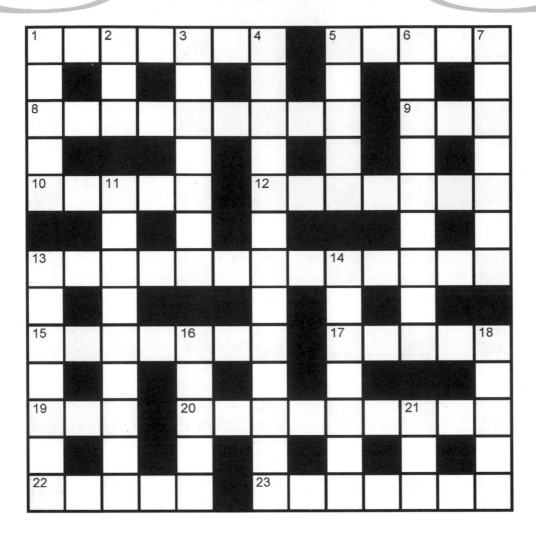

Across

1 Payment into a bank account (7)
5 Bed (5)
8 Every three years (9)
9 Upper limb (3)
10 What the "R" stands for in NRA (5)
12 Light (7)
13 Cantankerous (13)
15 Heavenly act (7)
17 Plant extract (5)
19 Female monk (3)
20 Makes more countrified (9)
22 The bride must walk up this (5)
23 ___ Branson, founder of Virgin (7)

Down

1 Dissuade (5)
2 Measurement of air pressure, in abbreviated form (3)
3 Shaft of light (3-4)
4 Practical method of experimentation (5-3-5)
5 Criminal (5)
6 Plays, but not comedies (9)
7 Candidate (7)
11 Carved models (9)
13 Yerevan is the capital of this landlocked Republic (7)
14 Synthetic fabric (7)
16 Sorceress of "The Odyssey" (5)
18 Meddled, snouted (5)
21 Belgian town and motor-racing track (3)

Difficult 2

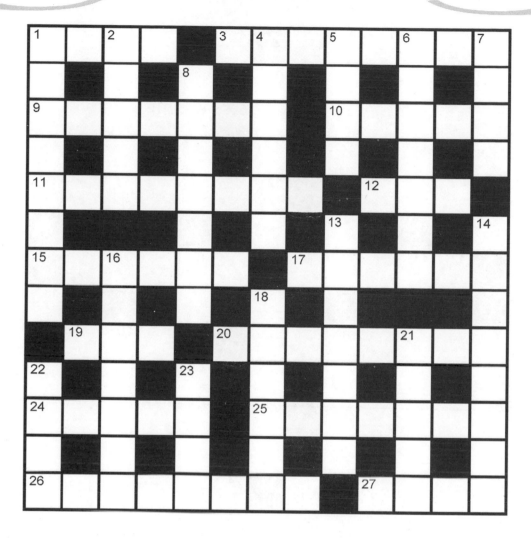

Across

1 Ferment (4)
3 Jail occupant (8)
9 Decadent (7)
10 Brazilian dance (5)
11 Broken hair (5,3)
12 Affectionate name for Abraham Lincoln (3)
15 Island off northern Scotland (6)
17 On fire (6)
19 Pig house (3)
20 Grip (8)
24 Respectful address used in colonial India (5)
25 Unsure (7)
26 Reduced (8)
27 Religious song (4)

Down

1 Fiction and non-fiction retail outlet (8)
2 Well matched (5)
4 Part of the eye (6)
5 Average (2-2)
6 African country bordering South Africa (7)
7 Loud noise, as made by a lion (4)
8 Water boilers (7)
13 Hide (7)
14 English poet, Alfred Lord ___ (8)
16 Red sauce (7)
18 Prize for third place (6)
21 Tusk, shade of white (5)
22 Second-hand (4)
23 Capable (4)

Difficult 3

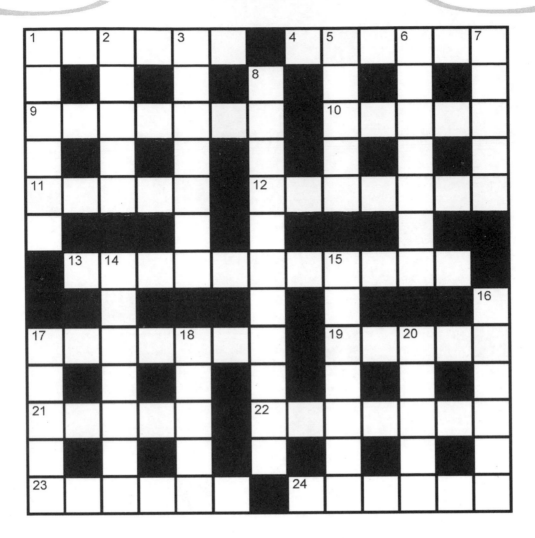

Across

1 Wooden tool (6)
4 Intonation (6)
9 Point of no return (7)
10 Directed at (5)
11 Spicy sauce (5)
12 Biological diffusion (7)
13 Dealer in clothing or dressmaking goods (11)
17 Unit of sound intensity (7)
19 Grind down (5)
21 Supportive shout (5)
22 Eight-armed sea creature without an internal shell (7)
23 Beat (6)
24 Youthful (6)

Down

1 Sullen (6)
2 Printed slander (5)
3 Distinct territory (7)
5 Deep opening (5)
6 Together (2,5)
7 Rises and falls of sea levels (5)
8 Ruthlessly (2,4,5)
14 Medieval science (7)
15 Ceremonial staff (7)
16 The ___ social system consisted of vassals and lords (6)
17 Interior design (5)
18 Dock (5)
20 Purplish-white flower (5)

Difficult 4

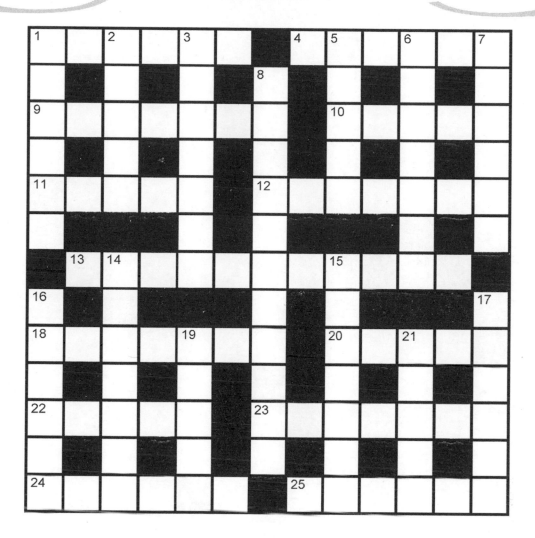

Across

1 Polish city (6)
4 Witch doctor (6)
9 Tempts (7)
10 Gratified (5)
11 Collectively, the human ankle and heel bones (5)
12 Planetary extremities (3-4)
13 Children of Adam and Eve (4,3,4)
18 Overlook (7)
20 Quality (5)
22 One of the senses (5)
23 Three-pronged spear (7)
24 White substance, part of a tooth (6)
25 Tranquil (6)

Down

1 Funeral garland (6)
2 Helicopter part (5)
3 Public sale (7)
5 Urgency (5)
6 Gas that makes Neptune blue (7)
7 Naturist (6)
8 Tasks (11)
14 Loss of memory (7)
15 Greed—one of the deadly sins (7)
16 Grass cutting tool (6)
17 Sculpture, often a memorial (6)
19 Dangerously overweight (5)
21 Blockade (5)

Difficult 5

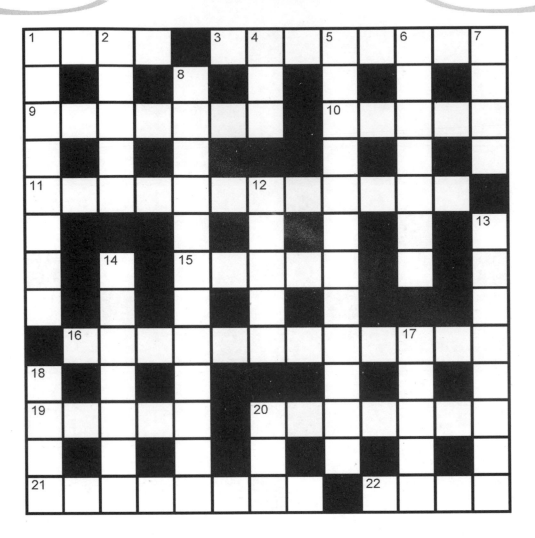

Across

1 Cheekbone (4)
3 Individual listing menu (1,2,5)
9 Withdraw (7)
10 Bioweapon (5)
11 Skirmish site (12)
15 ___ Parker is Spiderman (5)
16 Games or pursuits played on ice and snow (6,6)
19 Blood vessel (5)
20 Letter (7)
21 Slightly (8)
22 Person in charge (4)

Down

1 Void of energy (8)
2 Nineteenth century pianist and composer (5)
4 Container seal (3)
5 Related to map making (12)
6 Abjures (7)
7 Sea eagle (4)
8 Miniature people created by Swift (12)
12 Abbreviated name of an amphibious reptile (5)
13 Facial hair (8)
14 Head waiter (6,1)
17 Two quantities, relatively (5)
18 Ointment (4)
20 Long, thin marine creature (3)

Difficult 6

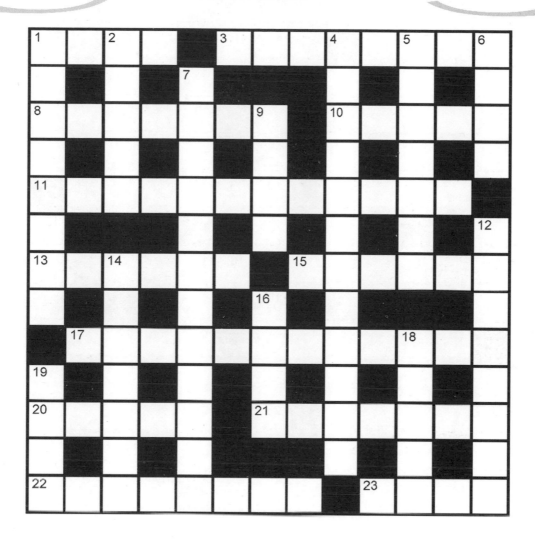

Across

1 Funeral fire (4)
3 Hatchet (8)
8 Novel by Daphne du Maurier (7)
10 Man-made fabric (5)
11 One hundred degrees (7-5)
13 Position (6)
15 Untidy handwriting (6)
17 Temperature gauges (12)
20 Italian explorer who searched for Asia (5)
21 Inhale (7)
22 Overthrow (8)
23 Fine-grained soil that goes hard when fired (4)

Down

1 Plane curve (8)
2 Jewish elder (5)
4 The fourth wife of Henry VIII (4,2,6)
5 Venue of the 1996 Olympic Games (7)
6 Monarch (4)
7 Broadcast author (6-6)
9 Basic marine plant, in singular (4)
12 Windy (8)
14 Live with someone, unmarried (7)
16 Burial place (4)
18 Glorify (5)
19 Corrosive liquid (4)

Difficult 7

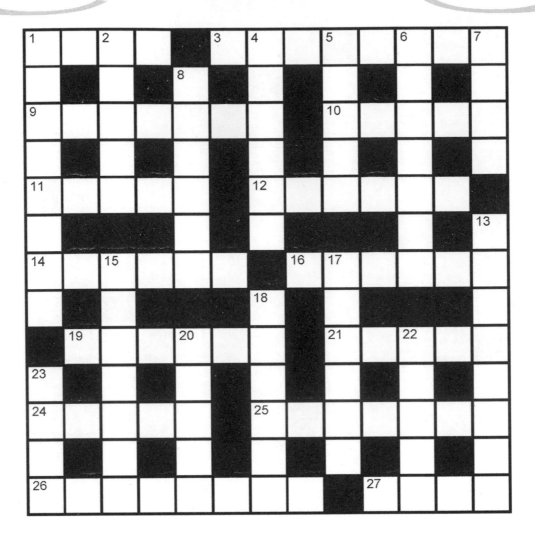

Across

1 Word that can precede money or our souls (4)
3 Australian city, capital of South Australia (8)
9 Attack (7)
10 Area of expertise (5)
11 Epic poem by John Milton (8,4)
13 Not late (2,4)
15 Mountaineer (6)
17 North European (12)
20 Author of Metamorphosis (5)
21 Month (7)
22 A false belief (8)
23 Large number of cattle (4)

Down

1 Washes hair (8)
2 Part of a helmet (5)
4 Hate (6)
5 Newspaper column in which single people advertise for companionship (6,6)
6 Sharpest human tooth (7)
7 Viewing organs (4)
8 Basics (12)
12 Gathered (8)
14 Sensitive (7)
16 Traditional robe (6)
18 Permeate (5)
19 Slide (4)

Difficult 8

Across

2 Infants (6)
5 Slightly open (4)
8 Against the law (7)
9 Exclude (5)
11 Nationality of a person from Prague (5)
12 Three-masted vessel (7)
13 Bubbles sat on the top of a beverage (5)
15 Limb joint (5)
20 Bath, for example (4-3)
22 Take exception (5)
24 Mike ___, star of the Austin Powers movies (5)
25 Overshadow (7)
26 Occupy (4)
27 Pestilence (6)

Down

1 Involuntary movement (6)
2 Protrude (5)
3 An important person, or someone who thinks they are important (3,4)
4 High praise (6)
6 Prison guards (7)
7 Face cover, as worn by a bride (4)
10 Female name (4)
14 Town in New Mexico, famous for alien visitations (7)
16 Danger sign (3,4)
17 Travel unaided across water (4)
18 Descend on a rope (6)
19 Take into custody (6)
21 "___ of the D'Urbervilles", classic novel by Thomas Hardy (4)
23 The leaf of this tree is the symbol of Canada (5)

Difficult 9

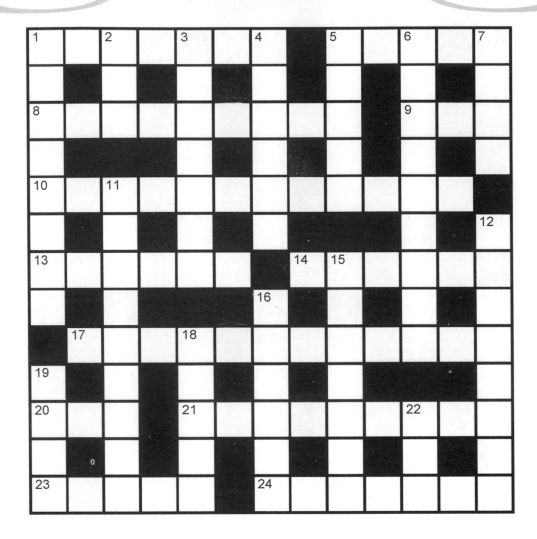

Across

1 Swamp (7)
5 One who is intolerant (5)
8 Army units (9)
9 Travel on foot (3)
10 Sleepwalker (12)
13 Exert (6)
14 Felons (6)
17 Great surprise (12)
20 We breathe it (3)
21 Victor (9)
23 Pol Pot led the ____ Rouge in Cambodia (5)
24 Doubter (7)

Down

1 Intensive course (8)
2 Small powerful boat (3)
3 Swimming aid (7)
4 European river (6)
5 Herb (5)
6 Spinning wheel that provides resistance (9)
7 Word that can follow think and water (4)
11 Whirlpool (9)
12 Knowledge confined to a small group (8)
15 Domiciled once more (7)
16 Nefarious persons (6)
18 Come to pass (5)
19 Medieval torture device (4)
22 Decay (3)

Difficult 10

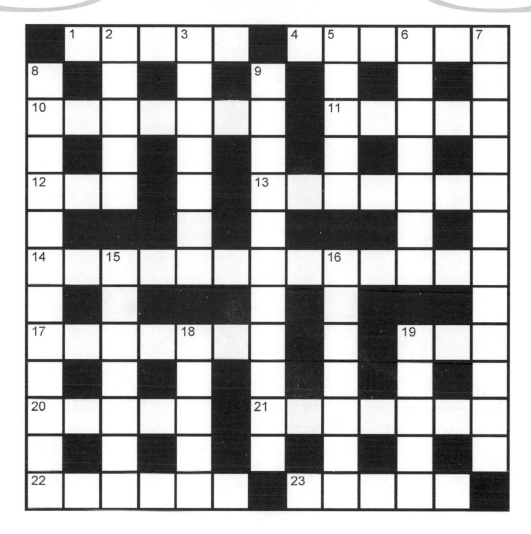

Across

1 Jules ___, author of "Around The World In Eighty Days" (5)
4 Artillery gun (6)
10 Hardy annual flower (7)
11 Addictive narcotic (5)
12 Outfit (3)
13 Wild West party (7)
14 Not significant (13)
17 Monarchy (7)
19 Slice (3)
20 Obviate (5)
21 More agile (7)
22 Type of seed often found on bread rolls (6)
23 Spy (5)

Down

2 African country with Mediterranean and Red Sea coasts (5)
3 Facial cosmetic surgery (4,3)
5 Home (5)
6 Kenyan city (7)
7 Terminology (12)
8 Golfer known as the Golden Bear (4,8)
9 Type of drug sometimes used to treat narcolepsy (11)
15 Fourteen-line poems (7)
16 Reporter (7)
18 Data, in singular (5)
19 Musical instrument (5)

Across

1 Word that can follow electric, and precede absorber (5)
4 Sword (5)
9 Southwestern Spanish city, famous for bullfighting (7)
10 Error (5)
11 Upper arm muscle (5)
12 Run away (7)
13 Supernova (9,4)
16 Impassioned (7)
18 Species of tree—its branches have been used as a whip (5)
20 Falls open (5)
21 Coincide (7)
22 Remains (5)
23 Line spoken by a stage actor to the audience (5)

Down

2 Chaos (5)
3 Sea nymph of "The Odyssey" (7)
5 Book of maps (5)
6 Compatibility (7)
7 Revenge (11)
8 Target audience (10)
9 Deception (10)
14 Low wall (7)
15 Chalices (7)
17 Analytical composition (5)
19 Annoyed (5)

Difficult 12

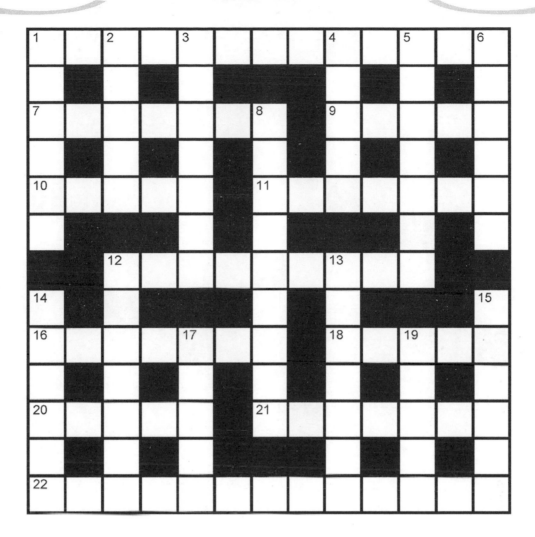

Across

1 Novel by James Joyce (9,4)
7 Newspaper story (5-2)
9 Disagree (5)
10 Resin used as incense (5)
11 Contemplate (7)
12 With good intentions (4-5)
16 Three-pointed hat (7)
18 Turf removed by a golf shot (5)
20 Runs without haste (5)
21 Sea creature (7)
22 Winter greeting (9,4)

Down

1 Submitted (6)
2 Sound (5)
3 Old Testament book of prophecies (7)
4 Item of winter clothing (5)
5 Enlarge (7)
6 Happenings (6)
8 Desire to cause fire (9)
12 Speak quietly (7)
13 Julie ___, actress who played Mary Poppins (7)
14 Slanted, when referring to writing (6)
15 Serve (6)
17 Safe shelter (5)
19 Musical instrument (5)

Difficult 13

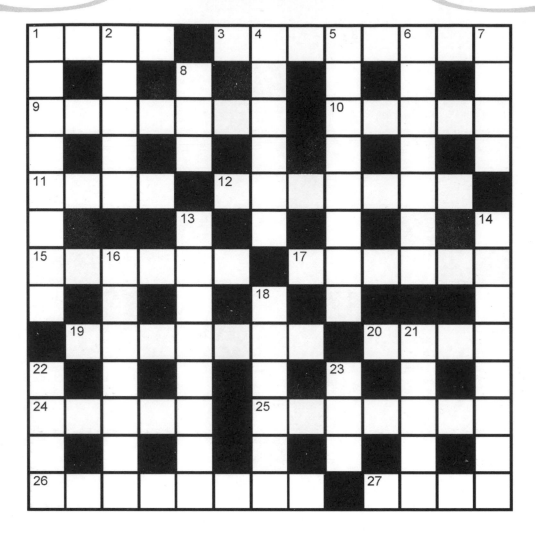

Across

1 Girlfriend of a gangster (4)
3 Outline (8)
9 Movie starring Tom Cruise (3,4)
10 Championship (5)
11 Roald ___, author of "Charlie and the Chocolate Factory" (4)
12 Intestinal disease (7)
15 Circumvolution (6)
17 Reasoning part of the brain (6)
19 Characteristic version of a language (7)
20 Particle (4)
24 Order (5)
25 Bolshevik (7)
26 Synthetic rubber (8)
27 Stylish (4)

Down

1 Bullfighters (8)
2 Parasite (5)
4 Japanese motorcycle manufacturer (6)
5 Perform significantly better than (8)
6 Sarcastically critical (7)
7 The ___ Canal links the Red Sea with the Mediterranean (4)
8 Movie starring Tom Hanks (3)
13 Sporty (8)
14 Airtight (8)
16 Unimportant (7)
18 Cool customer, like Val Kilmer's character in "Top Gun" (3,3)
21 Leg part (5)
22 Dick Turpin's horse was called Black ___ (4)
23 Arid (3)

Difficult 14

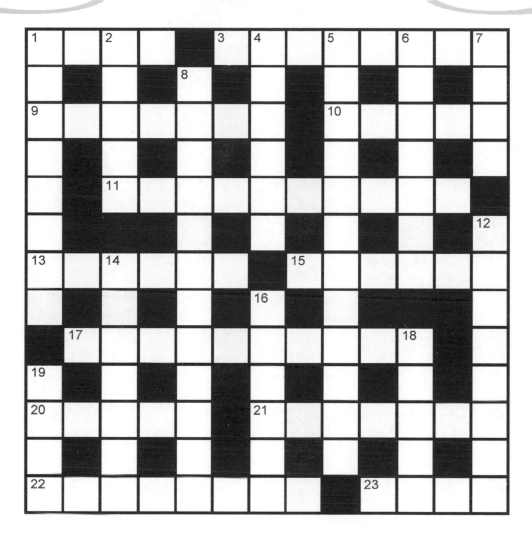

Across

1 Bones that protect the internal organs (4)
3 Whims (8)
9 Ballroom dance (7)
10 Soft white rock (5)
11 Removal of impurities (10)
13 ___ Hemingway, American author. His books include "For Whom The Bell Tolls" (6)
15 Lebanese capital (6)
17 Container (10)
20 ___ Mountains, African range extending into Morocco, Tunisia, and Algeria (5)
21 Subtle differences (7)
22 One who is not there (8)
23 Listen to (4)

Down

1 Umpires (8)
2 Fighter (5)
4 Fletcher Christian once led one (6)
5 Not profitable (12)
6 Wrench (7)
7 Rice wine (4)
8 Skilled worker (12)
12 Emphasized (8)
14 Sewing implements (7)
16 Position (6)
18 Compere (5)
19 Festival (4)

Difficult 15

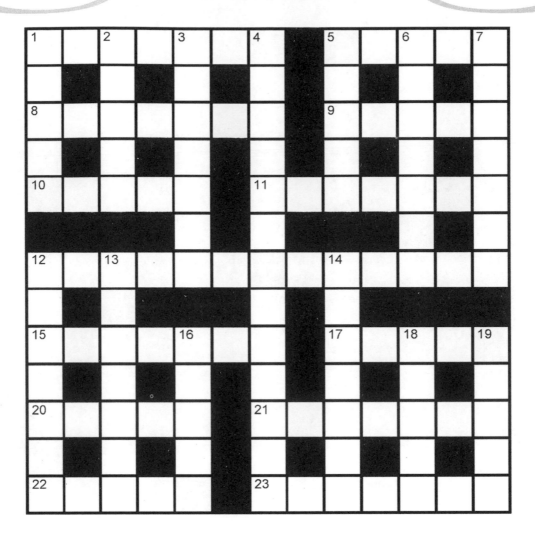

Across

1 Tuft of grass (7)
5 Brightest star in the constellation Cygnus (5)
8 17th century French writer. His works include "The Miser" (7)
9 Machine for trimming grass (5)
10 Genie (5)
11 To change the subject is to go off at a ___ (7)
12 Rubella (6,7)
15 Protein made from animal tissue (7)
17 Strong cotton yarn (5)
20 Woody climbing plant (5)
21 Payment made to an author before their book is published (7)
22 Lucifer (5)
23 Paces (7)

Down

1 Swollen (5)
2 Seasoned ragout made with game birds (5)
3 Continent that includes Polynesia (7)
4 Compulsive thieves (13)
5 Evil spirit (5)
6 Economic plan of President Roosevelt in 1930's USA (3,4)
7 Lambasts (7)
12 Eye protectors (7)
13 Dependent (7)
14 Finished (3,4)
16 Part of a bridal gown that needs to be carried (5)
18 Ecclesiastical council (5)
19 Pitchers (5)

Cryptic 1

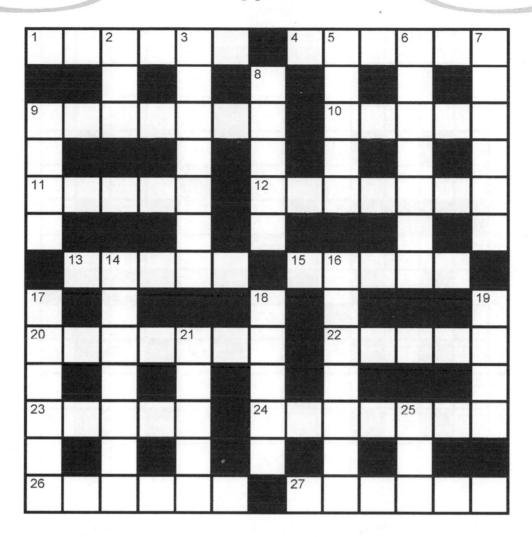

Across

1 Suffer bad cut and demand ransom, perhaps? (6)
4 Mashed sprout results in grogginess (6)
9 Packing material to add inside wing (7)
10 Loud bell causes dismay (5)
11 Flat in Rome contains dead language (5)
12 Snubs varied regions (7)
13 To embarrass, one party is held (5)
15 Even scores, there and back (5)
20 Offer money for aged lasso (3,4)
22 Bus used to train sportsmen (5)
23 Confused beaus suffer ill treatment (5)
24 Bovine fall produces yellow flower (7)
26 St. Ezra becomes a poor substitute (6)
27 Avoid ring road (6)

Down

2 North or south, he's your father (3)
3 Customers like broken stencil (7)
5 Strain is reduced to mode of transport (5)
6 Ripe air on grassy plain, possibly (7)
7 Rearranging misers is neglectful (6)
8 Once more, profit is earned (5)
9 Flow backward to see large canine (4)
14 Bud begs parasites to let them sleep (7)
16 Place a type of bet on left and right (4,3)
17 Or hiding in male raises spirits (6)
18 Extend to a little treachery (5)
19 Locate man within Indian bread (4)
21 Twisted voter keeps no secret (5)
25 Pasture reached by mixing ale (3)

Cryptic 2

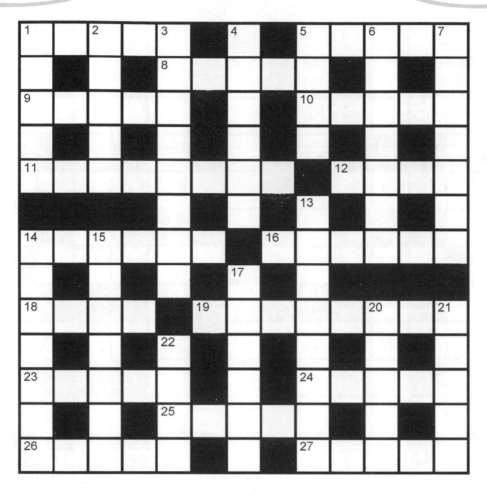

Across

1 Curtailed lunatic becomes an obsession (5)
5 Stranded whale is reduced to having suffered dull pain (5)
8 Broken flesh becomes a ledge (5)
9 Scandinavians who dwell in Andes (5)
10 Lager brewed backward has royal quality (5)
11 Tiny rims lead us to government department (8)
12 Shortened journey to collect currency (4)
14 Mist is omitted, we hear (6)
16 She, within cod, is struck viciously (6)
18 As lawn is cut, we hear a complaint (4)
19 As man wears sweater, a policeman tells him to stop the car, we hear (8)
23 Hilarity can be found in the slaughterhouse (5)
24 Reversible central principle (5)
25 Disguised couple had option to take on another's child (5)
26 Netherlander wants to go halves (5)
27 One very harbours all without exception (5)

Down

1 Brothel manageress, however you see her (5)
2 Listen in on topless silky fabric (5)
3 Sets aids in a different order by being helped (8)
4 Fastening strip lurks within level crossing (6)
5 Man disguises his hairstyle in a frown (4)
6 Rearrangement shows how gash makes false statement (7)
7 Dishonestly led dude into confusion (7)
13 Let in route to arrive at casino game (8)
14 Dumb elm, in a mess, did not speak clearly (7)
15 Twisted stud was creating wood particles (7)
17 No mutt can become sheep meat (6)
20 Meeting is held in shortened avenue (5)
21 Irritable rodent is tarty, perhaps? (5)
22 Hash is made of Iranian leader's title (4)

Cryptic 3

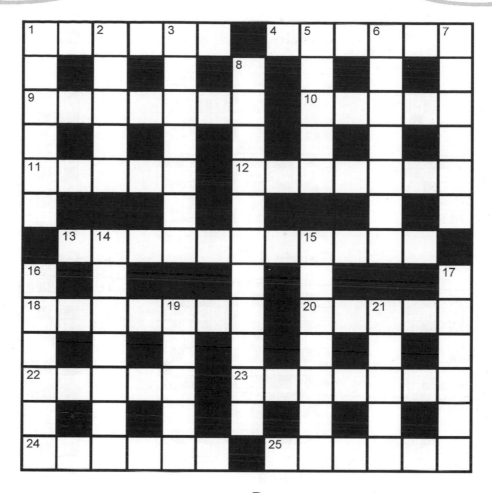

Across

1 Reversal prevents one from looking less embarrassed (6)
4 In cert, with an adjustment, looks like an idiot (6)
9 Side bus may sink as it breaks (7)
10 One is certain that this is the seafront (5)
11 Come in and join the competition (5)
12 Extreme camping trip (7)
13 Depart mogul, confused, after he made a formal declaration (11)
18 Distrust the one with no alibi (7)
20 Drove haphazardly in cab to a room on a boat (5)
22 Perhaps, M, reel in Mr Fudd (5)
23 Thespian may wish to carve variedly, and ham it up (7)
24 Gorgon woman was once amused (6)
25 Stiffening agent is buried as workers tar church (6)

Down

1 Job is done more recklessly than a strip of bacon (6)
2 Payment made is lost in bidet (5)
3 Grim pea is whipped into a quip (7)
5 Adjust to zero by demolishing trees (5)
6 Take a nut core and beat severely (7)
7 The dough was made consistent, as required (6)
8 Lawmaking is achieved by rearranging lit gasoline (11)
14 Re-begin summarized life story (7)
15 Very old history looks like nine cat (7)
16 Man meets E, going in the opposite direction, with much respect (6)
17 Chants are muddled as a kidnap takes place (6)
19 Laser twisting produces aristocracy, perhaps (5)
21 British Prime Minister's witch project? (5)

Answers

Gentle 1

```
M U L E   S O R C E R E R
A A M D   A E U
R E D H E A D   R A F T S
Z L R S   O U H
I D E A L   O B L O N G
P   O N   D A
A S T U T E   B E D S I T
N E D   L R
  U N T R U E   I G L O O
O D E V X L C
H A R E M   O R I G A M I
M I I U R M T
S O L I T A R Y   Z A N Y
```

Gentle 2

```
J O U R N E Y   F A C T S
U N U E E A W
N O V E L L A   A M P L E
T E L R S T D
A N   I L L A T E A S E
  T F Y   I N
H A I R Y   U S I N G
A L G H S
M E A N D E R   R E T C H
B T O O I A U
U P E N D   W I N E B A R
R D G U K L L
G   P E N P U S H E R S
```

Gentle 3

```
D A T A   A   E
H O U S E H O L D N A M E
  V L E T D U
B E V E R A G E   R I L E
  E T R E S
V A M P I R E   T W A I N
  U E A   O
S T A T E   S U R F I N G
  O U M S A
A B E L   O U T L I V E D
  A I U R N T
S H O P A S S I S T A N T
  N S E A S A
```

Gentle 4

```
P I N E   P A C K A G E
O O H A H L D
S E T S A I L   E A G L E
T E T T S E N
M I S E R   R E S O R T
A E Y I
N E V A D A   S P R A T S
  A C O T
  S C U R V Y   L A D L E
W C U C A R T
O N I O N   L I N G E R S
O N G E D A O
D R E S S E D   O D I N
```

Gentle 5

```
H O T A I R   P R O B E D
A O N H A R E
S E A T T L E   N E A R S
S S E L C I I
L A T I N   E X H A L E R
E S N L E
  W I N E B O T T L E S
B L F I C
A I L M E N T   P O U C H
L L R R S N A
B R U N O   O C T O P U S
O C D Y E E T
A N K L E S   P R A G U E
```

Gentle 6

```
  C A R V P T
D O U B L E F I G U R E S
  L S P P F A
B A G U E T T E   F I R E
  R I R I D
G O N D O L A   S N O R E
  V E D O
K E N D O   G E S T A P O
  R E S T O
S C A R   P Y R A M I D S
  A A A O A O
A S T I T C H I N T I M E
  T L E T O E
```

Gentle 7

```
  G S P S K D
B O T T L E   H E I F E R
  T E N O N C
C H O P   P A R A G U A Y
  A A E S D
E M E R A L D   C I D E R
  E S P Z
C H E S T   R E L E A S E
  E P C N C
B L O O D R E D   H E A L
  M N U A I R
C E N S U S   N O V I C E
  T E T T E E
```

Gentle 8

```
P R I N C E S   W A T C H
E F O U I E O
D I S T U R B E D   E B B
A R M E N B
L A N K A   A I R M A I L
  I G R G E
M A G N E T I C F I E L D
A H N A R
C O T T A G E   S U S H I
A M N C T S
B O A   G A R D E N E R S
R R R E S R U
E N E M Y   W A T T A G E
```

Gentle 9

```
H O P S   F R A C T U R E
E E O U L N A
L E A F L E T   I N F E R
L R D M O N
B E L O W T H E B E L T
E I I I D E
N E T   V E N I N   S O Y
T U E G G E
  C R O S S E D W I R E S
G M T A D
R I O J A   O R L A N D O
A I L U L G W
F A L S E T T O   V E I N
```

Gentle 10

```
  H E S S B C
S I G N E T   N O R W A Y
  T I I A U E
A M I D   L O C H N E S S
  A L K E A
E N T E R E D   S T O R Y
  V R F T
T R A I N   B O N E D R Y
  O L O R O
G U I D E D O G   C L U B
  S E D E A N
S E D A T E   R E M E D Y
  S D R Y P S
```

Gentle 11

```
  T S P I S F
W R I T E R   D R A G O N
  U O E I O
K E N O   S H A L L O T S
  L L S O W
F R I S B E E   B R I E F
  E Y W A
B L A C K   H I N D E R S
  E A Z S E
E V A C U A T E   A L P S
  A K I M D U
A N G L E R   E N L I S T
  T E E N Y H
```

Gentle 12

```
A B S O R B   C O R P S E
N W O B F H R
N I A G A R A   F L A I R
U R S T N A
A D M I T   H O U S T O N
L E I O T
  F I N D I N G N E M O
A N G I C
G O S P E L S   E X C E L
H T U L I
A W A K E   I N S T Y L E
S L Y T E D N
T E L L E R   I N F E C T
```

Answers

Gentle 13

Gentle 14

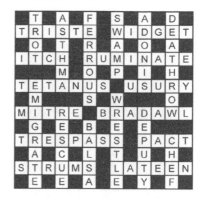

Gentle 15

Challenging 1

Challenging 2

Challenging 3

Challenging 4

Challenging 5

Challenging 6

Challenging 7

Challenging 8

Challenging 9

Answers

Challenging 10

```
C O P E   G R O U N D E D
A   R   B     N     E   U
S M O K E R S   D E S K S
E   U   A   E   P     K
M I D S U M M E R D A Y
E       T   I   G   I   C
N U T T Y   R   A O R T A
T   R   Q   U   R       U
  R E Q U I R E M E N T S
W   K   E   A   E   O   E
A N K L E   L O N G B O W
R   E   N     T   L     A
S I D E S H O W   L E V Y
```

Challenging 11

```
G A L A H A D   M A S A I
E   E   I   A   A   H   N
N   A L L E G A T I O N S
O   T   A   G     R   E
A S H   R H E U M A T I C
    E   I   R   O   A   T
  B R O O K   H O U N D
A   J   U   R   N   D
F L A G S H I P S   S I N
R   C   P   H   W   O
A S K I N G P R I C E   M
I   E   O   E   N   E   A
D A T E D   D U E T T E D
```

Challenging 12

Challenging 13

```
H A N D S U P   S C A L D
A   U   H   A   O   B   Y
L A R G E   L I N C O L N
V   S   L   A   R   A
E Y E   L A C E R A T E S
    E   F E E E T     T
U N P A I D   D E A D L Y
N   A   S   R   L   E
B I R D H O U S E   C A B
O   A   L   C   O   A
W E B S I T E   T O L L S
E   L   A   R   E   I   K
D R E A M   S E D U C E S
```

Challenging 14

Challenging 15

Difficult 1

```
D E P O S I T   F U T O N
E   S   U   R   E   R   O
T R I E N N I A L   A R M
E   B   A   O   G   I
R I F L E   L A N T E R N
  I   A   A   D   E
A R G U M E N T A T I V E
R   U   D   C   E
M I R A C L E   R E S I N
E   I   R   Y   O
N U N   R U R A L I S E S
I   E   C   O   I   P
A I S L E   R I C H A R D
```

Difficult 2

Difficult 3

```
M A L L E T   A C C E N T
O   I   N   I   H   N   I
R U B I C O N   A I M E D
O   E   L   C   S   A   E
S A L S A   O S M O S I S
E       V   L   S
  H A B E R D A S H E R
    L       B   C       F
D E C I B E L   E R O D E
E   H   E   O   P   R   U
C H E E R   O C T O P O D
O   M   T   D   R   I   A
R H Y T H M   V E R N A L
```

Difficult 4

Difficult 5

Difficult 6

Answers

Difficult 7

Difficult 8

Difficult 9

Difficult 10

Difficult 11

Difficult 12

Difficult 13

Difficult 14

Difficult 15

Cryptic 1

Cryptic 2

Cryptic 3

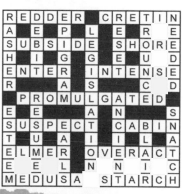

Sudoku

To solve a sudoku puzzle, every digit from 1 to 9 must appear in each of the nine vertical columns, in each of the nine horizontal rows, and in each of the nine boxes. They range in difficulty from easy to very hard, depending on the positioning of the numbers you're given to start with.

Row with numbers 1 to 9

5	8	7	4	9	3	1	6	2
6	4	3						
9	1	2						
3								
2								
8								
1								
4								
7								

Box with numbers 1 to 9

5	8	7	4	9	3	1	6	2
6	4	3						
9	1	2						
3								
2								
8								
1								
4								
7								

Column with numbers 1 to 9

5	8	7	4	9	3	1	6	2
6	4	3						
9	1	2						
3								
2								
8								
1							.	
4								
7								

For an 'Xtra' challenge, you will find an X-sudoku at the end of each section. In these puzzles, every digit from 1 to 9 must appear in each of the nine vertical columns, nine horizontal rows, nine boxes **and** in both of the highlighted diagonal lines that cross the entire grid!

Getting started

There's a 3 in the middle box, and a 3 in the box on the right – but the box on the left still needs a 3. At first glance you might think the 3 could go into any of the four empty cells. However, the 3 cannot go in the top row of the box, because the top row of the grid already has a 3. A grid-row has room for only one of each number. Nor can the 3 go in the second row of the box because the second row of the grid already has a 3.

There's only one square left for the 3 to go!

		6		③	1			
1	9						③	
2	③	8				4		

A tip: As you work through the sudoku, you can write all possible numbers in the corner of a box in pencil. Then, by process of elimination, as more numbers are found, it makes it easier to solve your sudoku.

Getting started

To continue with this theory, its possible to see where to place a 5 in the middle top box. This time, you have to look down the columns as well as across the rows. As before, by looking across the rows, it is possible to place a 5 in four of the squares in the top two rows of this box, which is not a great help! So, by looking down the columns, you can see that it is not possible to place a 5 in any of the squares in the first two columns of this box.

There's only one square left for the 5 to go!

				8	2	5		
	5	6		3	4		8	
8		7				3	9	
7	1		6		8			
3	6						2	8
			3		5		1	9
	2	4				9		1
	7		2	9		8	6	
		8	4	1				

		8	3				2	
6			8	2	7			
		2		4		7		6
	6		9		3		7	2
	4	9				6	3	
7	2		6		4		9	
1		4		3		9		
			4	6	1			8
	5				8	3		

6	3					4		7
			3	7		9		6
4	5		9		1			
		5	1		2	7	3	
	4						2	
	2	3	7		8	6		
			2		7		4	3
3		1		8	9			
2		4					7	9

9					8	7		2
	4		1	3			8	
8		6	9			5		
4			7		5	3	9	
	5						2	
	9	8	4		6			7
		4			1	9		5
	8			6	4		3	
1		5	2					8

Sudoku
'easy 5'

2				6			7	4
	8	7				5		
9			7		2			
3			5	7		4	1	
		8	2		3	7		
	7	1		8	9			2
			8		5			1
		2				8	3	
8	4			2				6

8			4		7		2	3
3		4						
	5	2	3	1	8			
	8			3			7	5
	2	5				3	4	
4	3			5			8	
			2	8	1	4	9	
						1		6
7	4		5		9			2

4			5		1		3	7
3			4	6		5		
	5	6				9		
2				4			9	8
	6		1		3		7	
8	1			7				6
		5				8	2	
		7		5	2			9
1	2		9		4			5

			6		2	3		
7			8				6	
		5		1		8		
6		7		4			8	
3	9	1	2		8	4	5	6
	8			3		7		2
		6		8		5		
	7				1			9
		2	3		7			

1		6		3			2	4
4				8	1			
		9	6			3		5
	7		4		3	2		
2	4						9	3
		5	9		2		4	
6		7			5	4		
			2	4				9
8	9			6		5		2

	6	8				7		9
	3		8	4	6			1
4		2					6	
		3		7		5	8	6
			3		2			
8	9	7		5		4		
	8					1		3
3			4	6	7		9	
9		5				6	2	

		3	7		1	5		
	4		9			3	8	
2	6	5				7		9
3				7			2	1
			4		5			
9	8			2				5
4		8				2	5	7
	1	9			7		3	
		7	5		4	1		

				8	3	4	5	
		5	2		1			3
3	1					8		
7			5	9				2
9	3	2				1	4	5
5				3	2			9
		8					3	6
2			8		6	7		
	7	6	3	5				

		5		1		2		
	8		7	6	4			1
3		6			2	8		
1			6	7				2
	2						3	
6				4	1			7
		1	8			7		5
5			4	3	7		1	
		7		9		6		

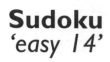

		4	1	2				
	3			8	7		6	
		7	5		9	4		3
	2	1				3		8
5	7						4	1
3		9				2	7	
8		6	9		5	7		
	5		2	1			8	
				7	8	5		

3		8	5				9	
6	5			4	1			
	9	4			8		6	
9				5	4			6
		1				7		
4			1	6				5
	1		4			2	8	
			6	8			3	7
	3				2	6		4

			8	2				
	3	9			6	2		7
1	2		7					8
	7			6		9	8	
		1				6		
	9	8		5			4	
2					5		3	9
9		5	6			7	2	
				8	2			

Sudoku
'medium 1'

			4		1	9		
5		1			8			
	8						5	1
8				2			4	5
1	2			7			9	6
7	6			4				8
4	5						6	
			7			5		3
		6	5		9			

			6		2		7	9
9		3		5				
	2		7	3				
	4	8	2		5		1	
	6						9	
	3		8		1	7	4	
				2	4		6	
				1		8		7
1	9		3		7			

3			7				6	2
4				6		9		
	5		3	9	4			
		5				2		4
	4	8				3	9	
9		2				1		
			9	4	6		7	
		3		5				1
7	6				8			9

		4		7	1			8
7					6			
3					8	7	5	1
4	7				2			
	9	2				6	3	
			8				7	2
9	1	7	2					6
			1					3
6			9	4		2		

3	9							5
2					8	1	3	
	8		3	6		9		
		5	8	2				
9		1				8		3
				3	1	7		
		3		9	2		4	
	6	2	4					1
4							6	8

		5	9				1	
4		8		7				
			4		5		9	2
		9		5		4		6
	8		1		4		7	
7		4		2		9		
5	3		7		9			
				1		3		7
	7				3	6		

6		2	7			3		1
		5	6	1				
4			2				6	9
						4	8	7
	3						9	
7	2	8						
2	7				3			4
				6	1	9		
9		1			2	6		3

Sudoku
'medium 8'

				1	6	5	4	
6		3				7		
2	5				4		3	
9		7		3				
5			6		8			7
				4		9		1
	3		5				7	4
		5				6		8
	9	2	4	6				

	5			2	6		4	
1						8		5
	4	6		5		7		
3			6		2			
8		5				1		4
			5		1			6
		4		7		6	1	
2		3						7
	9		4	1			5	

		4	9					
	9	3	4		7		2	
		8				4	3	9
	1			9			6	8
			8		3			
8	4			5			7	
6	3	7				2		
	2		3		5	7	8	
					6	3		

	9	3		5	6			
			2					6
		5	3		1	9		2
4		7				1	6	
1								5
	6	8				2		4
5		2	6		4	8		
9					3			
			1	8		5	2	

Sudoku
'medium 12'

4				5	2			
	6				9			5
	2		1			3	8	
		7		9		6		2
	8	2				7	9	
6		4		7		5		
	5	6			7		3	
3			4				7	
			3	2				9

	5	8	2					9
	3					6	1	
		4		3	6			
9			8	4				
3	7			5			8	2
				2	7			5
			4	7		2		
	4	9					5	
5					9	1	4	

		4		3			7	
9		7	5			8		
	6	2				3	5	4
			3		6		4	
3								8
	9		2		7			
8	4	1				5	2	
		9			3	4		7
	2			1		9		

7		5		4				1
	2				7		6	
		1	9			2		3
	5		8		6	1		
1								8
		4	5		1		3	
5		7			9	3		
	6		2				5	
2				8		6		9

1	4				9		6	
	9					7	3	
7					3			
	8	6	3	1				
2								6
				6	4	3	8	
			8					7
	1	7					5	
	5		4				1	2

		2		9	5		8	
9	3	7			8			
		8						4
	6	4	1			7		
			3		6			
		1			7	3	4	
2						4		
			2			5	1	7
	7		8	3		2		

							5	7
	4	1	7	8				
			6	1	5			
1	5					9		
		7	1		2	6		
		8					2	1
			2	4	3			
				7	6	4	8	
7	2							

9	2		3					1
			8	1	2			
3	1						6	
			1	9				
	6	9				4	7	
				7	4			
	4						5	7
			9	5	8			
6					7		1	3

4	5				1			2
						5		6
	7		2	8				
7			8		2	3		
		1				2		
		3	6		7			1
				9	4		3	
1		7						
9			1				2	8

Sudoku
'hard 5'

	6		1		9			5
	8			5			7	
			7			3		2
7		9	6		5			
			3		1	5		6
1		4			2			
	9			1			4	
5			4		3		6	

	1		3					
	4						5	8
		9	4	5		2		
			8		5	1		7
		1				5		
9		4	2		1			
		2		1	6	3		
5	3						7	
					3		6	

4							3	6
2		9		5		4		
	7				4		1	
		1	4		6			
	8						2	
			5		1	3		
	5		3				7	
		4		6		2		9
7	9							3

			6		2		1	
3	1							6
					4	7		3
	4	9	1	8				
		7				6		
				7	3	4	9	
9		1	2					
4							7	8
	5		9		7			

			7				3	
2		1	4			7		
	6	8				1	9	
				2			4	6
			1		3			
5	4			8				
	8	9				2	5	
		5			2	4		8
	7				4			

			8		6		9	
7		3			4			
		4			2	7	8	
1	7	6						4
3						6	5	9
	6	2	5			1		
			6			9		5
	5		2		9			

Sudoku
'hard 11'

		5			2	6		
				8		7		
8	4							2
5			8		6			
	1						8	
			2		9			5
9							2	3
		8		6				
		7	3			8		

Sudoku
'expert 1'

		8		4				
	6				3		2	
7			1		2	6		
5			6					4
		7				5		
2					5			8
		1	7		8			6
	3		2				9	
				3		1		

	3				1			7
8		4						
			9	7			8	
5				4		3		
9								2
		6		1				9
	1			6	2			
						7		5
3			7				1	

Sudoku
'expert 3'

3						2		4
			1		7		8	
6			5					
	3				5	9		
	9			2			4	
		8	9				2	
					9			7
	5		7		1			
4		9						8

1		8		5			9	
		9			7			
			2	1			5	
7					4		3	
		5				2		
	6		7					5
	2			7	1			
			3			6		
	4			2		3		8

		8			2	4	3	
5				6		2		
			3	7				
						9		6
			1		6			
8		5						
				3	9			
		9		5				1
	7	3	2			6		

			6			7		4
9				2		6		
6		1	3					
	1		9					
3	2						9	8
					5		7	
					3	2		7
		7		5				9
5		6			7			

	8					1		2
6				5		8		
			8				3	
3		5	9					
					7	6		1
	5				9			
		8		6				9
7		9					4	

Answers

Easy 1

1	9	3	7	8	2	5	4	6
2	5	6	9	3	4	1	8	7
8	4	7	5	6	1	3	9	2
7	1	9	6	2	8	4	5	3
3	6	5	1	4	9	7	2	8
4	8	2	3	7	5	6	1	9
6	2	4	8	5	7	9	3	1
5	7	1	2	9	3	8	6	4
9	3	8	4	1	6	2	7	5

Easy 2

4	7	8	3	1	6	5	2	9
6	9	5	8	2	7	1	4	3
3	1	2	5	4	9	7	8	6
5	6	1	9	8	3	4	7	2
8	4	9	1	7	2	6	3	5
7	2	3	6	5	4	8	9	1
1	8	4	2	3	5	9	6	7
9	3	7	4	6	1	2	5	8
2	5	6	7	9	8	3	1	4

Easy 3

6	3	9	8	2	5	4	1	7
8	1	2	3	7	4	9	5	6
4	5	7	9	6	1	3	8	2
9	6	5	1	4	2	7	3	8
7	4	8	6	9	3	5	2	1
1	2	3	7	5	8	6	9	4
5	9	6	2	1	7	8	4	3
3	7	1	4	8	9	2	6	5
2	8	4	5	3	6	1	7	9

Easy 4

9	1	3	6	5	8	7	4	2
5	4	2	1	3	7	6	8	9
8	7	6	9	4	2	5	1	3
4	2	1	7	8	5	3	9	6
6	5	7	3	1	9	8	2	4
3	9	8	4	2	6	1	5	7
2	3	4	8	7	1	9	6	5
7	8	9	5	6	4	2	3	1
1	6	5	2	9	3	4	7	8

Easy 5

2	3	5	9	6	8	1	7	4
6	8	7	3	4	1	5	2	9
9	1	4	7	5	2	6	8	3
3	2	9	5	7	6	4	1	8
4	6	8	2	1	3	7	9	5
5	7	1	4	8	9	3	6	2
7	9	6	8	3	5	2	4	1
1	5	2	6	9	4	8	3	7
8	4	3	1	2	7	9	5	6

Easy 6

8	1	6	4	9	7	5	2	3
3	7	4	6	2	5	9	1	8
9	5	2	3	1	8	7	6	4
6	8	9	1	3	4	2	7	5
1	2	5	8	7	6	3	4	9
4	3	7	9	5	2	6	8	1
5	6	3	2	8	1	4	9	7
2	9	8	7	4	3	1	5	6
7	4	1	5	6	9	8	3	2

Easy 7

4	8	2	5	9	1	6	3	7
3	9	1	4	6	7	5	8	2
7	5	6	3	2	8	9	4	1
2	7	3	6	4	5	1	9	8
5	6	9	1	8	3	2	7	4
8	1	4	2	7	9	3	5	6
9	4	5	7	1	6	8	2	3
6	3	7	8	5	2	4	1	9
1	2	8	9	3	4	7	6	5

Easy 8

8	4	9	6	5	2	3	7	1
7	1	3	8	9	4	2	6	5
2	6	5	7	1	3	8	9	4
6	2	7	1	4	5	9	8	3
3	9	1	2	7	8	4	5	6
5	8	4	9	3	6	7	1	2
1	3	6	4	8	9	5	2	7
4	7	8	5	2	1	6	3	9
9	5	2	3	6	7	1	4	8

Easy 9

1	5	6	7	3	9	8	2	4
4	3	2	5	8	1	9	6	7
7	8	9	6	2	4	3	1	5
9	7	8	4	1	3	2	5	6
2	4	1	8	5	6	7	9	3
3	6	5	9	7	2	1	4	8
6	2	7	3	9	5	4	8	1
5	1	3	2	4	8	6	7	9
8	9	4	1	6	7	5	3	2

Answers

Easy 10

1	6	8	5	2	3	7	4	9
7	3	9	8	4	6	2	5	1
4	5	2	7	1	9	3	6	8
2	1	3	9	7	4	5	8	6
5	4	6	3	8	2	9	1	7
8	9	7	6	5	1	4	3	2
6	8	4	2	9	5	1	7	3
3	2	1	4	6	7	8	9	5
9	7	5	1	3	8	6	2	4

Easy 11

8	9	3	7	6	1	5	4	2
7	4	1	9	5	2	3	8	6
2	6	5	3	4	8	7	1	9
3	5	4	8	7	6	9	2	1
1	7	2	4	9	5	8	6	3
9	8	6	1	2	3	4	7	5
4	3	8	6	1	9	2	5	7
5	1	9	2	8	7	6	3	4
6	2	7	5	3	4	1	9	8

Easy 12

6	2	7	9	8	3	4	5	1
8	4	5	2	7	1	9	6	3
3	1	9	6	4	5	8	2	7
7	6	1	5	9	4	3	8	2
9	3	2	7	6	8	1	4	5
5	8	4	1	3	2	6	7	9
1	9	8	4	2	7	5	3	6
2	5	3	8	1	6	7	9	4
4	7	6	3	5	9	2	1	8

Easy 13

4	7	5	3	1	8	2	6	9
2	8	9	7	6	4	3	5	1
3	1	6	9	5	2	8	7	4
1	5	8	6	7	3	4	9	2
7	2	4	5	8	9	1	3	6
6	9	3	2	4	1	5	8	7
9	3	1	8	2	6	7	4	5
5	6	2	4	3	7	9	1	8
8	4	7	1	9	5	6	2	3

Easy 14

6	9	4	1	2	3	8	5	7
2	3	5	4	8	7	1	6	9
1	8	7	5	6	9	4	2	3
4	2	1	7	5	6	3	9	8
5	7	8	3	9	2	6	4	1
3	6	9	8	4	1	2	7	5
8	4	6	9	3	5	7	1	2
7	5	3	2	1	4	9	8	6
9	1	2	6	7	8	5	3	4

Easy 15

3	7	8	5	2	6	4	9	1
6	5	2	9	4	1	8	7	3
1	9	4	3	7	8	5	6	2
9	2	7	8	5	4	3	1	6
5	6	1	2	9	3	7	4	8
4	8	3	1	6	7	9	2	5
7	1	6	4	3	5	2	8	9
2	4	5	6	8	9	1	3	7
8	3	9	7	1	2	6	5	4

Easy 16

5	6	7	8	2	1	4	9	3
8	3	9	5	4	6	2	1	7
1	2	4	7	3	9	5	6	8
3	7	2	1	6	4	9	8	5
4	5	1	3	9	8	6	7	2
6	9	8	2	5	7	3	4	1
2	1	6	4	7	5	8	3	9
9	8	5	6	1	3	7	2	4
7	4	3	9	8	2	1	5	6

Medium 1

6	7	3	4	5	1	9	8	2
5	4	1	2	9	8	6	3	7
9	8	2	6	3	7	4	5	1
8	3	9	1	2	6	7	4	5
1	2	4	8	7	5	3	9	6
7	6	5	9	4	3	1	2	8
4	5	7	3	1	2	8	6	9
2	9	8	7	6	4	5	1	3
3	1	6	5	8	9	2	7	4

Medium 2

8	1	5	6	4	2	3	7	9
9	7	3	1	5	8	4	2	6
6	2	4	7	3	9	1	8	5
7	4	8	2	9	5	6	1	3
2	6	1	4	7	3	5	9	8
5	3	9	8	6	1	7	4	2
3	8	7	5	2	4	9	6	1
4	5	2	9	1	6	8	3	7
1	9	6	3	8	7	2	5	4

Medium 3

3	8	9	7	1	5	4	6	2
4	1	7	8	6	2	9	3	5
2	5	6	3	9	4	7	1	8
1	3	5	6	7	9	2	8	4
6	4	8	5	2	1	3	9	7
9	7	2	4	8	3	1	5	6
5	2	1	9	4	6	8	7	3
8	9	3	2	5	7	6	4	1
7	6	4	1	3	8	5	2	9

Medium 4

5	2	4	3	7	1	9	6	8
7	8	1	5	9	6	3	2	4
3	6	9	4	2	8	7	5	1
4	7	3	6	5	2	1	8	9
8	9	2	7	1	4	6	3	5
1	5	6	8	3	9	4	7	2
9	1	7	2	8	3	5	4	6
2	4	5	1	6	7	8	9	3
6	3	8	9	4	5	2	1	7

Medium 5

3	9	7	2	1	4	6	8	5
2	5	6	9	7	8	1	3	4
1	8	4	3	6	5	9	7	2
7	3	5	8	2	9	4	1	6
9	2	1	7	4	6	8	5	3
6	4	8	5	3	1	7	2	9
8	1	3	6	9	2	5	4	7
5	6	2	4	8	7	3	9	1
4	7	9	1	5	3	2	6	8

Medium 6

3	2	5	9	8	6	7	1	4
4	9	8	2	7	1	5	6	3
1	6	7	4	3	5	8	9	2
2	1	9	3	5	7	4	8	6
6	8	3	1	9	4	2	7	5
7	5	4	6	2	8	9	3	1
5	3	2	7	6	9	1	4	8
9	4	6	8	1	2	3	5	7
8	7	1	5	4	3	6	2	9

Medium 7

6	8	2	7	5	9	3	4	1
3	9	5	6	1	4	7	2	8
4	1	7	2	3	8	5	6	9
1	6	9	3	2	5	4	8	7
5	3	4	1	8	7	2	9	6
7	2	8	9	4	6	1	3	5
2	7	6	5	9	3	8	1	4
8	5	3	4	6	1	9	7	2
9	4	1	8	7	2	6	5	3

Medium 8

7	8	9	3	1	6	5	4	2
6	4	3	8	5	2	7	1	9
2	5	1	9	7	4	8	3	6
9	6	7	2	3	1	4	8	5
5	1	4	6	9	8	3	2	7
3	2	8	7	4	5	9	6	1
1	3	6	5	8	9	2	7	4
4	7	5	1	2	3	6	9	8
8	9	2	4	6	7	1	5	3

Medium 9

7	5	8	3	2	6	9	4	1
1	3	2	7	9	4	8	6	5
9	4	6	1	5	8	7	3	2
3	7	1	6	4	2	5	8	9
8	6	5	9	3	7	1	2	4
4	2	9	5	8	1	3	7	6
5	8	4	2	7	9	6	1	3
2	1	3	8	6	5	4	9	7
6	9	7	4	1	3	2	5	8

Medium 10

2	5	4	9	3	8	6	1	7
1	9	3	4	6	7	8	2	5
7	6	8	5	2	1	4	3	9
3	1	2	7	9	4	5	6	8
5	7	6	8	1	3	9	4	2
8	4	9	6	5	2	1	7	3
6	3	7	1	8	9	2	5	4
9	2	1	3	4	5	7	8	6
4	8	5	2	7	6	3	9	1

Medium 11

2	9	3	8	5	6	4	7	1
8	1	4	2	9	7	3	5	6
6	7	5	3	4	1	9	8	2
4	5	7	9	3	2	1	6	8
1	2	9	4	6	8	7	3	5
3	6	8	7	1	5	2	9	4
5	3	2	6	7	4	8	1	9
9	8	1	5	2	3	6	4	7
7	4	6	1	8	9	5	2	3

Medium 12

4	7	3	8	5	2	9	6	1
8	6	1	7	3	9	4	2	5
9	2	5	1	6	4	3	8	7
1	3	7	5	9	8	6	4	2
5	8	2	6	4	1	7	9	3
6	9	4	2	7	3	5	1	8
2	5	6	9	1	7	8	3	4
3	1	9	4	8	5	2	7	6
7	4	8	3	2	6	1	5	9

Medium 13

6	5	8	2	1	4	3	7	9
2	3	7	5	9	8	6	1	4
1	9	4	7	3	6	5	2	8
9	2	5	8	4	3	7	6	1
3	7	6	9	5	1	4	8	2
4	8	1	6	2	7	9	3	5
8	1	3	4	7	5	2	9	6
7	4	9	1	6	2	8	5	3
5	6	2	3	8	9	1	4	7

Medium 14

5	8	4	6	3	2	1	7	9
9	3	7	5	4	1	8	6	2
1	6	2	9	7	8	3	5	4
2	1	8	3	9	6	7	4	5
3	7	6	1	5	4	2	9	8
4	9	5	2	8	7	6	3	1
8	4	1	7	6	9	5	2	3
6	5	9	8	2	3	4	1	7
7	2	3	4	1	5	9	8	6

Medium 15

7	3	5	6	4	2	9	8	1
9	2	8	1	3	7	4	6	5
6	4	1	9	5	8	2	7	3
3	5	2	8	7	6	1	9	4
1	7	6	3	9	4	5	2	8
8	9	4	5	2	1	7	3	6
5	8	7	4	6	9	3	1	2
4	6	9	2	1	3	8	5	7
2	1	3	7	8	5	6	4	9

Medium 16

1	4	3	7	2	9	5	6	8
5	9	2	1	8	6	7	3	4
7	6	8	5	4	3	9	2	1
4	8	6	3	1	5	2	7	9
2	3	5	9	7	8	1	4	6
9	7	1	2	6	4	3	8	5
3	2	4	8	5	1	6	9	7
8	1	7	6	9	2	4	5	3
6	5	9	4	3	7	8	1	2

Hard 1

6	4	2	7	9	5	1	8	3
9	3	7	4	1	8	6	5	2
5	1	8	6	2	3	9	7	4
3	6	4	1	8	2	7	9	5
7	5	9	3	4	6	8	2	1
8	2	1	9	5	7	3	4	6
2	9	6	5	7	1	4	3	8
4	8	3	2	6	9	5	1	7
1	7	5	8	3	4	2	6	9

Hard 2

8	9	6	3	2	4	1	5	7
5	4	1	7	8	9	2	3	6
2	7	3	6	1	5	8	9	4
1	5	2	4	6	8	9	7	3
9	3	7	1	5	2	6	4	8
4	6	8	9	3	7	5	2	1
6	8	5	2	4	3	7	1	9
3	1	9	5	7	6	4	8	2
7	2	4	8	9	1	3	6	5

Hard 3

9	2	4	3	6	5	7	8	1
5	7	6	8	1	2	3	4	9
3	1	8	7	4	9	5	6	2
4	5	7	1	9	6	2	3	8
1	6	9	2	8	3	4	7	5
2	8	3	5	7	4	1	9	6
8	4	2	6	3	1	9	5	7
7	3	1	9	5	8	6	2	4
6	9	5	4	2	7	8	1	3

Hard 4

4	5	8	3	6	1	9	7	2
3	1	2	4	7	9	5	8	6
6	7	9	2	8	5	4	1	3
7	6	4	8	1	2	3	5	9
5	8	1	9	4	3	2	6	7
2	9	3	6	5	7	8	4	1
8	2	6	7	9	4	1	3	5
1	3	7	5	2	8	6	9	4
9	4	5	1	3	6	7	2	8

Answers

Hard 5

2	6	7	1	3	9	4	8	5
3	8	1	2	5	4	6	7	9
9	4	5	7	8	6	3	1	2
7	1	9	6	2	5	8	3	4
6	5	3	9	4	8	7	2	1
4	2	8	3	7	1	5	9	6
1	3	4	8	6	2	9	5	7
8	9	6	5	1	7	2	4	3
5	7	2	4	9	3	1	6	8

Hard 6

2	1	5	3	6	8	7	9	4
3	4	7	1	2	9	6	5	8
8	6	9	4	5	7	2	1	3
6	2	3	8	9	5	1	4	7
7	8	1	6	3	4	5	2	9
9	5	4	2	7	1	8	3	6
4	9	2	7	1	6	3	8	5
5	3	6	9	8	2	4	7	1
1	7	8	5	4	3	9	6	2

Hard 7

4	1	5	8	7	2	9	3	6
2	6	9	1	5	3	4	8	7
8	7	3	6	9	4	5	1	2
3	2	1	4	8	6	7	9	5
5	8	6	9	3	7	1	2	4
9	4	7	5	2	1	3	6	8
6	5	2	3	4	9	8	7	1
1	3	4	7	6	8	2	5	9
7	9	8	2	1	5	6	4	3

Hard 8

7	8	4	6	3	2	5	1	9
3	1	2	7	9	5	8	4	6
6	9	5	8	1	4	7	2	3
5	4	9	1	8	6	2	3	7
1	3	7	4	2	9	6	8	5
2	6	8	5	7	3	4	9	1
9	7	1	2	6	8	3	5	4
4	2	6	3	5	1	9	7	8
8	5	3	9	4	7	1	6	2

Hard 9

9	5	4	7	1	8	6	3	2
2	3	1	4	9	6	7	8	5
7	6	8	2	3	5	1	9	4
1	9	3	5	2	7	8	4	6
8	2	6	1	4	3	5	7	9
5	4	7	6	8	9	3	2	1
4	8	9	3	6	1	2	5	7
3	1	5	9	7	2	4	6	8
6	7	2	8	5	4	9	1	3

Hard 10

2	1	5	8	7	6	4	9	3
7	8	3	1	9	4	5	6	2
6	9	4	3	5	2	7	8	1
1	7	6	9	8	5	2	3	4
5	2	9	4	6	3	8	1	7
3	4	8	7	2	1	6	5	9
9	6	2	5	3	7	1	4	8
4	3	7	6	1	8	9	2	5
8	5	1	2	4	9	3	7	6

Hard 11

1	7	5	4	9	2	6	3	8
6	2	9	1	8	3	7	5	4
8	4	3	6	5	7	9	1	2
5	9	2	8	3	6	4	7	1
3	1	6	5	7	4	2	8	9
7	8	4	2	1	9	3	6	5
9	6	1	7	4	8	5	2	3
2	3	8	9	6	5	1	4	7
4	5	7	3	2	1	8	9	6

Expert 1

1	2	8	9	4	6	7	5	3
9	6	4	5	7	3	8	2	1
7	5	3	1	8	2	6	4	9
5	8	9	6	2	7	3	1	4
3	1	7	8	9	4	5	6	2
2	4	6	3	1	5	9	7	8
4	9	1	7	5	8	2	3	6
8	3	5	2	6	1	4	9	7
6	7	2	4	3	9	1	8	5

Expert 2

6	3	9	4	8	1	5	2	7
8	7	4	3	2	5	6	9	1
1	5	2	9	7	6	4	8	3
5	2	1	8	4	9	3	7	6
9	8	3	6	5	7	1	4	2
7	4	6	2	1	3	8	5	9
4	1	7	5	6	2	9	3	8
2	9	8	1	3	4	7	6	5
3	6	5	7	9	8	2	1	4

Answers

Expert 3

3	1	5	6	9	8	2	7	4
9	4	2	1	3	7	5	8	6
6	8	7	5	4	2	1	3	9
2	3	4	8	7	5	9	6	1
7	9	1	3	2	6	8	4	5
5	6	8	9	1	4	7	2	3
1	2	6	4	8	9	3	5	7
8	5	3	7	6	1	4	9	2
4	7	9	2	5	3	6	1	8

Expert 4

1	3	8	4	5	6	7	9	2
2	5	9	8	3	7	4	6	1
4	7	6	2	1	9	8	5	3
7	1	2	5	8	4	9	3	6
9	8	5	1	6	3	2	7	4
3	6	4	7	9	2	1	8	5
8	2	3	6	7	1	5	4	9
5	9	1	3	4	8	6	2	7
6	4	7	9	2	5	3	1	8

Expert 5

6	1	8	5	9	2	4	3	7
5	3	7	8	6	4	2	1	9
9	2	4	3	7	1	5	6	8
3	4	1	7	8	5	9	2	6
7	9	2	1	4	6	8	5	3
8	6	5	9	2	3	1	7	4
1	5	6	4	3	9	7	8	2
2	8	9	6	5	7	3	4	1
4	7	3	2	1	8	6	9	5

Expert 6

8	5	2	6	1	9	7	3	4
9	7	3	5	2	4	6	8	1
6	4	1	3	7	8	9	2	5
7	1	8	9	3	2	5	4	6
3	2	5	7	4	6	1	9	8
4	6	9	1	8	5	3	7	2
1	9	4	8	6	3	2	5	7
2	3	7	4	5	1	8	6	9
5	8	6	2	9	7	4	1	3

Expert 7

5	8	7	4	9	3	1	6	2
6	4	3	1	5	2	8	9	7
9	1	2	8	7	6	4	3	5
3	6	5	9	2	1	7	8	4
2	7	1	6	8	4	9	5	3
8	9	4	5	3	7	6	2	1
1	5	6	2	4	9	3	7	8
4	3	8	7	6	5	2	1	9
7	2	9	3	1	8	5	4	6

World Capitals
wordsearch

Find the capital cities of the countries below. Words can go horizontally, vertically and diagonally, and can read forwards and backwards.

```
L  I  L  W  L  H  M  W  J  Z  L  C  B  H  T
I  H  S  Q  H  O  N  A  O  P  D  E  B  Y  I
Y  L  G  Q  B  L  N  I  D  N  E  M  E  E  K
I  T  V  R  F  A  T  D  O  R  T  O  R  S  D
H  I  I  H  P  U  L  T  O  T  I  R  L  I  D
J  M  S  C  X  G  G  G  O  N  H  D  I  R  G
X  V  R  A  O  N  X  D  X  R  I  A  N  A  T
N  S  I  M  I  C  O  V  H  U  R  E  H  P  E
D  D  A  H  K  Z  I  M  N  R  J  K  H  T  S
A  W  S  W  N  L  W  X  E  W  O  C  S  O  M
X  A  C  I  O  O  D  B  E  O  T  D  M  I  T
W  A  W  L  C  T  N  G  T  M  M  V  N  B  V
I  N  Z  S  Z  A  T  P  T  M  U  M  P  T  E
T  G  P  O  C  T  U  O  Z  W  L  A  K  H  I
```

1. Capital of Germany
2. Capital of Australia
3. Capital of England
4. Capital of Spain
5. Capital of Mexico
6. Capital of Russia
7. Capital of Canada
8. Capital of France
9. Capital of Italy
10. Capital of USA

Jobs wordsearch

Find the words listed below. Words can go horizontally,
vertically and diagonally, and can read forwards and backwards.

```
G V F T I L E O N B R X Q T D R F E H C
S J T Y E N S X X E J B O Q E O T Y L N
T S E N I L J P N X A L C V U Y F C B H
I P E R A H E A I R I X I L A R N E X H
N T A D Y T E P T P J R E E E X E Q D J
D M S I R L S E H M D C J L H D D N J L
V T K I C A N I E O T H I W O A R Q R G
N X C U N D W C S U N P S C K O A S O B
I W T N E O H E R S M I T W E T W B T D
X K I R A A I E T O A O S N S S C E A E
X N J U N M R T C S R P A T N I I R R S
M A Y I O X E E P P V I O X Z L F E O I
N M C C L T L C L E C J R H R A F T C G
X E S A U Z E U I I C E U E S N A N E N
T R R A Z R M A R L D E I F L R R E D E
O I X U N B A T C L O D R A K U T P W R
S F P U E O C T I H L P W J A O H R X K
Y W R R C E X U O O E Y V V Y T J Q A N X
P S Z Q L R B T S R E R I L R Q H C E X
E I V E L X C Y M R A N A M S E L A S O
```

BARTENDER	DOCTOR	MECHANIC	SHOP ASSISTANT
BUILDER	DRIVER	NURSE	SOLDIER
CARPENTER	ELECTRICIAN	PILOT	STEWARDESS
CHEF	FIREMAN	PLUMBER	TEACHER
CLEANER	JOURNALIST	POLICEMAN	TELEPHONIST
CURATOR	LAWYER	PUZZLE COMPILER	TRAFFIC WARDEN
DECORATOR	LECTURER	RECEPTIONIST	
DESIGNER	MARINE	SALESMAN	

Roald Dahl
wordsearch

Find the words listed below. Words can go horizontally, vertically and diagonally, and can read forwards and backwards.

```
L M B O R A U I T Q H E T W R F R J G H
Y R U Y N Z D Y P E A N H H D B J Z X V
B J Y S K H T V E N P I P E E A L Q V L
B J J B V C U F Y O M C E S B T N F F Q
O M N I W K J A D R O I T I W Z W N N C
W D K G R A D N V M O D E O H H C I Y I
A A Z F C R I T I O L E K T C C K S T X
U M O R E I E A C U H M C R W A B W Z S
G I Q I A N V S N S A S U O D E A P U F
U K V E D R I T G C P U B T L P M Q M K
S E E N G N N I I R M O E M A T Z Z L W
T T R D C C I C X O O L I D S N V N K A
U E W L B C C M M C O L L N U A P J D U
S E I Y Z A B R B O L E R D N I C L J Y
G V T G L Y D F W D I V A L N G I O P I
L E C I Q H I O Z I N R H X I T Y M F Y
O E H A Q Q L X E L W A C V A M L T E R
O A E N H D L C P E D M Y M C V Y A G X
P E S T C H O C O L A T E F A C T O R Y
W I L L Y W O N K A M R Z S W O W H Y G
```

AUGUSTUS GLOOP   ESIO TROT   OOMPAH LOOMPAH

BIG FRIENDLY GIANT   FANTASTIC MR FOX   THE TWITS

CHARLIE BUCKET   GIANT PEACH   WILLY WONKA

CHOCOLATE FACTORY   MARVELLOUS MEDICINE   WITCHES

DANNY   MATILDA

ENORMOUS CROCODILE   MIKE TEEVEE

South America
wordsearch

Find the words listed below. Words can go horizontally, vertically and diagonally, and can read forwards and backwards.

```
N W I J Z G N H R L V P W U D E X J P E
W R N L H N B Y Q G G Q F P P E A A M V
U E O Q P V A U T X S U W B J O R A A D
R Y Y H X O Q N E R A L Y J A A X B T Z
V S S K E R F C Y N A R V A G V B I Y B
R F A O P P B B E Q O M A U N G O P M O
A Q Z N E B A A Y B W S A M J A L O W W
U Y Z G T K T C X X R Y A R Y X I N M K
G E Q T Y I M A M A Z O N I M A V M F Q
D E O J D A A J R L W O A K R O I A J C
B P J J P N A G J E Z W G Z L E A J V V
D M M U L S R O A N D E S D O S P E Y
Q N C P N Y D T G A I B M O L O C N G U
S H M J M N B L Q E C I F Y A Z E I R H
E F L U A D H V D V D N U D Z C U Y A
H W T W E C U A D O R T H A U B G N T E
W H R Z C A T M V A S C I E R U E O U L
B R A Z I L X E P Y E C L N A A G A R I
Q X H H J D A W O U O A D Y A O U I E H
F H E X Y V X O Q A I Y C S B A U G P C
```

ABIPON	BOLIVIA	ECUADOR	QUECHUA
AMAZON	BRAZIL	GUARANI	SANTIAGO
ANDES	BUENOS AIRES	GUYANA	URUGUAY
ARGENTINA	CAPE HORN	MAPUCHE	VENEZUELA
AYMARA	CHILE	PARAGUAY	
BOGOTA	COLOMBIA	PERU	

Actresses wordsearch

Find the names of the actresses. Words can go horizontally, vertically and diagonally, and can read forwards and backwards.

```
S E Q D D E J U L I A R O B E R T S H N
E S Q L E N I V L G Z Z N Y G K W E P M
E R M U Y G R L P H Q V R P T D L L J X
R V O B V S Q T O D O R G J P E N E V P
E E I M W K X R S J E A R L N G N T B Q
Q X E X Y L I U R B A P X A J N R V S L
D U C S V R K M E C Y N B A I Y N J H H
N W L A E O R L B J N O I F K T M Z H N
C E F S E W L A A A N I E L E E R A E O
K E L N D A I F B H S R U L E N S L N R
O Q A B H F H T A W A I S T A G J H O D
D U E G I T I M H N E N N M I K N U T Q
I T Z L B D C Z I E I R R G F C G A S N
Z X K N Z A P S X W R U D Y E E L R N T
Q J Z U R Y T F E T H S X W G R Z Q O D
Z Z H T H O S T Q T T T P H U B G P R L
L T E N N P A M A L N L A O D N Y Y A K
A R G B E K B M A I T T N M O H K N H Y
H Y N B S X U P H S T K M B P N L C S O
T G D S G R E G E W L L E Z E E N E R Y
```

1. Starred in "Tomb Raider"
2. Starred in "Never Been Kissed"
3. Starred as Catwoman
4. Starred in "Corpse Bride"
5. Starred in "Bruce Almighty"
6. Starred in "The Mexican"
7. Starred as young Iris Murdoch
8. Starred in "L A Confidential"
9. Starred in "Just Like Heaven"
10. Starred as Bridget Jones
11. Starred in "Basic Instinct"
12. Starred in "Kill Bill"

Actors
wordsearch

Find the names of the actors. Words can go horizontally, vertically and diagonally, and can read forwards and backwards.

```
L V M I C W S W E E E G X I X Z R S S G
K M L G E O R G E C L O O N E Y C D K V
O E E E R E G D R A H C I R P A L I A T
K E O Q I O F V R K L U H C S S C T Y N
I Q N H I D V D F L W T K I M M U A R A
X I A N O M A D T T A M L N P A G Z L R
K C R Q V P B I D D W L R I Z I B C P G
K Z D Z A E H R R V I K E I S L U D U H
X T O E U A R T A W O R S N C L P S D G
J A D S K H L U E D C Z I H M I O V P U
O U I W C B U C S E P B E S I W H K R H
H K C D X I U Y B S B I U B R N R T I P
N U A P V R W R J O E X T W Z I K G S G
N R P M B D O T R E I L V T I B A O I Y
Y S R B O S X M T P O Q L S Y O S H P S
D M I H N M I R W M R H S C Q R X N S E
E B O A B T Q V Z D L K V H R X S C A D
P G N Y R E N N O C N A E S T O K G T M
P K M F K C A S U C N H O J M C W I Z T
G D I M C Q J P P O J H G I O B I E S L
```

1. Starred in "Troy"
2. Starred in "Die Hard" movies
3. Starred in "Three Kings"
4. Starred in "Nine Months"
5. Starred in "High Fidelity"
6. Starred as Willy Wonka
7. Starred in "Titanic"
8. Starred as Will Hunting
9. Starred in "Die Another Day"
10. Starred in "Pretty Woman"
11. Starred as Mrs Doubtfire
12. Starred in "Gladiator"
13. Starred in "The Rock"
14. Starred in "Jacob's Ladder"

Tom Cruise wordsearch

Find the words listed below. Words can go horizontally, vertically and diagonally, and can read forwards and backwards.

```
M C L K S M T O P G U N R B C O D Z M A
S T T I A D I J F Q Q L Y O O A C I N F
U S G R G T P M A W U D C D Y L S N Y E
S H E C U U I U I P D K C S U S P Z V W
L C H N I O S E R R T V O W I O T U N G
N L I P I T C V H A O F G O I U H A E O
O D V E C S N N I O T G N K H M M Y R O
K V U L N K U L O H L I E S M D Z A I D
R O X E J T J B U I M M E R I I C W U M
A R A P B O O N Y P L D E K S I D A G E
I A H P M V D L O K I E E S V I H D A N
N O Z C R E T S O W S L D O J K P N M C
M D H P R H S C S G O I K T N Y T A Y W
A Q P Q E I S E T C Y N R T A I T R R S
N E X F B N Y U I E O C F M R T T A R H
P F I L V E S N I R S J P I Q C S F E Q
I R E C O L O R O F M O N E Y I R E J C
M X G B Z U R C E P O L E N E P L L L E
M C Z Y K S A L L I N A V K I G C P W O
S G C P E J C J V Q Z Q A M F S M Z G P
```

A FEW GOOD MEN

COCKTAIL

COLOR OF MONEY

DAYS OF THUNDER

EYES WIDE SHUT

FAR AND AWAY

JERRY MAGUIRE

KATIE HOLMES

LESTAT DE LIONCOURT

MIMI ROGERS

MISSION IMPOSSIBLE

NICOLE KIDMAN

PENELOPE CRUZ

RAIN MAN

RISKY BUSINESS

RON KOVIC

SCIENTOLOGY

THE FIRM

TOP GUN

VANILLA SKY

Underwater wordsearch

Find the words listed below. Words can go horizontally,
vertically and diagonally, and can read forwards and backwards.

```
L E V R C X K I Y K X Z B E D M W K G B
X M Z K S D C E T T T N O V E M F I X Y
W I X R K A S R U G U D A Z V W G W L E
I K A A U L L C A N Y W I O Q D Y K T N
H V Q H K W O M U B Z X Z A O V D Y O O
T S Q S S H L B O B H S I F R A T S O M
G T O E H A Z F S N A S P A H L E C A E
P I W M I L J K J T E D S W H A T M C N
O N J H P E K L P A E E I X X O W Z W A
R G J M W Z Z U B S A R F V P O C X X B
E R D P R C X E S H L E L U E L H A K E
T A T D E A D H O S V Y S R O R A H E Q
S Y R R C T O R A R P M D W S Z Q Y B I
Y A O E K A S O X S J W N L Q F U H M O
O R U F L E M H Y K X F N O T K N A L P
B T T N S C Z E P J I S H V P J Y V E E
B L U E T A N G C S S U C T E V G T O D
P J K U R E V Q H J U O I A W M O J E L
W I D S F E E R L A R O C I J M N C B M
W K Z S S F H C R O P L E E Y A R O M P
```

ANEMONE

BLUE TANG

CLOWNFISH

CORAL REEF

CRAB

HAKE

LOBSTER

MORAY EEL

OCTOPUS

OYSTER

PLANKTON

SALMON

SCUBA DIVER

SEA HORSE

SEABED

SHARK

SHIPWRECK

SHOAL

STARFISH

STING RAY

TROUT

WHALE

120

Dinosaur wordsearch

Find the words listed below. Words can go horizontally,
vertically and diagonally, and can read forwards and backwards.

```
Y P M X Y N O Y R A B S V J C D X K Y S
V T T I O S P J S Q U N E H I V N A T U
E E T G C C T A H P G S A P V U I U R H
L R R R Q R V E R Y S T L U P A K K I C
O A Q O A V O A G N K O E J U O G X C Y
C N P Q L I C D O O D O O U I M E S E N
I O I I H E M D O O C J Y Q W R R U R O
R D H G T K O M C N O E I Z S Y U E A N
A O W A U R D U A V T T R U E L A M T I
P N L M T A S B I W N O R A C H S O O E
T P S E W H N R B U Q U S L S Q O R P D
O O M T B H A O Z P A O K A Y S I D S U
R I D G G P V I D S W C N X U G L O V P
D M D W T O X C O O Q P T C M R P R L Y
U Q J O S A O N G D N X P M W Z U O H P
Y E R H G D N S U R U A S A I A M S J P
C N I J G A S U R U A S O L Y K N A O S
M R N S R H E L I C O P R I O N C U P M
N V D Y L V V I C W J H Z N O I S P Q K
L S T G U H E I H H O E R T J B M U R M
```

ANKYLOSAURUS	IGUANODON	PLIOSAUR
BARYONYX	MAIASAURUS	PTERANODON
DEINONYCHUS	MICRODONTOSAURUS	STEGOCERAS
DIMETRODON	ORODROMEUS	TRICERATOPS
DIPLODOCUS	OVIRAPTOR	TYRANNOSAURUS REX
HELICOPRION	PLATECARPUS	VELOCIRAPTOR

Detective wordsearch

Find the words listed below. Words can go horizontally, vertically and diagonally, and can read forwards and backwards.

```
T S T P Q Y W C G K B X I C D T F H M Y
T S I U Y X H Y R A V N F E E R E O S C
D Z E T F W M U B H V S Q Y O R O I P A
V G X R A U Q H V E O T Y C C N M N Y R
B E U J R Z N E S G B M K U L Y C J G T
J X U M C A M T V O R F L I V E A F L K
K N F A D K I B D B O E G H Z N S I A C
D S X K I G K P Y R P H T W N E E R S I
R L W Y A A F J D O T O I G B C F E S D
A E F T J Y K I I I E U H R F S I C S D
G U E O R O L R N M A G N U M E L I G I
N T K E D Y O G J A Z H E Q T M E L E U
E H T N L T B O S O U H J D Y I G O A C
T S H E R L O C K H O L M E S R I P N O
Q A Z D H V E L H J Y Z D Q C C F A O L
S W G T V B X P G N O S A M Y R R E P U
A N X R Z F Z C U N P I K M T H C Q K M
N S O S L E G N A S E I L R A H C L Q B
G H P O M O D H G N E C U Q B P H H U O
L D H K P A H F M K T J M T P Q S W G E
```

ARREST

CASE FILE

CHARLIES ANGELS

CLUE

COLUMBO

CRIME SCENE

DICK TRACY

DRAGNET

HERCULE POIROT

INVESTIGATE

KOJAK

MAGNUM

MOONLIGHTING

PERRY MASON

POLICE

ROCKFORD

SHERLOCK HOLMES

SLEUTH

SNOOP

SPYGLASS

Beatles
wordsearch

Find the words listed below. Words can go horizontally,
vertically and diagonally, and can read forwards and backwards.

```
S Q G B F G X B X Q N B R V E P B Y V N
F D P E P T I F U N K Z N K A L E R P T
T S L O O Y W Q J L B F J P R L X L Q L
N I J E H R L R G J E I E U L N H O U G
F P C J I E G F K D C R C O U D A O M I
L R X K T F A E U C B P W T R F R P X R
Z L E I E B Y J H A X S D I P Y D R S I
L D T L F T Y R C A U T B A E N D E U N
A B Q O E E T K R B R A R N G Z A V O G
E B U P H A W O M E S R T M I F Y I Y O
Z R Q Q G R N A R A B R I N G Y S L S S
I D X S I C R O E I A W M S U T N S E T
X V C T F I M E R C D L A S O V I O V A
U Y E X N S R U C R M E O R B N G U O R
O R B E B F P M M H I S X V T O H M L R
P O U M O M L T R C M G P U E S T J E A
T S O M H U Q O P J A M B K S M P Q H F
A I Y G A R E V O L V E R Y C X E L S V
J I M P C A V E R N C L U B P X Z D E N
O T E N A L Y N N E P D B O G I F U O H
```

CAVERN CLUB

ELEANOR RIGBY

FAB FOUR

FREE AS A BIRD

GEORGE HARRISON

HARD DAYS NIGHT

HELP

HEY JUDE

LET IT BE

LIVERPOOL

LOVE ME DO

PAPERBACK WRITER

PAUL MCCARTNEY

PENNY LANE

REVOLVER

RINGO STARR

SHE LOVES YOU

STRAWBERRY FIELDS

TICKET TO RIDE

YELLOW SUBMARINE

John Wayne
wordsearch

Find the words listed below. Words can go horizontally, vertically and diagonally, and can read forwards and backwards.

```
K U Y S O Q V M V W W V K D M S Z M H C
S G Z O T D U D U O Z C S F A Y F J Z A
R U X A M O R I J S O A O V R O Y L K W
P O S K G U N G E T I R R T I B W U P J
D I N S A R K Y N T T H R X O W G L V C
O L B A Y L O I B A M U C B N O T A J I
R L S L V T L A P R E A A S M C Q U Q R
E B D A G C G A I G O C N J O E B O F C
G I G O M H C H R K K O V H R H Z O L U
O G D T P H M I D T P W K L R T O N Y S
N J Z H E H T C O F T U M E I M C P I W
T A B T G H B B U X G F Q J S K I B N O
R K B R E Q A P S M D F R K O P E F G R
A E G O W T Q O S V V G C K N Z Z I T L
I Z G N A W Y O M I N G O U T L A W I D
L Y M A B I G S T A M P E D E D E P B H G W
I W N T Y A D J C W R I O B R A V O E H
G G O M Q N F P U A I H I W T J C F R N
X R G P K I T C H N F Y S T N A X J S P
W A R W A G O N G T Z I D X H F O T O Z
```

BACK TO BATAAN	MARION MORRISON	THE COWBOYS
BIG JAKE	MCLINTOCK	TRUE GRIT
BIG STAMPEDE	NORTH TO ALASKA	WAR WAGON
CHISUM	OREGON TRAIL	WYOMING OUTLAW
CIRCUS WORLD	QUIET MAN	
FLYING TIGERS	RIO BRAVO	
FORT APACHE	STONY BROOKE	

WWE Superstars
wordsearch

Find the words listed below. Words can go horizontally, vertically and diagonally, and can read forwards and backwards.

```
V E R H G P E S A I B I D D E T K E L O
B M V E R O D D Y P I P E R O B G A L N
A K F C Y N A I T S I R H C T A K K W J
T C V J E M P T R I P L E H V G U U C R
I G P N E Z Y W Z R S I P A U V R N T Z
S K A G N L G S X O T D S H N D T S I J
T K D S R V R U T M Q Y J A D P A Y T E
A E C L R B E B J E D U Q R E F N M O S
H G A E I R G R I N R Z H D R H G M S S
O U R A A L O J A I B I Q C T Y L I A E
B Q L H L F R R O M I M O O A D E J N V
Z X I C F S Y K N V G Z J R K R Z J T E
V F T I C E H C N I S S X E E A Z O A N
F B O M I A E A R Z H D F H R H M H N T
P A J N R F L B A Z O I I O Z T A N A U
W L T W O F M I D O W S P L U T Y C I R
O R V A V L S V Y F S Z P L Q A U E G A
O O M H H U L K H O G A N Y M M E N C F
L S Y S A V I N C E M C M A H O N A C S
T R E K O O B F T I O N E B S I R H C Z
```

BATISTA	GREGORY HELMS	KURT ANGLE	TED DIBIASE
BIG SHOW	HARDCORE HOLLY	MATT HARDY	TITO SANTANA
BOOKER T	HULK HOGAN	RANDY SAVAGE	TRIPLE H
CARLITO	JESSE VENTURA	REY MYSTERIO	UNDERTAKER
CHRIS BENOIT	JIMMY SNUKA	RIC FLAIR	VINCE MCMAHON
CHRISTIAN	JOHN CENA	RODDY PIPER	
EDGE	KANE	SHAWN MICHAELS	

Music Bands
wordsearch

Find the words listed below. Words can go horizontally,
vertically and diagonally, and can read forwards and backwards.

```
N A A R Y W N Y X E A I A L B M S R T C
Y S F B J B Z A G R E E N D A Y O O P M
N C E P Z D A V R B O D P Z E L X I C S
M E M E H O X C O U P G S H L S N P Y Z
W P J M R K C L K E D D D I D K F T I G
E F V U Q G E E B S N N N K F G O P J S
C Z T H N F E K V O T G A L U X U B P J
N Y Q S P B K D M I S R O R M X R P H P
B M F T D P N S E T F Y E U U T T Z F E
S S X N I U O I O E D N B E V D O Q S A
Y J E I V R C N B I R H O E T N P H W R
E E J T S H E W I O G H K S A B S K Y L
T N Y S I S D Z Y H Z S T H K T O M S J
O U I V N O X A L W H N I N Q C L Y L A
M A T R S V L T B E D Z E E R G A E S M
S Z Z H V P X Z W H B E O N X H L J S C
M S F W D A E I L T U Q F A X V N I D U
S D P L R M N O T Q X R V A W D J M U J
I G O B L M Z A J T D S J E D R O H S X
Y C O D G P H U Q X C P D M K M V P L O
```

BACKSTREET BOYS	INXS	QUEEN
BEATLES	JACKSON FIVE	ROLLING STONES
COLDPLAY	NIRVANA	THE WHO
DURAN DURAN	OSMONDS	THREE DEGREES
FOUR TOPS	PEARL JAM	
GREEN DAY	PINK FLOYD	

Musicals
wordsearch

Find the words listed below. Words can go horizontally, vertically and diagonally, and can read forwards and backwards.

```
J U E C C G V A T E R A B A C I R N V R
S V P S O Z P B M T U D T T O J A C L T
G T R F A Y K G H O K R D D V T D W E R
O U A M Y E P C N F H S M I S E H A H P
S D J R X R R G Q G T A N K L I R T R P
M R E B L X O G T A S R L H S E Z Q X S
C A D T N I K T C I O Y T K P E I N N A
Z S M B A K G L S G W C F O O Y E B S B
U Z D M E I J H A E A E E Y T V C I N R
H B O V A J I C T D D H Z H Y I D L I F
W E I F I M I F K E T I E Q S E N L P D
P S X F O H I C D F X K S U J M K Y P W
W P T G C D E A O U I P M T M A D E O W
A T I V E O R M U N Z F R A S F Y L P R
C D O P I O O A G P O Y S E U E H L Y E
Y L M F U T U A Z D L N D D S P W I R V
H T N A N I N H N I U U P C J S X O A I
H T X A R D Z U C X W X D X U X N T M L
H K H O I R O Y D A L R I A F Y M M L O
L P T A U S Q Q X N O G I A S S S I M F
```

ANNIE	GREASE	PHANTOM OF THE OPERA
BILLY ELLIOT	MAMMA MIA	SOUND OF MUSIC
CABARET	MARY POPPINS	STARLIGHT EXPRESS
CATS	MISS SAIGON	THE KING AND I
CHICAGO	MY FAIR LADY	WEST SIDE STORY
EVITA	OKLAHOMA	WIZARD OF OZ
FAME	OLIVER	

Hollywood
Legends wordsearch

Find the words listed below. Words can go horizontally,
vertically and diagonally, and can read forwards and backwards.

```
E X P M T T J B K T T R V R N Z L X O R
S L I B U H B X G G V O E O V S I R Y J
W L B S A H A V Y Z J T Y C E A Q A C N
N T O A O R C W V H B Y X K R L U F H V
I M O P G N B T F E Y V C H G G N A A K
V C A N O K O A I Z Y S J U F U A O R A
R V D E L M R T R M P S N D L O E B L Q
A D Y G W O V A S A T I V S H D D R E K
M L N J M E M Q L E S R H O O K S A S C
E B N K I U S N O C H T E N F R E G B E
E S F G W U L T T I Q N A B J I M A R P
L B F X Y O O K L H E P O N O K A T O Y
E O R N O M N Y L I R A M T W R J E N R
E L P M E T Y E L R I H S O L Y C R S O
X S U U S I V A D E T T E B E R C G O G
W D D U A R T A N I S K N A R F A K N E
F R E D A S T A I R E L N X M F J H E R
J N J Q T D L E I F S N A M E N A J C G
C U W D D Y G I N G E R R O G E R S Z T
E T Z A S O G T N A R G Y R A C P U G E
```

BARBARA STANWYCK	FRED ASTAIRE	LEE MARVIN
BETTE DAVIS	GINGER ROGERS	MAE WEST
CARY GRANT	GREGORY PECK	MARILYN MONROE
CHARLES BRONSON	GRETA GARBO	ROBERT MITCHUM
CHARLTON HESTON	JAMES DEAN	ROCK HUDSON
CLARK GABLE	JANE MANSFIELD	SHIRLEY TEMPLE
FRANK SINATRA	KIRK DOUGLAS	

Royal Family
wordsearch

Find the words listed below. Words can go horizontally,
vertically and diagonally, and can read forwards and backwards.

```
T I W M S L R E J O N V D J B W N Q N E
N C A G U E H M B C Y E U X E T V O O L
E R J B T Q L X X N V M H S Y D K B D T
M Z Q E L H C R D A G K T A E Z U E N S
A P J E R W E I A I I M G K Z C L U O A
I V Z F W X A Q C H I R E U K G L E L C
L S C E C N X X U N C L B I N R Q X F R
R F R A A R D C S E A E N X Q H H T O O
A O K T V Y O T J Z E G C C C J M A R S
P U S E N N E W G I H N Q N U P V E E D
X S T R I C F N A N Q K Y I F P F W N
V W I S A A X S M Q Z J E D X R G W O I
L A H B G T U P Z T E N I A Q U P Q T W
R F B G A J A P R I N C E P H I L I P M
T E F U Q L E N N A S S E C N I R P X Y
Y I H M A Y R R A H D N A M A I L L I W
K L H C O F S W U S F J X U X G J S D T
E G E X B K J H P T H R O N E A C X C C
L P U C S B N O D N O L E V W B W P S L
J N H D H L D Q C F N U R F Y H T C K I
```

BEEFEATERS   PARLIAMENT   THRONE
BUCKINGHAM PALACE   PRINCE CHARLES   TOWER OF LONDON
CROWN   PRINCE PHILIP   WESTMINSTER ABBEY
DIANA   PRINCESS ANNE   WILLIAM AND HARRY
LONDON   THE QUEEN   WINDSOR CASTLE

Elvis Presley
wordsearch

Find the words listed below. Words can go horizontally,
vertically and diagonally, and can read forwards and backwards.

```
J A I L H O U S E R O C K I R Z K G V I
A P D V A E K N Q N O R P E N Q W T H L
B P I O I D V T G V E X T A J P H M A Q
A U R C N D S N A D X U O G Q S G R R U
E K J M S T I R N V R K S I P D R J D H
S O G B A K B E B N C T W B P N P P H N
Q O T P E L R E T D U F L Y T I T S E M
K H G H G R B O C C L U W R E M B B A W
G S T R U T S K K R E Z A F G S Z U D S
J L L S A E R O G S U E B O M U X I E T
E L O G N C N K U Z H E D B U O W T D E
J A Y D D Y E E H N D D L W B I O E W Y
S I E X O V D L E N N R B A N C B D O O
I R L U S E N D A U U X N G H I L D M G
H N O U S H O N O N M D F F V P I Y A B
C O K H T O F H I T D P F R F S O B N C
Q L O B W J B J E O Q N V I U U M E K E
A E K U M U L K K F D V A B U S V A S I
S Y L E T O H K A E R B T R A E H R X F
F I L Q T L O V E M E T E N D E R P C V
```

ALL SHOOK UP   JAILHOUSE ROCK   THE KING
BLUE SUEDE SHOES   LOVE ME TENDER   WOODEN HEART
DON'T BE CRUEL   RETURN TO SENDER
GRACELAND   STUCK ON YOU
HARD HEADED WOMAN   SURRENDER
HEARTBREAK HOTEL   SUSPICIOUS MINDS
HOUND DOG   TEDDY BEAR

American States
wordsearch

Find the words listed below. Words can go horizontally,
vertically and diagonally, and can read forwards and backwards.

```
N G G Z D I T D N A L Y R A M C Y Y S X
O U S F S L W U D K B S N J U W N A Z K
T X T S D L E E C I Q Y A A Q W S M F E
G H Y A R I K L V I W B D C A N W N T N
N F V U H N R W M H T I I N A Y J E S T
I A E A H O O D M O R C O K G H N W A U
H A N X W I Y X N O N Z E X A O C M S C
S Z S A S S W D L A I T N N R N E E N K
A V U S I A E F E R L N A T N N S X A Y
W Z G F A S N W A O E S H N I O G I K A
A Y J Z C Q I S M W O D I A A O C C R L
O I T E V A T U E C A I M E K F Z O A A
H N N W G E B N O K R R H W D E S M A B
A O C R X K G H O L L U W O D O D E L A
D G N A O L H T T N O M R E V C H W A M
I E S N A F A C A K H A W A I I A R S A
Q R P N U T I S O U T H D A K O T A K Q
I O D L L Q O L N P A M O H A L K O A P
I D V P O Q A L A K K P A D A V E N R E
Q O W M K P K Z G C H A Z Q L B B B I X
```

ALABAMA	IDAHO	NEVADA	RHODE ISLAND
ALASKA	ILLINOIS	NEW ENGLAND	SOUTH DAKOTA
ARIZONA	KANSAS	NEW MEXICO	TEXAS
ARKANSAS	KENTUCKY	NEW YORK	UTAH
CALIFORNIA	LOUISIANA	NORTH DAKOTA	VERMONT
CONNECTICUT	MAINE	OHIO	WASHINGTON
FLORIDA	MARYLAND	OKLAHOMA	
HAWAII	MONTANA	OREGON	

Car Makers
wordsearch

Find the words listed below. Words can go horizontally,
vertically and diagonally, and can read forwards and backwards.

```
E H U K L O A P Z C J B X D P C T C B K
K Z M J K G L V M M D T W G A C Z K T W
Q I M S T T O C P T P A A R I W A A T D
W G T Z F L V P H Y E O D T E E S F W F
D K H R V U M Q M R G T R N R V K E O D
N C F O A A M K E C Y O R S L L O R C A
J X N W P N N T R E E H X O C U D R J D
F V P S A E S Q C N V S S V A H A A I O
K S F H X R U T E G I Y R Z C O E R W K
K W I B D S E G D O D E E I S N H I P N
F D N B Z Z A L E X U S P D S D T H Q Y
Y O N I Z W A A S O A Q Z V V A S O N Y
S I J O S T Q J B Y T I T X R K V H M Q
Q T G K T S C H E V R O L E T M P X Y J
X T L W F I A D N U H S U M C N F T K
T O A J T Z H N Z O U A C I S V F C F Q
V U J M I B A V T F M H I W W W X Z I J
R T L B P J J A Q U F I J N L R O V U R
I U A N E D I J I R D X A D D A P K P K
H X X L Y F U K J N L E K B C M M E C D
```

AUDI	FORD	PEUGEOT	TOYOTA
CHEVROLET	HONDA	PORSCHE	VOLKSWAGEN
CHRYSLER	HYUNDAI	RENAULT	VOLVO
CITROEN	LEXUS	ROLLS ROYCE	
DODGE	MASERATI	ROVER	
FERRARI	MERCEDES BENZ	SAAB	
FIAT	NISSAN	SKODA	

Harry Potter
wordsearch

Find the words listed below. Words can go horizontally,
vertically and diagonally, and can read forwards and backwards.

```
C G H I P E E X G K U F C J I P Y T O R
A X N C P A F H A U S T A N G N A O B Y
O L I P T H M F U V A L J R U H B M S O
Q D H E R I O S F O P F Y E L D U D O I
H B D A H C D E R I F F O T E L B O G K
Z U S M G U Q D N E F O H T H K D E M F
B X N Y W R R W I I D F Z O E E B N O W
I P J B I W I G N U X U C P G S R O J L
F Q A G M P D D M R Q L A Y I W N I N Y
E L N Z X D O B O B O N Q R R V A M N X
C H G P N R L S Z E S V I R A N B R U M
M U B S B E S I X C W U O A E M A E T X
K F A X D E D A E M S G O H K V K H J S
J F Y O F L A M U B U E I O E L Z G U P
L L R O P R Y E L S A E W N O R A V X F
S E R X Q B X A P L P L C Z H S F E U P
W P X Z N D C O H V O L X Y U C B S N O
P U F P E K R L F D A F I I A V A Z E B
A F C N U R N N Y W P Q D T Q H Z Q E U
F F G L R L K S K C I P O H S B B Z B T
```

AZKABAN
DUDLEY
DUMBLEDORE
GOBLET OF FIRE
GRYFFINDOR
HAGRID

HARRY POTTER
HERMIONE
HOGSMEADE
HOGWARTS
HUFFLEPUFF
MALFOY

MARAUDERS MAP
PHOENIX
PROFESSOR
QUIDDITCH
RAVENCLAW
RON WEASLEY

SIRIUS BLACK
SLYTHERIN
SNAPE

Olympic Sports
wordsearch

Find the words listed below. Words can go horizontally,
vertically and diagonally, and can read forwards and backwards.

```
O B M D I V I N G N I L C Y C V R U A R
M L G A Y B V O F J E O S Q V N R C H H
W B E A H G P A W T G N I L I A S N Z N
K D E C A T H L O N P G G C H Q O S E B
Y T T A I W G Y Q M J J O Q R H O T Y M
N O Q Q C I V G D C S U U H T H X D B N
O X U Q L H I G H J U M P A D H P P H D
Y Z A D S J V B Y P H P R G P Q H U O M
P B Z M G C R O Z N A A Y G E M R K K O
S A J X R V Y W L O M I G L T D K R V J
E D L N V Q T P I L M B V W L E P J C Y
R M S I N A I R T S E U Q E U C B Z U A
S I N N E T T T W J R Y S V A A B S C H
J N N T Y B U I A C T J B H V R D C Z N
V T Q F V P M V J S H Z N A E Y I E T H
P O V Y T M E A U A R G G L L A W I H Q
P N P O I L O V E H O C Q W O L H C N H
A V H N I D O H I W W B R A P E X J Y R
X S G N I T O O H S O C C E R R G M Q B
I G M V P D O J K O Q S O O F E R H L N
```

BADMINTON	HAMMER THROW	POLE VAULT	SWIMMING
BEACH VOLLEYBALL	HIGH JUMP	RELAY RACE	TENNIS
CYCLING	HURDLES	SAILING	
DECATHLON	JAVELIN	SHOOTING	
DIVING	LONG JUMP	SHOT PUT	
EQUESTRIANISM	MARATHON	SOCCER	

Bird
wordsearch

Find the words listed below. Words can go horizontally,
vertically and diagonally, and can read forwards and backwards.

```
I  D  C  J  O  T  W  O  R  R  A  P  S  H  D
S  R  S  E  A  G  U  L  L  M  F  S  W  A  N
E  I  R  K  T  W  C  N  R  H  L  B  R  R  A
A  B  K  E  O  O  I  J  Y  C  A  K  D  E  W
G  G  U  L  H  O  R  J  Z  N  M  R  U  K  X
L  N  G  T  S  S  K  R  K  I  I  O  L  C  Z
E  I  X  W  S  K  I  A  A  F  N  T  O  E  O
P  M  N  M  O  A  W  F  B  P  G  S  D  P  S
E  M  I  C  R  U  S  R  G  U  O  W  G  D  T
L  U  F  O  T  D  O  V  E  N  R  B  E  O  R
I  H  F  V  A  R  S  O  X  G  I  R  M  O  I
C  Y  U  D  B  Y  R  A  N  A  C  K  A  W  C
A  O  P  B  L  P  E  A  C  O  C  K  D  S  H
N  Q  O  A  A  V  U  L  T  U  R  E  H  A  U
I  E  R  U  N  O  C  T  O  U  C  A  N  P  Y
```

ALBATROSS	FLAMINGO	PEACOCK	SWAN
CANARY	HUMMINGBIRD	PELICAN	TOUCAN
CONURE	KINGFISHER	PUFFIN	VULTURE
DOVE	KOOKABURRA	SEAGULL	WOODPECKER
EAGLE	OSTRICH	SPARROW	
FINCH	PARROT	STORK	

Snake wordsearch

Find the words listed below. Words can go horizontally,
vertically and diagonally, and can read forwards and backwards.

```
C M O N E V J F F A N G S R R
K O U O C I C G W B P Z O B E
C G M C H P Z W O E W T U G C
E H R M L D R D J Z C N R R A
N M T G O V H U Q I T E N A R
G C N U S N A L R X E K K T K
N I S M O D G T W N B I A T C
I G G N L M S A M X N Z N L A
R O W Q R N N A R G A E A E L
N R L K O E M O C T D L C S B
T U X C K B P O T S E F O N D
H O A Y A D B I E T I R N A O
J O R C E R O K V L O T D K J
B Y E W A X E M X E M C A E Y
O R E H T I L S N O H T Y P V
```

ANACONDA	FANGS	RATTLESNAKE
BLACK RACER	GREEN MAMBA	RINGNECK
BOA CONSTRICTOR	KING COBRA	SLITHER
COMMON GARTER	MEX MEX	VENOM
COTTONMOUTH	PYTHON	VIPER

Wedding wordsearch

Find the words listed below. Words can go horizontally, vertically and diagonally, and can read forwards and backwards.

```
Y  J  P  R  E  T  U  B  S  T  N  E  R  A  P
P  P  V  X  C  Y  E  E  V  R  A  T  L  A  Q
N  U  C  F  I  I  N  S  P  A  G  E  B  O  Y
X  Y  O  K  F  P  W  T  T  O  D  T  Q  L  D
R  E  N  Z  F  N  U  M  G  A  H  O  M  N  I
D  H  F  W  O  A  B  A  V  C  R  A  K  C  A
I  V  E  X  Y  G  Z  N  R  W  E  S  B  H  M
S  Y  T  Y  R  E  W  U  Z  N  C  T  R  E  S
F  T  T  G  T  P  H  M  L  Y  E  M  I  I  E
V  P  I  R  S  C  U  R  P  U  P  A  D  J  D
V  J  D  O  I  E  L  S  I  A  T  S  E  Z  I
U  O  V  O  G  R  I  N  G  S  I  T  I  H  R
T  G  W  M  E  X  T  V  K  F  O  E  N  I  B
G  N  K  S  R  A  V  P  K  V  N  R  W  R  G
T  H  G  I  N  G  N  I  D  D  E  W  C  F  V
```

AISLE	CONFETTI	RINGS
ALTAR	GROOM	TOASTMASTER
BEST MAN	PAGE BOY	VOWS
BRIDE	PARENTS	WEDDING NIGHT
BRIDESMAID	RECEPTION	
CHURCH	REGISTRY OFFICE	

Airport
wordsearch

Find the words listed below. Words can go horizontally, vertically and diagonally, and can read forwards and backwards.

```
V K C O S D N I W F S Y J S X
P I N D P T Z S L H A T S Y D
I Y E E F H R I U W M A O E R
L R H W S W G O N I P F P W K
O O O B I H E U P G T A D P N
T R L V T N R D N S R C A E S
P E I O S R G I U T S I A M A
E G D N X L D G U T R A O S R
G N A V I R A R A L Y T P W E
A E Y A A K E N I L S F H J H
G S F O N G C N I U L Q R U L
G S B U A J E E C M Q E K E P
U A Z T H C Q B H P R G R N E
L P E A W U U N L C J E I Y Z
S S E D R A W E T S J A T A Y
```

AIRLINE
BOARDING PASS
CHECK IN
CUSTOMS
DEPARTURE GATE
DUTY FREE

FLIGHT
HOLIDAY
LUGGAGE
PASSENGER
PASSPORT
PILOT

RUNWAY
STEWARDESS
SUITCASE
TERMINAL
VIEWING GALLERY
WINDSOCK

Mythology
wordsearch

Find the words listed below. Words can go horizontally,
vertically and diagonally, and can read forwards and backwards.

```
J Z O J O D I N Q N P V T O L
M S W U K B E X H M M N S T G
T U M I N O T A U R A I U P V
R E S N Y K X E U R C V P R A
D S N O H O R M C A H A M O L
A S N G B O M I R E P S Y M H
C Y I R S B S U L H S U L E A
H D A O L S S E R R U S O T L
I O L G U T N O V O P A T H L
L L U S N I D X K T I G N E A
L B H X I I I N N D E U U N
E V C O T D D L S E E P O S L
S X U E L E X W I M O L M A Q
K A C S I N O D A A H O M E R
S T T W I D I Y S B D V D D R
```

ACHILLES   HOMER   ODIN
ADONIS   ICARUS   ODYSSEUS
APHRODITE   ILIAD   OEDIPUS
CUCHULAINN   MENTOR   PEGASUS
EROS   MINOTAUR   PROMETHEUS
GORGON   MOUNT OLYMPUS VALHALLA
HELEN   NARCISSUS

Caribbean wordsearch

Find the words listed below. Words can go horizontally, vertically and diagonally, and can read forwards and backwards.

```
P M S B A E V N M R U D C P Q
O P N R B C U C G X O X O O H
G P I I L Q I A R M G R T C N
A W A A E I Z A I I T T A W O
B G T D S E A N M O C R T T T
O H N A I O I T F A I K M Q R
T U U N N C D S K B J I E Q I
O V O E A R P A B C L B L T N
F P M R M A R E B E O T T E I
Y J E G I K A C S R N C U V D
W D U N G N X I S K A H M O A
D H L P S R E G G A E B B U D
N E B E Q A L L I U G N A E R
K S A E X O T A N T I G U A C
P L B H G E I W M B O M I Q E
```

ANGUILLA
ANTIGUA
BARBADOS
BLUE MOUNTAINS
CARIBBEAN SEA

CRICKET
DOMINICA
GRENADA
JAMAICA
PORT OF SPAIN

REGGAE
RUM COCKTAIL
TOBAGO
TRINIDAD

Camping
wordsearch

Find the words listed below. Words can go horizontally,
vertically and diagonally, and can read forwards and backwards.

```
X G L N E M A H Q I Y R F V C
E E N B A C K P A C K L H M L
D T S O Y D P V H E A Y Q E I
A Q I S S Y A B A S B R O J W
R S E S L G J Z H H N U G A F
M T R V P S N L G A S A T T A
Y O I G Y M I I V N B E R A C
K V F E I G A A S G R B O R I
N E P I H M R C N P Q Q P P L
I O M T T A B I R G Q Z E A I
F L A S C B P O I P L Z G U T
E V C A S E O Y U E P N L L I
Z L Y G E F L A N T E R N I E
W Y D L S M A T C H E S T N S
I T S K Y T E N T D L Q O A B
```

ARMY KNIFE

BACKPACK

CAMP FIRE

CAMPSITE

CARAVAN

FACILITIES

FLASHLIGHT

LANTERN

MATCHES

ROPE

SING SONG

SLEEPING BAG

STOVE

TARPAULIN

TENT

WATERPROOFS

Rivers
wordsearch

Find the words listed below. Words can go horizontally, vertically and diagonally, and can read forwards and backwards.

```
E R N V Q P G Y Y O F M E E O
Q V E U G Y A U D S M B R N N
S O C W O N K A E O U R C I H
J L S S G O R V C N R O R E D
Z G D T N O E O A I N K Z S T
A A Z L L R N D O G Q N E T L
M E O O N I B G O W M J M V L
B A C H R T R A G M S M X A A
E M P O G A E U P H R A T E S
Z A T J N N S S E G N A G N T
I Z U D T X A E I M C A O N I
O O E Y O H Y U M N Q S V I G
W N S L T L G N H A D Y Q L R
F J D H S T L V X U H Y P E I
P A R A N A G B H J F T H L S
```

AMAZON	HUDSON	THAMES
COLORADO	NILE	TIGRIS
CONGO	ORINOCO	VOLGA
DANUBE	PARANA	YANGTZE
EUPHRATES	RIO GRANDE	YUKON
GANGES	SEINE	ZAMBEZI
HUANG HO	SEVERN	

Mountains wordsearch

Find the words listed below. Words can go horizontally, vertically and diagonally, and can read forwards and backwards.

```
M M C K I N L E Y Y S K S D L
L J I W K R T Q G R I F U J I
T W F K L H O E Y L P N S T K
S K Z I V F V C I C R N N G J
E E Y C S U G M K O I I E N V
R A L C K S A M H I O E M L C
E V U J I N A R H P E H Y N K
V T K G J Z E M A U Q S A Z A
E R N A A T Y M N H F L E E E
U N R Q T C A G H O B F S N P
L O N A O R N L L T S T T F H
A E M N O G Q O N M O N W M A
K R X N G F N O C H Z W I P R
A K A H P A M J L A M U Y V O
M P M O U N T C O O K V C D B
```

ACONCAGUA
BORAH PEAK
EVEREST
FUJI
KILIMANJARO

LHOTSE
MAKALU
MATTERHORN
MCKINLEY
MONT BLANC

MOUNT COOK
PANORAMA POINT
ROCKIES
VINSON MASSIF

American
Government wordsearch

Find the words listed below. Words can go horizontally,
vertically and diagonally, and can read forwards and backwards.

```
C F N V L U O B R P O E R Q R
C B O L O Z V X T C S J W E S
D T I Z T T C T O U N R P Y U
N N T G Z U E N O W E R F R C
O E C T D L G H W P E R Q A U
T D E Z E R E A U S C P N M A
G I L Z E T P B E K V U T I C
N S E S I A L N W T D X R R Y
I E S H W I T E T A N E S P G
H R W M C A D E M O C R A T S
S P W A T O K V B S D N Q O O
A N N I H U U Z G R Q U M R Y
W S V T R U O C E M E R P U S
P E V C Z V Z A V B K F N A C
S C A P I T O L H I L L O V E
```

CAPITOL HILL
CAUCUS
CONGRESS
DEMOCRATS
ELECTION

PRESIDENT
PRIMARY
REPRESENTATIVES
REPUBLICANS
SENATE

SUPREME COURT
VOTE
WASHINGTON DC
WHITE HOUSE

Where were they Born? wordsearch

Find the places where these people were born. Words can go horizontally, vertically and diagonally, and can read forwards and backwards.

```
B H U S I Q J T D A T C F S A
N E W Z E A L A N D D R E I T
F T I D R X T F B C A A S M C
G A N N C S E F T N O S N Q R
H U D A M O Y Y C G U H G A M
O S I L N U Z E T R A H A Q C
N T A E X T A U S T R A L I A
G R R R T H D N A L G N E X P
K I P I W A S C O T L A N D P
O A A A D F A C I A M A J N R
N I L Z G R L E G Q E U O X L
G E T R W I A R G E N T I N A
S O L A Y C B K U Y M P X F K
J N G L L A S P P B T C O X B
J R O E L Y A D U N L I L B Q
```

1. Che Guevara	7. Jackie Chan	13. Lenin
2. Paul Hogan	8. Mahatma Gandhi	14. Sean Connery
3. Arnie Schwarzenegger	9. Bono from U2	15. Nelson Mandela
4. Celine Dion	10. Christopher Columbus	16. Catherine Zeta-Jones
5. The Beatles	11. Bob Marley	
6. Gerard Depardieu	12. Sir Edmund Hillary	

Narnia
wordsearch

Find the words listed below. Words can go horizontally,
vertically and diagonally, and can read forwards and backwards.

O	X	T	L	D	S	U	R	K	R	K	O	H	S	Y
V	K	S	E	N	P	B	S	A	S	J	G	U	Z	Z
D	I	U	E	U	E	A	L	U	B	J	N	Q	E	A
T	B	Q	I	M	T	I	S	W	I	M	L	I	O	N
G	A	U	P	D	E	E	A	L	U	E	G	V	Y	G
I	D	D	P	E	R	R	K	T	A	N	R	J	A	L
N	T	L	Q	D	D	Y	R	G	C	N	L	O	T	D
A	M	D	O	R	I	E	I	K	Y	E	O	T	V	W
R	I	S	O	K	T	A	J	O	R	Q	O	S	X	V
R	N	B	I	S	W	H	I	T	E	W	I	T	C	H
B	E	A	I	W	U	Z	Q	L	J	V	S	Y	L	D
R	J	M	R	Z	E	H	Y	S	Y	U	Z	C	O	I
I	O	A	V	N	I	L	L	U	S	U	T	U	I	V
K	D	Q	P	A	I	D	S	A	J	B	M	L	J	R
Q	M	P	G	A	L	A	N	C	X	S	A	Q	X	P

ASLAN

C S LEWIS

EDMUND

GINARRBRIK

LION

LUCY

MISTER TUMNUS

NARNIA

OREIUS

PETER

SUSAN

WARDROBE

WHITE WITCH

Carnival wordsearch

Find the words listed below. Words can go horizontally,
vertically and diagonally, and can read forwards and backwards.

```
W N X Y Q R E G R U B M A H T
R A N M H N R L J K E W A U Z
B E Q G M S U Q L L S U N F C
Y W T S I M T O A S S N Z E K
P O V S E A G U O B E O Z L G
A K R R A F N L N L S L S P H
B X G E L O F T O O S S J P O
I O P U T Y C F S I C O Z A S
G P M S D S L R D L W O K E T
W E O N K O I E E L I D C E T
H O A Y V B S W Q L H D A F R
E C D E Q H W R T B L S E F A
E Q W T O I J Y J X Z O X O I
L I O W S M E G D O D T R T N
H M S K T E A C U P R I D E T
```

BIG WHEEL

CANDY FLOSS

COCONUT SHY

DODGEMS

GHOST TRAIN

GIANT SLIDE

HAMBURGER

LOG FLUME

ROLLER COASTER

SIDESHOW

TEACUP RIDE

TOFFEE APPLE

TUNNEL OF LOVE

TWISTER

Art
wordsearch

Find the artists. Words can go horizontally,
vertically and diagonally, and can read forwards and backwards.

```
A T E L R V X Z H J P V O Y U
N K U C E L O G H E E L A M P
X I S X B A O D R S E Y Z Y R
A T C E Y G H W A G B A Q Z C
X O A M N T G P N B K O M E V
W K C A N M D A A W V K W C I
H L V O O A L D T R N U S Y J
I I L N N E Z E U Q Z A L E V
S E E P H S E S P H R H X S X
T T W C P W T D A V I N C I L
L R I N E Z D A Z B A N L O T
E M T T Z B X M B C M M G M T
R K B Z B I T Y X L N W I Q G
I R E M B R A N D T E L C V M
O W A H H O Q O M V K N V C J
```

1. Painted "The Haywain"
2. Painted "Mona Lisa"
3. Painted "The Kiss"
4. Painted "The Creation of Adam"
5. Painted "Water Lilies"
6. Painted "Sistine Madonna"
7. Painted "The Money Changer"
8. Painted "Starry Night"
9. Painted "Venus at Her Mirror"
10. Painted "Portrait of the Artist's Mother"

Criminals
wordsearch

Find the words listed below. Words can go horizontally, vertically and diagonally, and can read forwards and backwards.

```
U U L A G E S Y S G U B G B Z
M J D L M K S N W L L M O N S
R R A Z L U R S J J O N L O D
P O O C M I X A O H N Q N O R
D X B M K H H H Y I V A C G A
E I S E L T N Y E T I L U O W
N I C O R G H P R C W Y D V D
O U H K O T A E U N F I E C E
P B Z T T R S L R A E M N K R
A L T C K U Y T W I Z H X S E
C I L E S K R K R G P O Y I T
L D R B C I E P X O H P E Y S
A X Z U B S L J I Y U U E E U
L H L D L L O S H N R D X R B
W O R R A B E D Y L C A A M H
```

AL CAPONE

BONNIE PARKER

BUGSY SEGAL

BUSTER EDWARDS

CLYDE BARROW

DICK TURPIN

GUY FAWKES

HENRY HILL

JACK THE RIPPER

JOHN GOTTI

KRAY TWINS

LUCKY LUCIANO

ROBERT STROUD

DIY
wordsearch

Find the words listed below. Words can go horizontally, vertically and diagonally, and can read forwards and backwards.

```
S C R E W D R I V E R J G T Q
V R D R I L L V T C N G G A R
W I O V M A E H B Z D G Y P K
A H N E N Q A S R N P M K E A
L J X T P M T E B B P O H M H
L I U I M A P B S Q O B P E S
P G T E P A T O L H S J U A U
A S R D P S C G E A C S I S R
P A W D D R X R N D D U N U B
E W N L A G U C Z I B D J R T
R A I U A T Q I R T K Y E E N
S A J S C P L I E R S S G R I
N L I I B R A D A W L O A M A
A C P H C N E B K R O W B M P
S V B L E V E L T I R I P S Q
```

BRADAWL

DRILL

HAMMER

JIGSAW

LADDER

MASKING TAPE

NAIL

PAINTBRUSH

PICTURE HOOK

PLIERS

SANDPAPER

SCREWDRIVER

SPIRIT LEVEL

TAPE MEASURE

WALLPAPER

WORKBENCH

Jewelry wordsearch

Find the words listed below. Words can go horizontally, vertically and diagonally, and can read forwards and backwards.

```
O W V Y Q N I A H C D L O G T
B T T B M L Y I B C O D Y R D
Y R E J V L E O V L A B B L O
D S O C N F M A A T I K H V M
U T V O A F F T R C X N B J P
T D P Y C L W L X R T X G O V
S I O J I H K B K K I G D S P
E A G O H V S C R D L N M D E
S M E J G S K G E A L C G G N
O O N P I W G K L N C R R O D
N N L L Y X P D B A H E E J A
P D V G M K H S V Q M S L M N
R E W N P L A T I N U M C E T
R R W E D D I N G R I N G Z T
H C U B I C Z I R C O N I A P
```

BLING
BRACELET
BROOCH
CHAIN
CUBIC ZIRCONIA

DIAMOND
EARRING
GOLD
NECKLACE
NOSE STUD

PENDANT
PLATINUM
SILVER
WEDDING RING

Cafe drinks
wordsearch

Find the words listed below. Words can go horizontally, vertically and diagonally, and can read forwards and backwards.

```
R O S C R E A M S O D A K A B
E J N A V F D M T I N B I Z J
T N M I E Q W E H J O H C R F
A A E B C M A X L T C O Q E V
W A N D X C J Y T I W T X Q C
L R E G A A U L B A G C X E Z
A R G E C N E P E Q O H F Z M
R B T U F O O M P X D O I N W
E F R Q F F B M V A Y C C G E
N H W B J X O C E W C O E Z O
I N E S Z V L C L L X L D O P
M E M I L K S H A K E A T P Q
R E I H T O O M S R C T E L F
A L O C Z L N D D B O E A J Q
E J F R U I T J U I C E S G Q
```

BOTTLE OF BEER

CAPPUCCINO

COFFEE

COLA

CREAM SODA

FRUIT JUICE

HOT CHOCOLATE

ICED TEA

LEMONADE

MILK SHAKE

MINERAL WATER

SMOOTHIE

Chinese food wordsearch

Find the words listed below. Words can go horizontally, vertically and diagonally, and can read forwards and backwards.

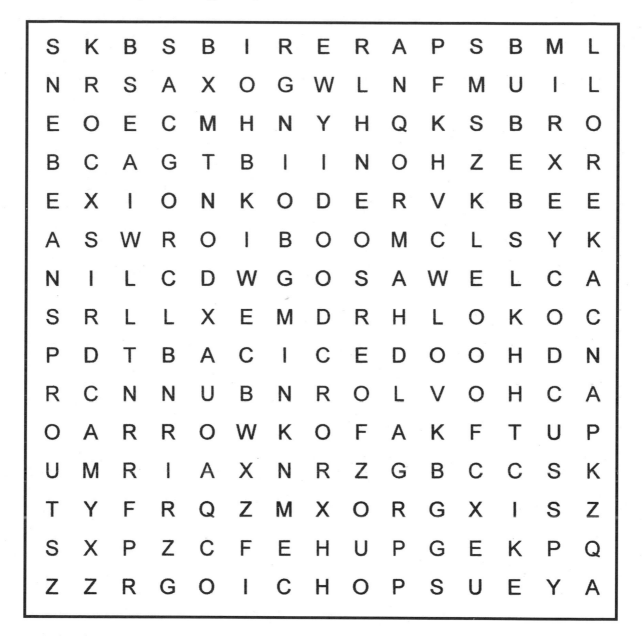

```
S  K  B  S  B  I  R  E  R  A  P  S  B  M  L
N  R  S  A  X  O  G  W  L  N  F  M  U  I  L
E  O  E  C  M  H  N  Y  H  Q  K  S  B  R  O
B  C  A  G  T  B  I  I  N  O  H  Z  E  X  R
E  X  I  O  N  K  O  D  E  R  V  K  B  E  E
A  S  W  R  O  I  B  O  O  M  C  L  S  Y  K
N  I  L  C  D  W  G  O  S  A  W  E  L  C  A
S  R  L  L  X  E  M  D  R  H  L  O  K  O  C
P  D  T  B  A  C  I  C  E  D  O  O  H  D  N
R  C  N  N  U  B  N  R  O  L  V  O  H  C  A
O  A  R  R  O  W  K  O  F  A  K  F  T  U  P
U  M  R  I  A  X  N  R  Z  G  B  C  C  S  K
T  Y  F  R  Q  Z  M  X  O  R  G  X  I  S  Z
S  X  P  Z  C  F  E  H  U  P  G  E  K  P  Q
Z  Z  R  G  O  I  C  H  O  P  S  U  E  Y  A
```

BAMBOO SHOOTS
BEAN SPROUTS
CHOP SUEY
CHOW MEIN

EGG FRIED RICE
NOODLES
PANCAKE ROLL
PICKLED GINGER

PORK BALLS
PRAWN CRACKER
SPARE RIBS

Friends TV show wordsearch

Find the words listed below. Words can go horizontally, vertically and diagonally, and can read forwards and backwards.

```
G T U R S Z J C A A S V N N F
M R C H A N D L E R H X D G G
L O N N A A N I S T O N K O Y
Z S Z R P P O F M J D H U Z R
K S V R L I S A K U D R O W R
S R R A C H E L Z F O L S T E
J C E M A T T L E B L A N C P
B X H P X O G Z M Y B R P F W
W P M W L K R O Y W E N H K E
P R R O I A P T X P Z U O P H
K S R J N M R A X G A E E S T
H S O Q Y I M T I O S X B X T
K E S T H N C E N E E W E V A
Y D X N O U Y A R E M L D X M
F F R V Q M V V P Y C W N G J
```

ANISTON

CENTRAL PERK

CHANDLER

JOEY

LISA KUDROW

MATT LE BLANC

MATTHEW PERRY

MONICA

NEW YORK

PHOEBE

RACHEL

ROSS

SCHWIMMER

Famous Americans
wordsearch

Find the words listed below. Words can go horizontally,
vertically and diagonally, and can read forwards and backwards.

```
V A S W B J X L W X T M J A A
F P Q C I O G A M D O A D G Q
B R G Y L H L E A I M L M E R
A A T E L N V N Y T C C N O Q
N X V R G N I O A I R O W R E
D S N F A Y G E A G U L J G I
Y T E N T C O L N E I M A E L
R E A I E A M L G R S X Y W M
O S Z W S S I I E W E S L B A
D K I H V H N U L O P S E U D
D I W A X B O Q O O N B N S O
I M N R D Q R A U D C S O H N
C K R P Y G E H J S Y I V U N
K V W O F C G S X B B P A H A
S M A I L L I W S U N E V X X
```

ANDY RODDICK	JOHNNY CASH	SHAQUILLE ONEAL
BILL GATES	MADONNA	TIGER WOODS
GEORGE W BUSH	MALCOLM X	TOM CRUISE
GERONIMO	MAYA ANGELOU	VENUS WILLIAMS
JAY LENO	OPRAH WINFREY	

155

Disney
wordsearch

Find the words listed below. Words can go horizontally,
vertically and diagonally, and can read forwards and backwards.

```
H I J O S N O W W H I T E U B
C E F V G N I B M A B I D P C
K Y R W G A Z S S Q L K G M C
J F J B H D O F T M W I L E N
O Y G U I Z W O Q F L G S C I
A J A G M E L V U I V U D I S
D O N A L D D U C K O D N N R
T N N N A N C O J M H N A D E
H O C I Z C R X Y J A Y L E T
N W Y F D P B E W Z E F Y R S
D E K S P D K W R T Z O E E N
O E O W T C A A R I E O N L O
S A K O I O T L L S V G S L M
X T Z M Y L R Y A Z F B I A S
C D O V A S M Y O X T H D K U
```

ALADDIN	DONALD DUCK	MONSTERS INC
BAMBI	GOOFY	SNOW WHITE
CINDERELLA	HERBIE	TARZAN
DISNEYLAND	MICKEY MOUSE	TOY STORY

X words
wordsearch

Find the words listed below. Words can go horizontally,
vertically and diagonally, and can read forwards and backwards.

```
W  G  B  Z  I  D  R  X  N  J  Y  I  J  J  S
N  Z  S  C  H  J  T  C  O  P  Y  T  N  C  I
M  L  W  W  K  Z  F  M  N  M  F  M  N  X  J
Z  X  X  R  A  T  E  D  E  B  M  Z  X  E  C
R  Y  E  N  Z  P  W  O  X  X  R  E  W  R  J
E  C  T  R  I  D  D  H  D  B  N  R  C  X  Y
L  F  W  G  O  Q  E  R  T  O  B  I  S  E  A
I  M  E  X  S  G  X  I  P  O  Y  N  X  S  R
J  U  E  C  A  Y  R  H  U  E  L  C  U  X  X
G  T  M  L  Q  X  O  A  J  K  Z  N  O  K  J
Z  V  H  X  Y  B  I  V  L  P  R  V  R  Y  L
N  Z  Z  W  I  X  B  W  Y  H  I  W  C  U  K
P  Y  D  A  X  V  G  X  Z  M  Y  R  B  T  S
B  B  V  S  E  N  O  H  P  O  L  Y  X  H  Z
P  G  N  G  J  V  C  Q  F  G  J  C  K  U  W
```

X RATED	XENOPHOBIA	XYLEM
X RAY	XEROGRAPHY	XYLOPHONE
XENON	XERXES	

Novelists wordsearch

Find the words listed below. Words can go horizontally, vertically and diagonally, and can read forwards and backwards.

```
C  L  T  S  E  T  N  A  V  R  E  C  W  E  D
H  H  N  O  H  G  R  G  E  F  V  D  A  D  D
Y  Q  A  C  I  Q  O  M  B  J  P  D  Z  G  O
G  D  Q  R  O  L  I  E  A  M  A  W  J  A  S
Y  G  R  H  L  L  E  M  T  N  F  A  J  R  T
I  O  O  A  E  E  E  I  H  N  N  E  A  O
N  W  T  Z  H  S  S  E  G  E  E  D  K  L  Y
V  R  O  S  J  S  L  D  A  R  L  K  K  L  E
B  L  E  O  L  D  A  U  I  I  O  B  D  A  V
A  R  Y  C  E  O  S  M  W  C  U  E  A  N  S
V  C  T  F  U  T  T  R  O  W  K  G  G  P  K
E  Q  O  A  E  A  A  O  I  H  R  E  E  O  Y
Z  E  T  N  U  C  H  A  E  O  T  W  N  E  R
Y  X  P  R  S  A  M  C  G  L  C  W  Y  S  L
G  M  D  O  N  I  A  W  T  K  R  A  M  T  S
```

CERVANTES	EDGAR ALLAN POE	JANE AUSTEN
CHARLES DICKENS	EMILE ZOLA	LEO TOLSTOY
CHAUCER	GEORGE ELIOT	MARK TWAIN
DANIEL DEFOE	GOETHE	OSCAR WILDE
DOSTOYEVSKY	JAMES JOYCE	THOMAS HARDY

Scooby Doo
wordsearch

Find the words listed below. Words can go horizontally,
vertically and diagonally, and can read forwards and backwards.

```
I  C  S  A  P  E  S  K  Y  K  I  D  S  M  Z
X  P  O  C  K  S  W  T  E  E  F  U  Y  C  P
P  N  D  L  O  K  R  O  S  Y  F  S  G  L  N
D  A  E  N  Z  O  X  E  G  O  T  I  O  F  V
J  V  R  B  A  V  B  H  P  E  H  O  L  R  O
B  L  M  E  E  L  P  Y  R  E  K  G  O  E  O
E  G  B  L  B  U  S  Y  S  F  E  T  M  D  D
X  N  M  H  S  R  M  I  O  N  Y  J  P  G  Y
Z  A  H  E  D  A  A  R  Y  Y  A  R  U  A  B
M  Q  K  P  C  E  C  B  U  K  G  C  H  E  O
Z  I  H  H  A  L  B  E  A  T  O  G  K  S  O
Y  Q  I  L  U  D  P  N  U  N  L  O  A  S  C
H  N  O  E  S  C  X  R  A  O  N  P  P  H  S
E  O  S  Y  A  B  B  A  D  O  O  A  O  S  S
O  O  D  Y  P  P  A  R  C  S  K  W  H  M  C
```

DAPHNE	MYSTERY MACHINE	SPOOKY ISLAND
FRED	PESKY KIDS	VELMA
GHOST	SCOOBY DOO	YABBA DOO
HANNA BARBERA	SCOOBY SNACKS	YIKES
JEEPERS	SCRAPPY DOO	
LOOK FOR CLUES	SHAGGY	

Body Parts
wordsearch

Find the words listed below. Words can go horizontally,
vertically and diagonally, and can read forwards and backwards.

```
D  X  T  W  B  Y  K  F  L  N  F  M  N  T  R
R  B  V  Q  F  N  C  I  P  I  J  A  A  B  V
E  V  F  X  Y  G  E  T  V  U  M  O  R  G  H
D  H  S  E  Z  N  N  R  B  K  R  B  E  N  G
N  N  E  L  L  U  K  S  E  H  E  X  V  H  C
A  M  F  V  Z  A  Q  P  T  G  Y  N  I  E  C
H  N  F  A  C  E  L  H  H  E  N  M  L  A  T
N  H  N  X  X  M  C  N  J  C  N  I  T  R  S
I  C  A  R  T  I  L  A  G  E  A  I  F  T  E
H  T  P  D  P  L  K  N  E  M  K  M  P  R  H
S  H  A  S  U  A  N  K  L  E  U  N  O  S  C
C  I  D  N  T  E  Y  B  R  N  H  S  E  T  F
A  G  G  O  N  M  N  A  X  L  F  Y  C  E  S
L  H  O  O  A  S  H  O  U  L  D  E  R  L  L
F  F  B  M  Z  E  B  Q  W  O  B  L  E  A  E
```

ANKLE	FACE	LIMB	SHOULDER
BONE	FINGER	LIVER	SKULL
CALF	FOOT	LUNG	SPINE
CARTILAGE	HAND	MUSCLE	STOMACH
CHEST	HEART	NECK	THIGH
ELBOW	KNEE	SHIN	THROAT

Family
wordsearch

Find the words listed below. Words can go horizontally,
vertically and diagonally, and can read forwards and backwards.

```
P  X  A  W  B  M  O  T  H  E  R  Y  P  Y  G
H  Y  B  N  I  S  U  O  C  H  H  X  M  D  T
B  P  J  R  Y  H  H  K  E  I  B  S  Y  O  P
N  V  Y  R  R  N  M  Q  A  G  Y  C  L  I  V
W  X  G  Y  A  E  B  A  R  W  E  H  P  E  N
Q  W  I  N  T  L  O  A  U  N  J  T  Q  Z  A
N  T  N  D  H  Q  N  X  Z  A  L  U  Q  B  N
A  A  W  L  S  D  P  E  U  H  U  X  R  R  Q
F  C  T  I  A  V  W  E  J  Z  Z  N  S  Z  N
A  Y  A  D  B  R  O  T  H  E  R  I  T  I  X
T  Z  H  M  N  U  Q  C  D  B  S  W  E  I  P
H  U  X  A  X  U  N  V  U  T  C  C  O  R  E
E  B  A  B  Y  E  N  C  F  P  F  Q  P  J  V
R  W  N  L  N  O  A  R  L  K  C  E  Z  K  M
P  Q  M  R  L  U  E  V  C  E  A  O  D  P  U
```

AUNTIE	FATHER	NEPHEW
BABY	GRANDAD	NIECE
BROTHER	MOTHER	SISTER
COUSIN	NANNA	UNCLE

Answers

World Capitals
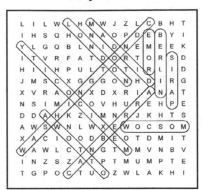

Jobs
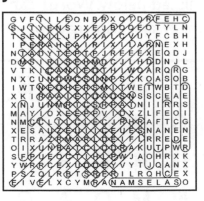

Roald Dahl
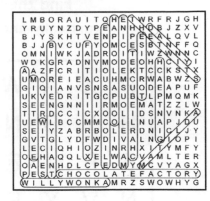

South America
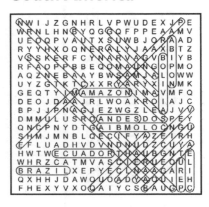

Actresses
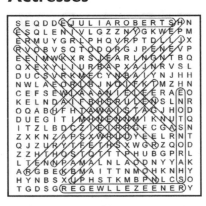

Actors
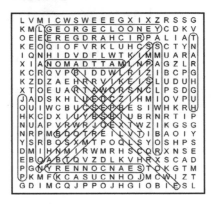

Tom Cruise
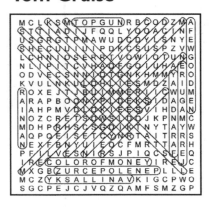

Underwater
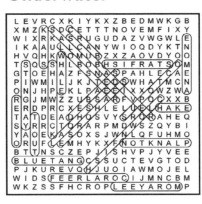

Dinosaur
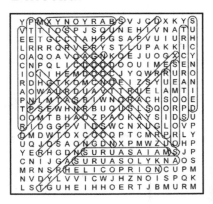

Answers

Detective

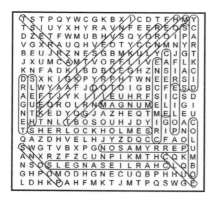

Beatles

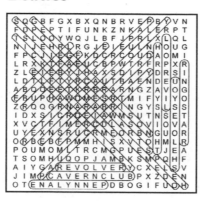

John Wayne

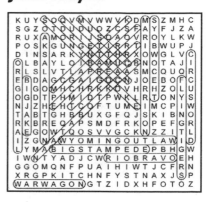

WWE Superstars

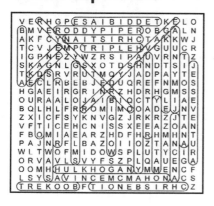

Music Bands

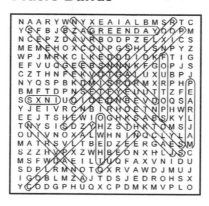

Musicals

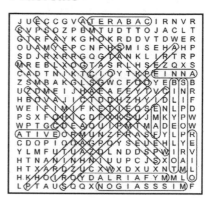

Hollywood Legends

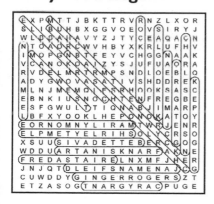

Royal Family

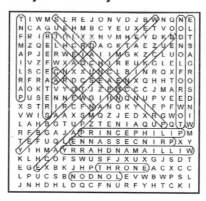

Elvis Presley

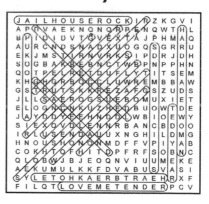

Answers

American States

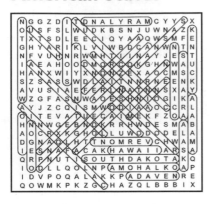

Car Makers

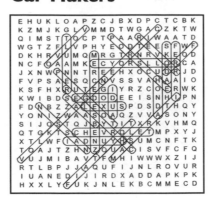

Harry Potter

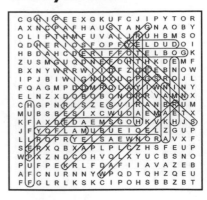

Olympic Sports

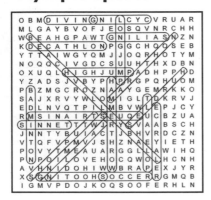

Bird

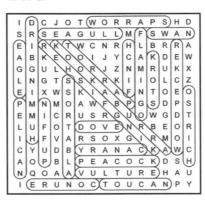

Snake

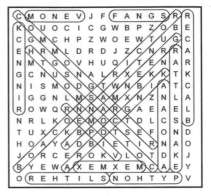

Wedding

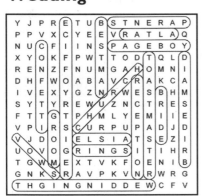

Airport

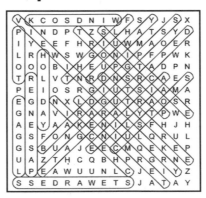

Mythology

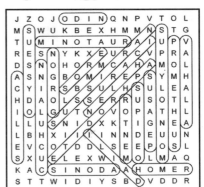

Answers

Caribbean

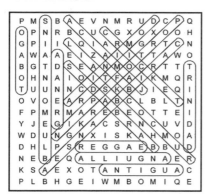

Camping

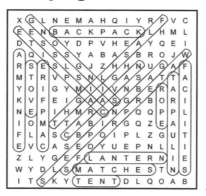

Rivers

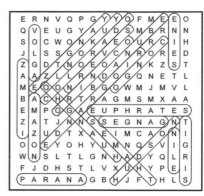

Mountains

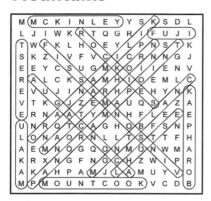

American Government

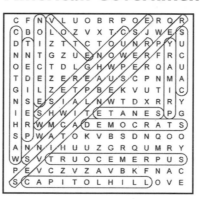

Where were they Born?

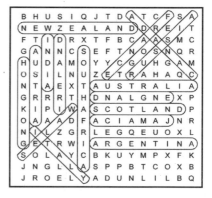

Narnia

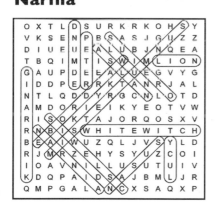

Carnival

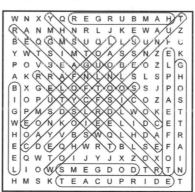

Art

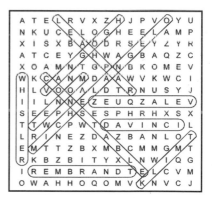

Answers

Criminals

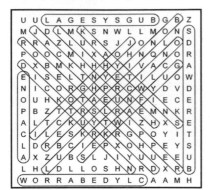

DIY

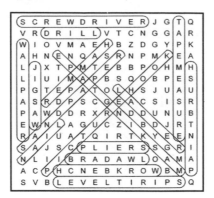

Jewelry

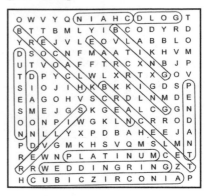

Cafe drinks

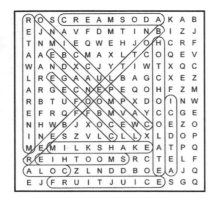

Chinese food

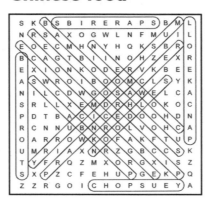

Friends TV show

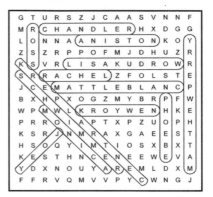

Famous Americans

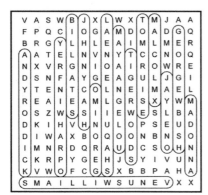

Disney

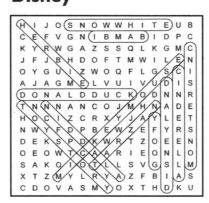

X words

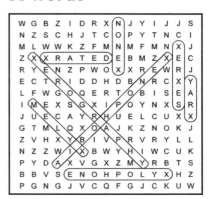

Answers

Novelists

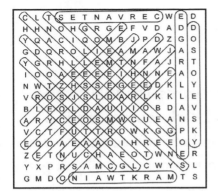

Scooby Doo

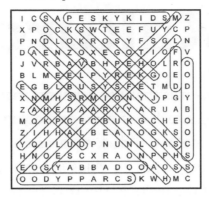

Body Parts

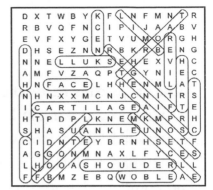

Family

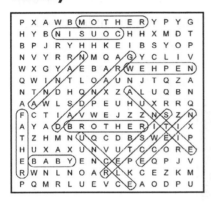

Kakuro

Kakuro puzzles resemble crosswords that use numbers instead of words. The kakuro grid, unlike in sudoku, can be of any size. It has rows and columns, and dark squares like in a crossword. Like a crossword, some of the dark squares contain numbers and some contain two numbers. Unlike a crossword, you get no clues in kakuro, these numbers are all you get! The numbers denote the total of the digits in the row or column referred to by the position of the number. Within each collection of squares in either a row or a column, called a run, any of the numbers 1 to 9 may be used, but like sudoku, each number may only be used once.

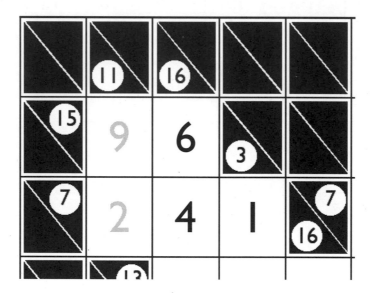

You can work out the combination through elimination and cross-referencing. For example, as you work out the answers elsewhere in the grid, you will naturally limit the number of combinations that it could be, helping you find the answer for the run you are focusing on.

Look at the diagram on the the left. The 15 in the top diagonal is the total of the squares in the row to the right of the 15. The 11 in the bottom diagonal is the total of the squares in the column below the 11, as with the adjacent 16 in the bottom diagonal. All numbers in the top diagonal refer to the row to the right of the number, and all numbers in the bottom diagonal refer to the column below the number.

So, as we are only dealing with a small part of the first sudoku puzzle, some numbers are already filled in to illustrate this example. If you were doing the whole puzzle, you would see that the 16 refers to a column of 5 numbers and this limits the number combinations. Likewise, the 3 refers to a column of 2 numbers and the square below it can only be a 2 or a 1.

The 15 refers to the row and as the 6 is filled in,
we know that the other number in this row must be a 9, (9 + 6 = 15).

The 11 refers to the column and as the 9 is now filled in,
we know that the other number in this column must be a 2, (9 + 2 = 11).

K Tips

i The best way to ease yourself into a kakuro puzzle is to
look for the cells with the least potential valid combinations.
For example, runs composing of two cells or with low numbers
will be a good place to start.

ii Look for where two runs cross each other,
therefore sharing a square and hence the same number.

iii Use a pencil, if you know a square can only contain a 3 or a 6,
write both in the corner of the square. Then, using cross-elimination,
you will be able to place the right number with certainty,
when you have more information.

iv Finally, as you do more and more kakuro, you will start to learn
the various combinations that can be used to make up each number!

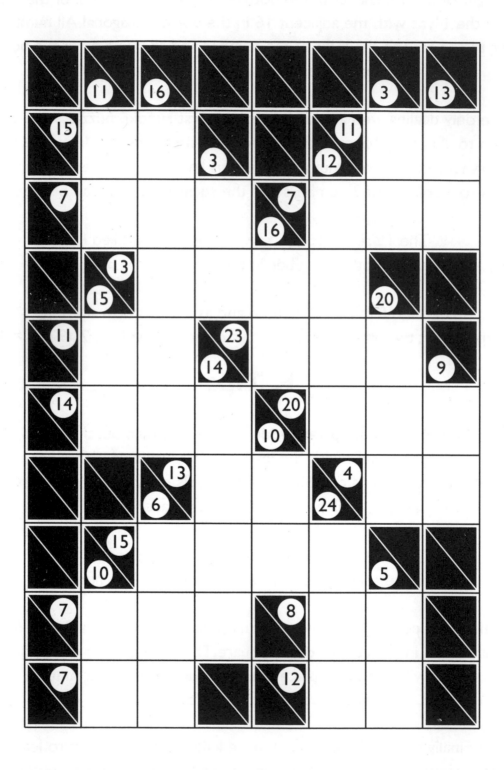

Kakuro for beginners 2

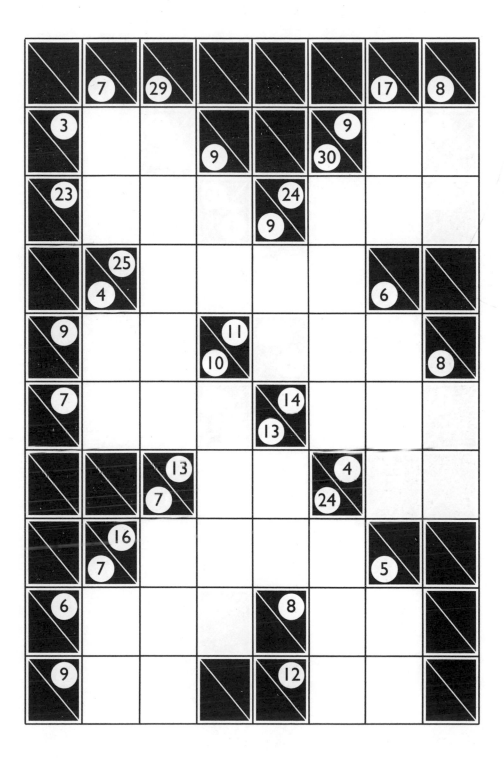

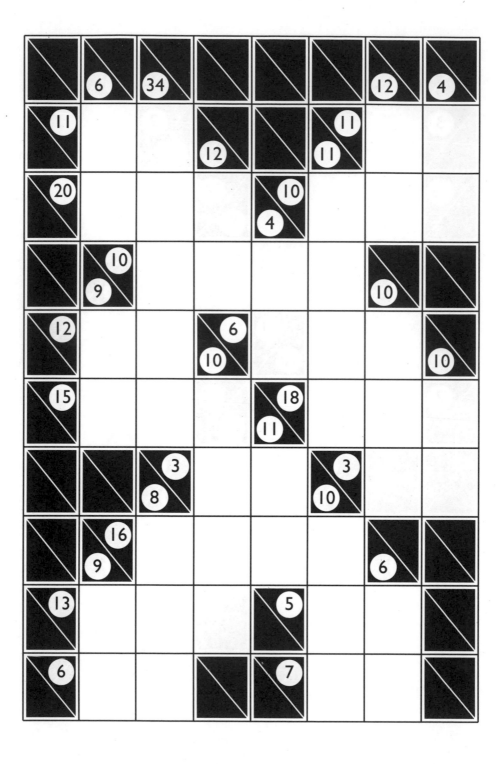

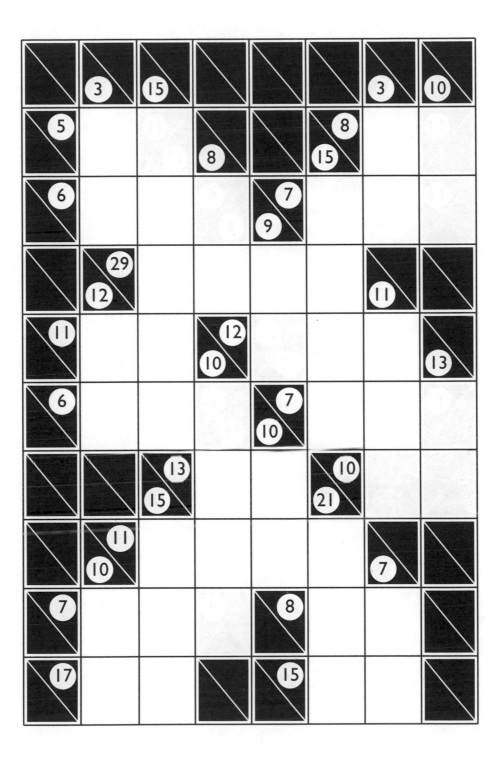

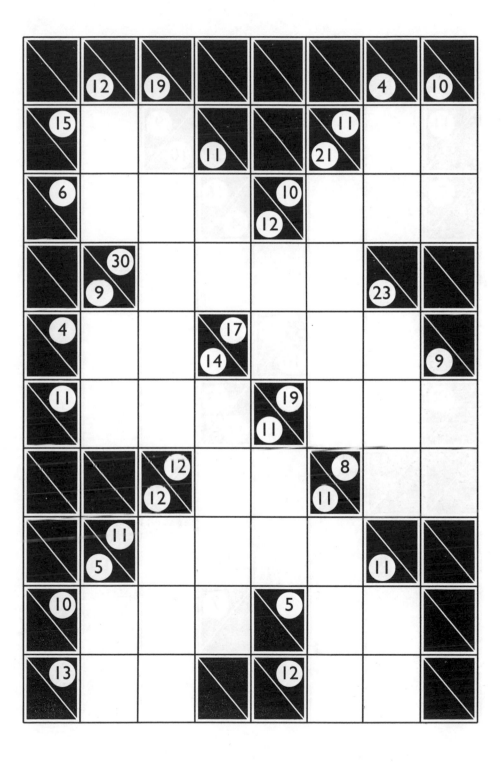

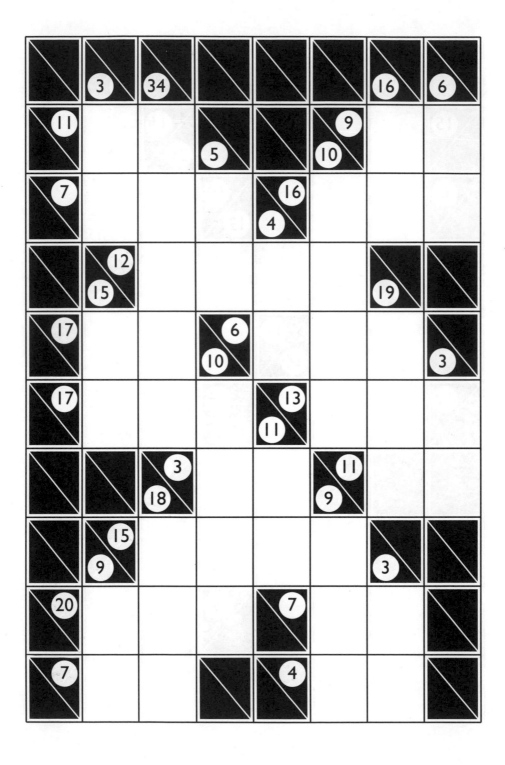

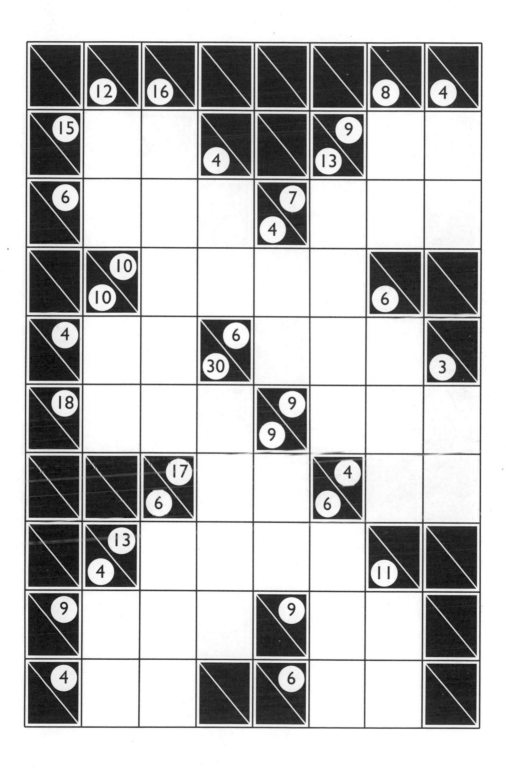

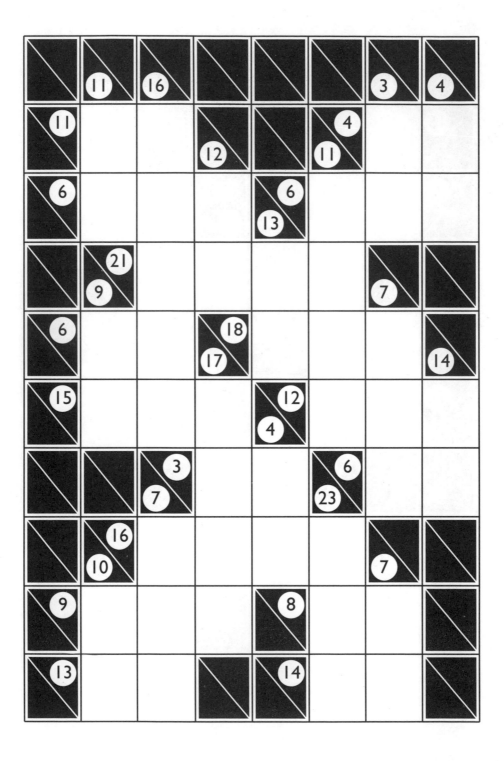

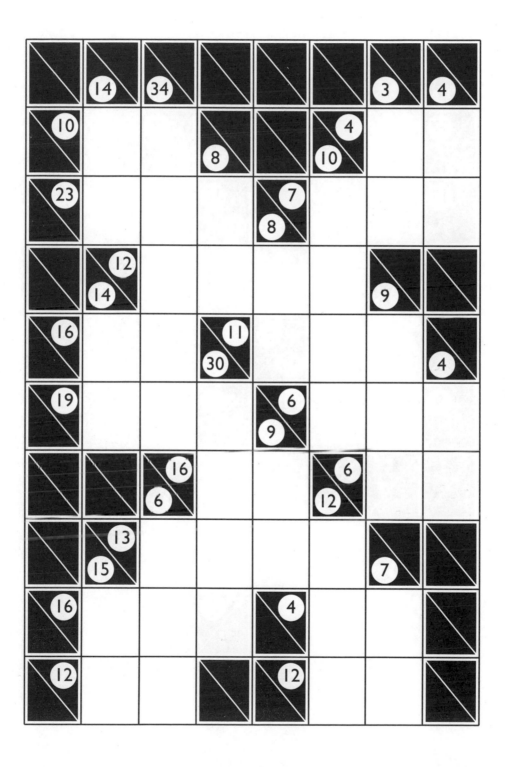

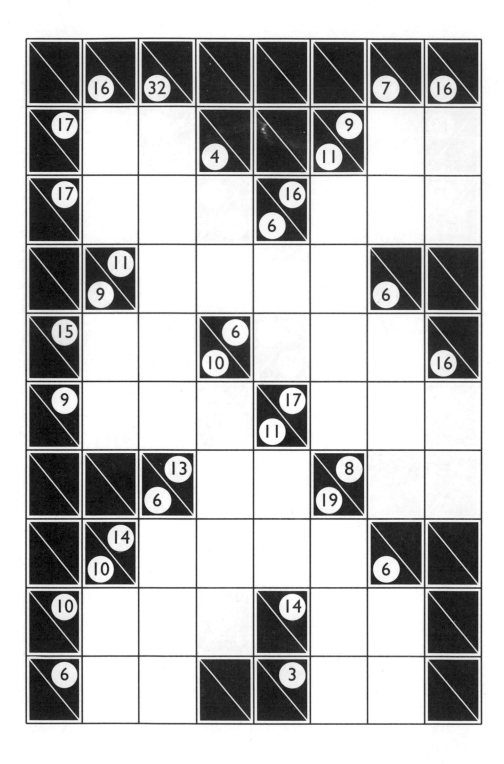

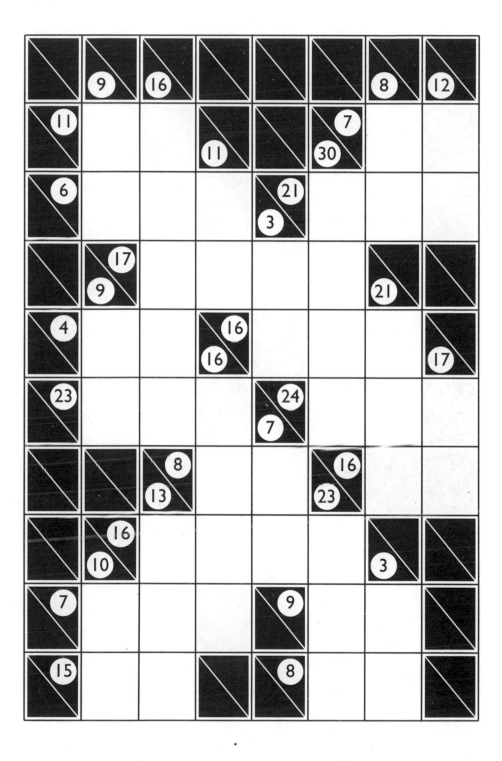

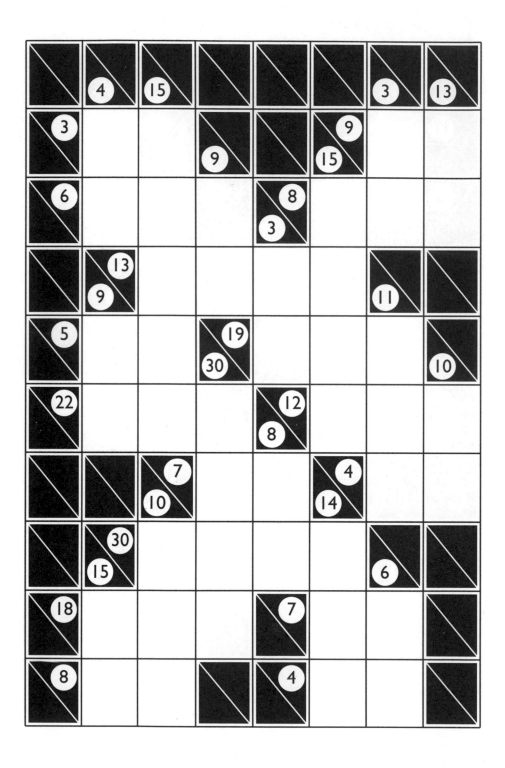

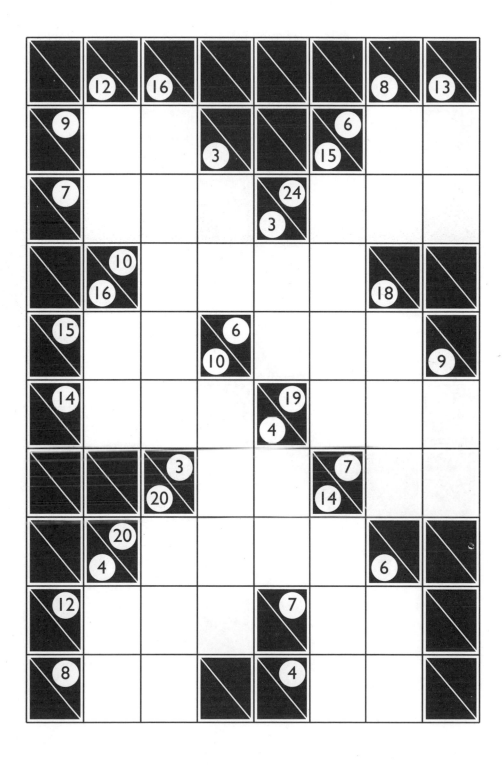

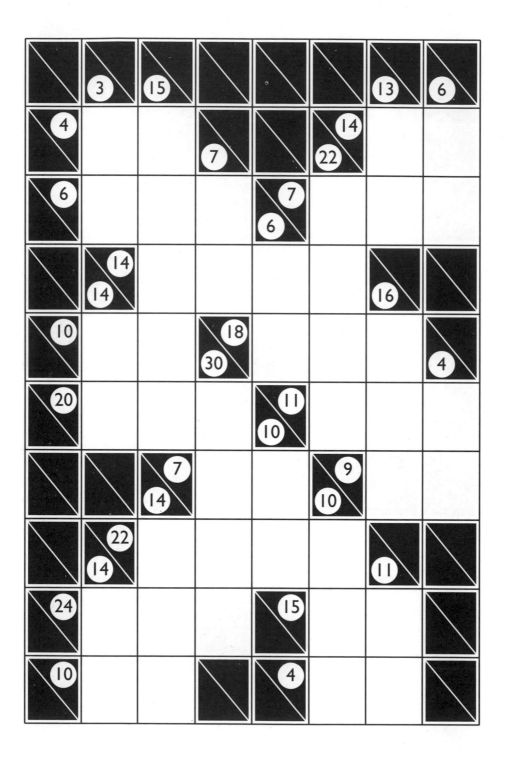

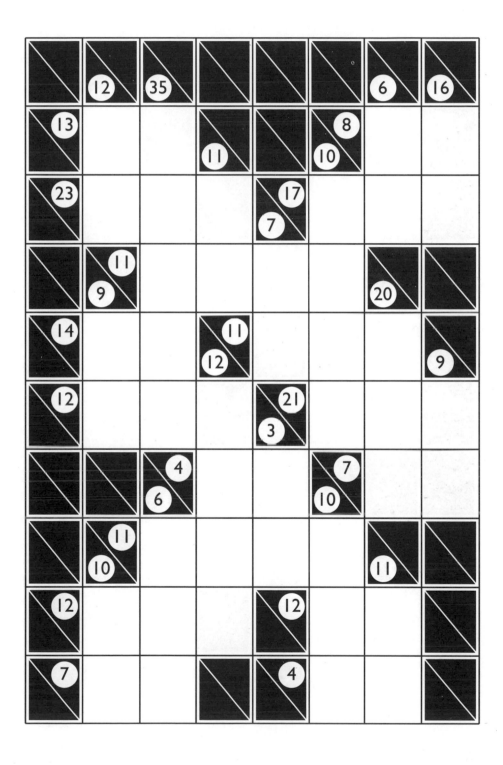

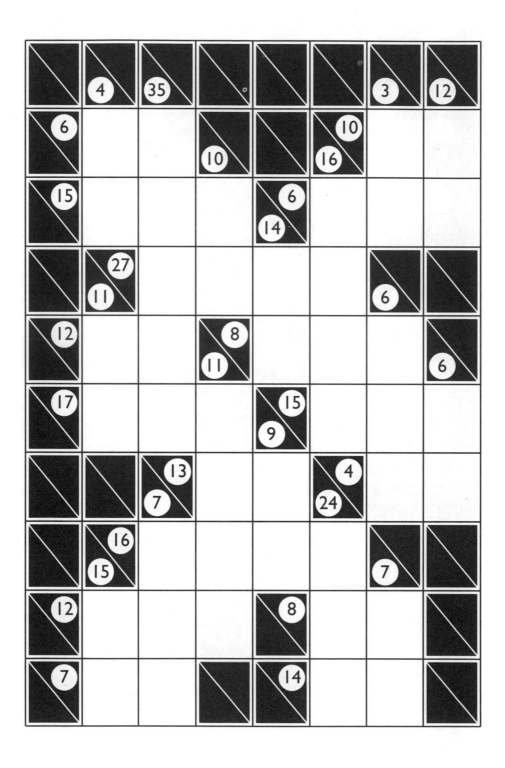

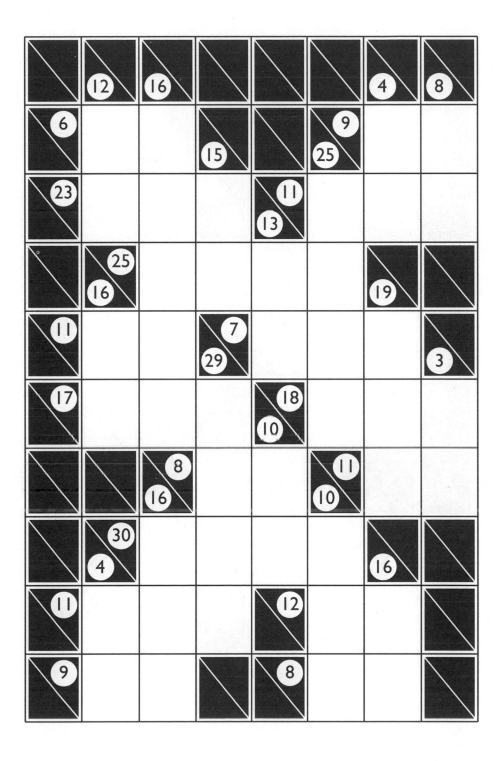

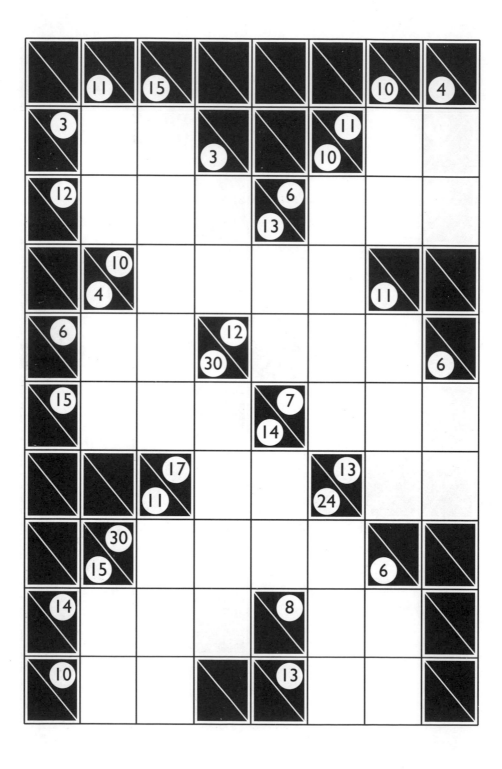

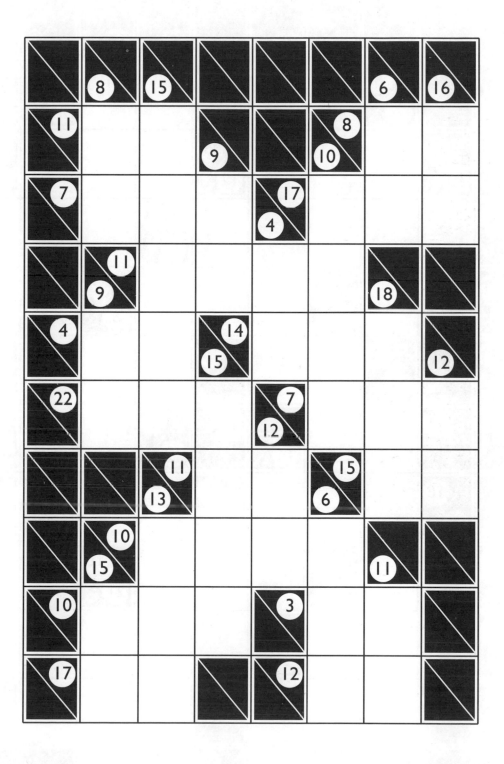

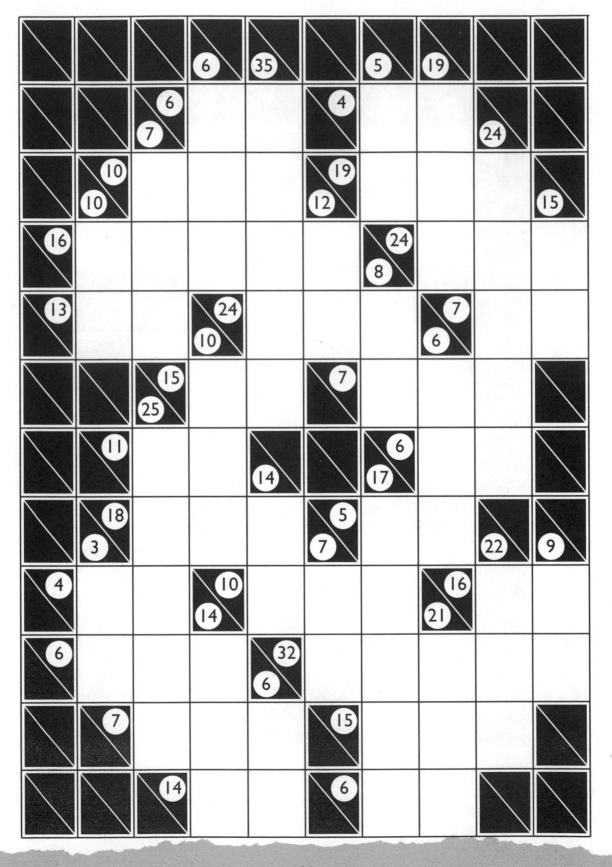

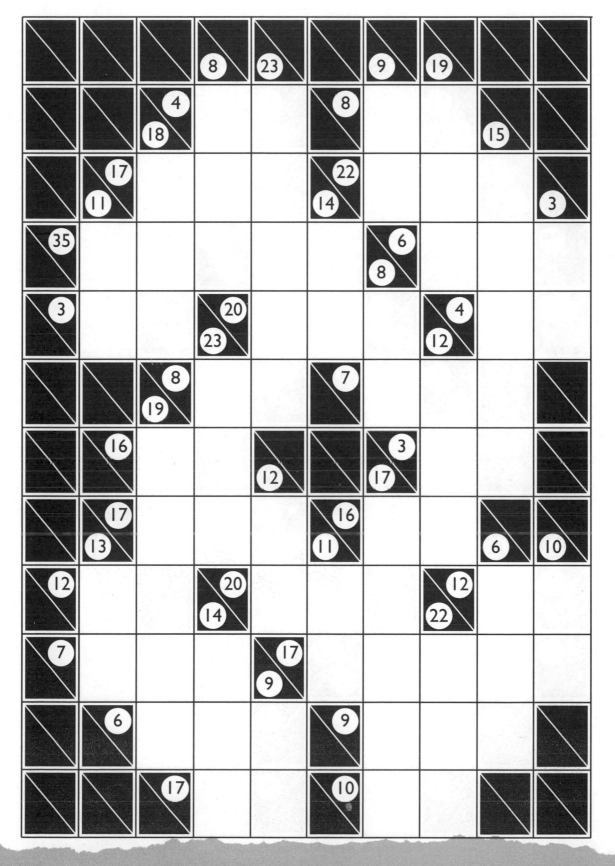

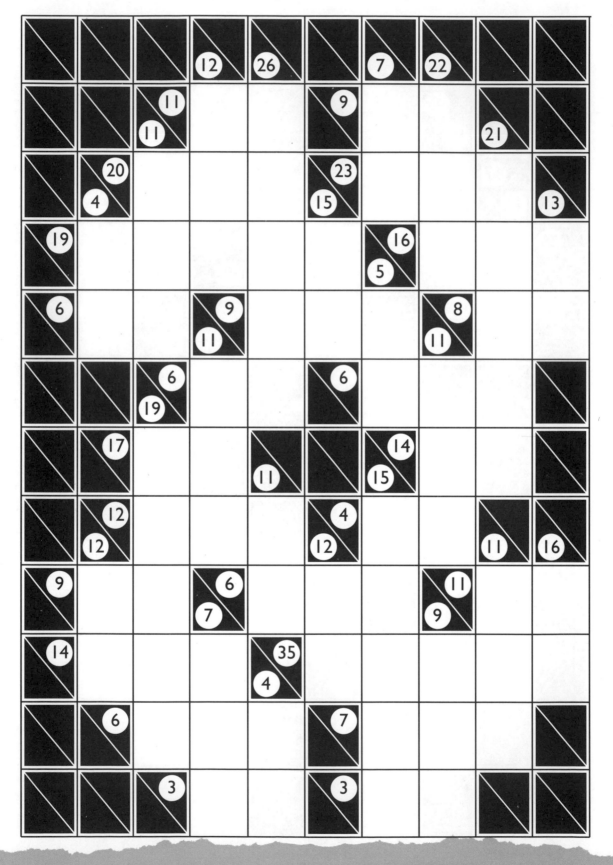

Kakuro for masters 24

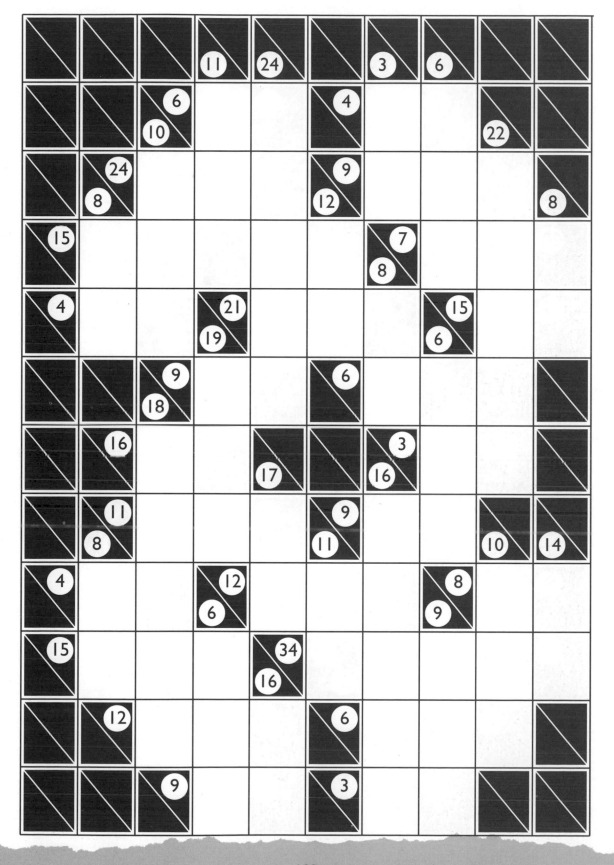

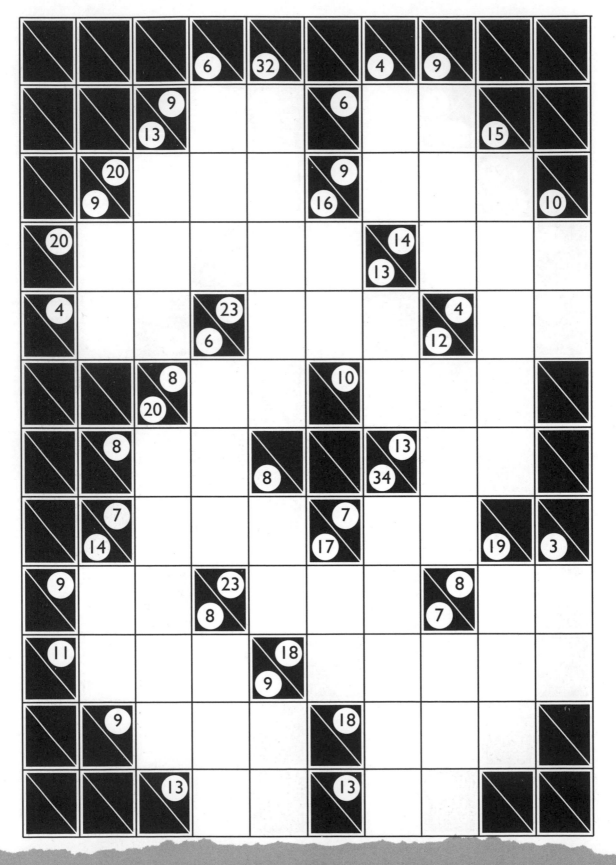

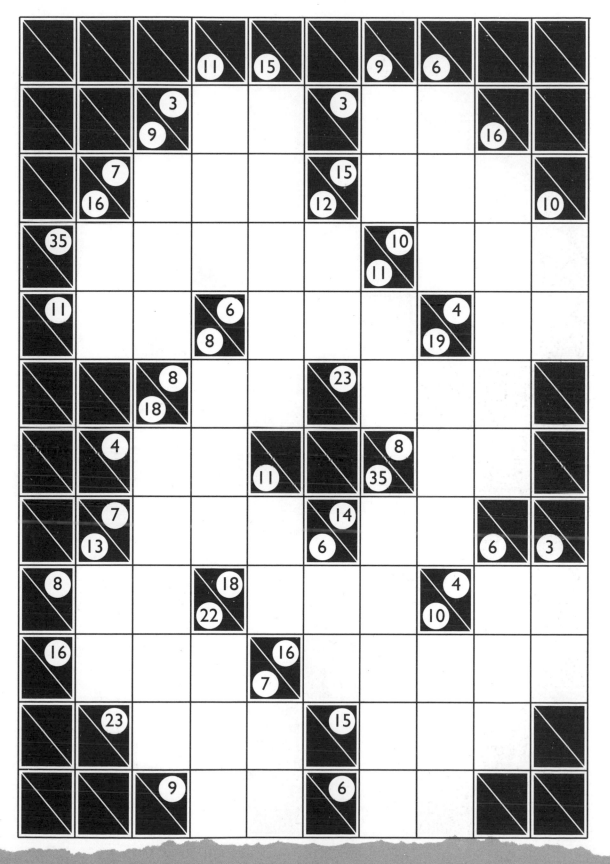

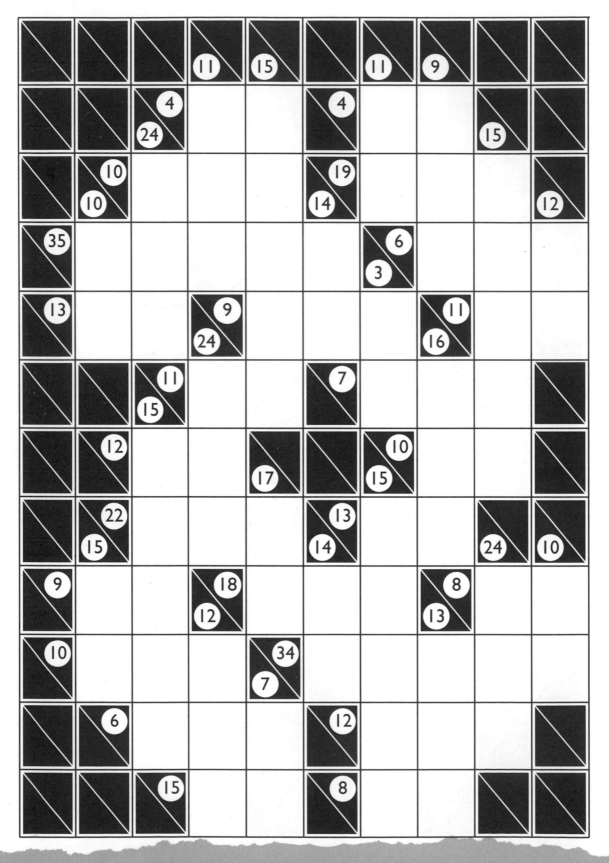

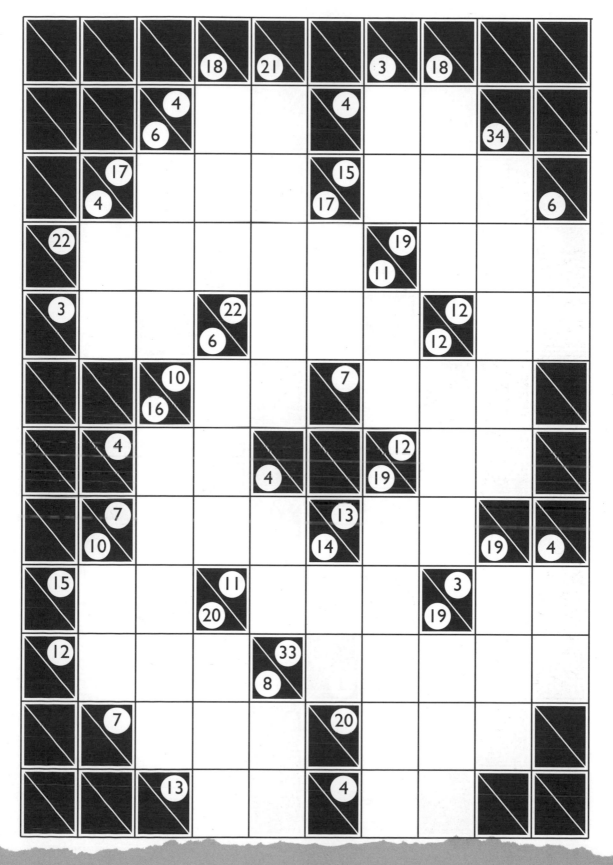

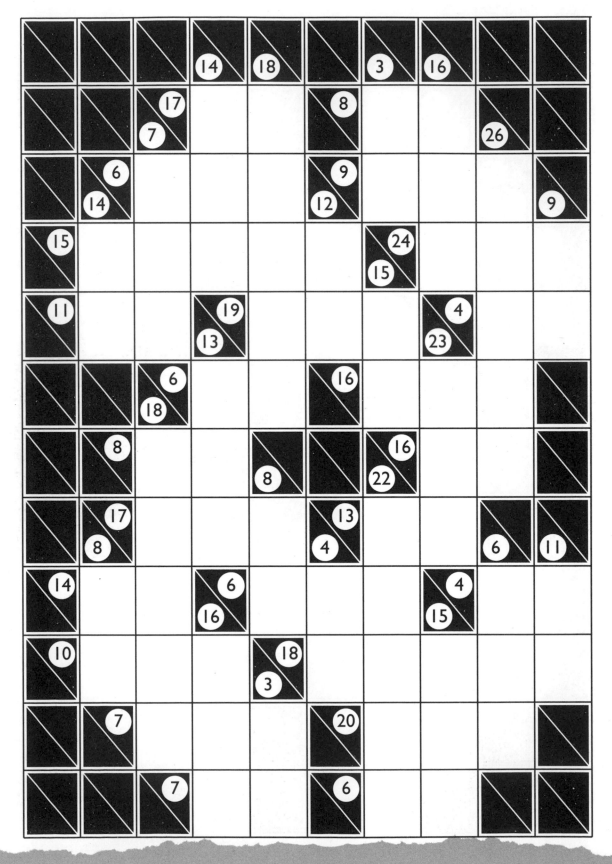

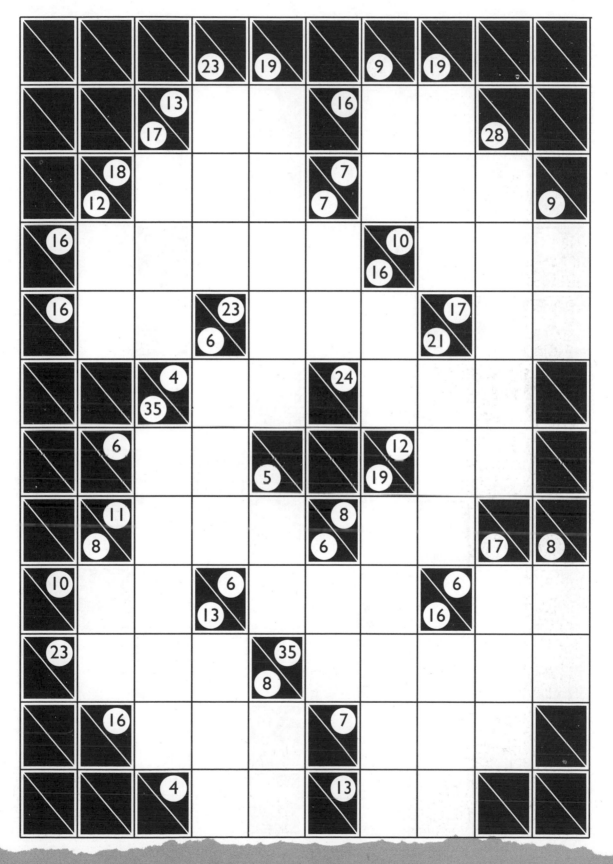

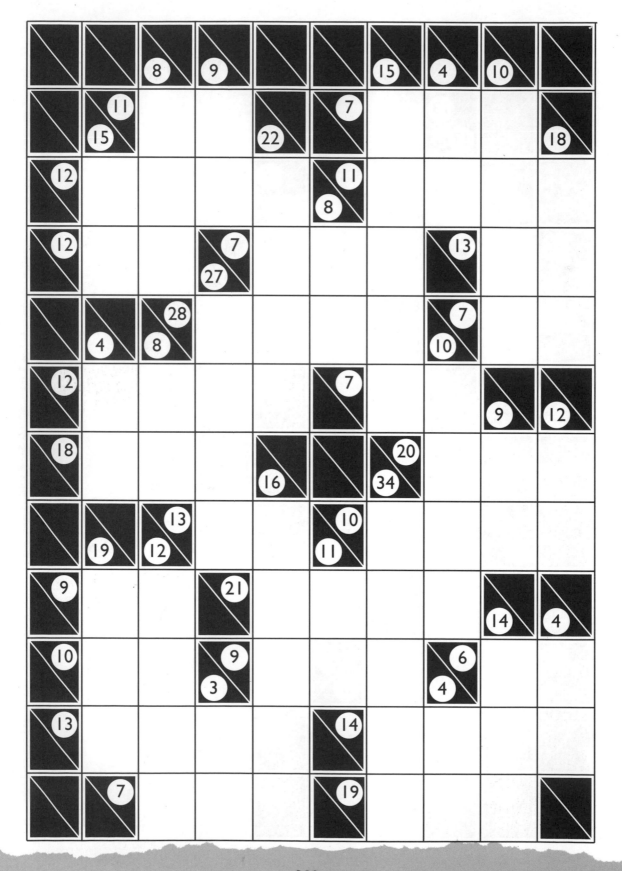

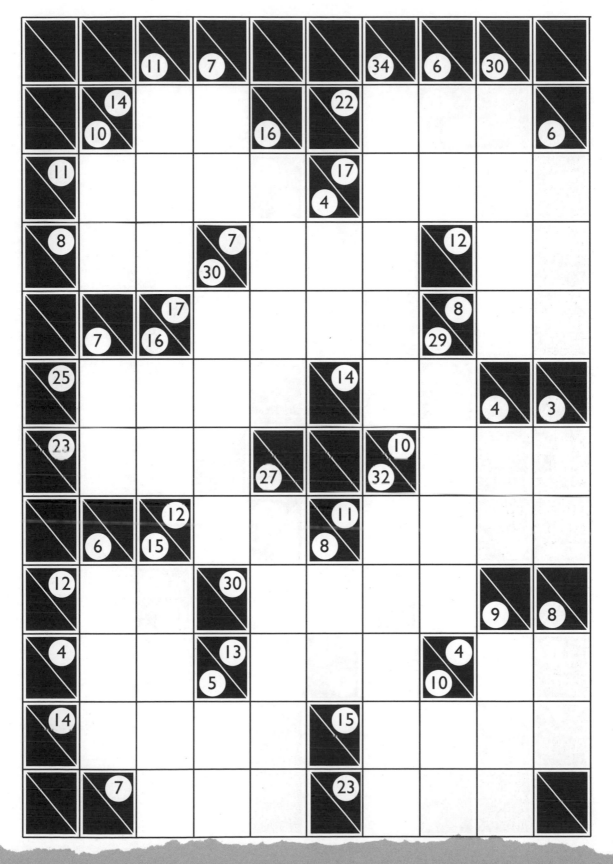

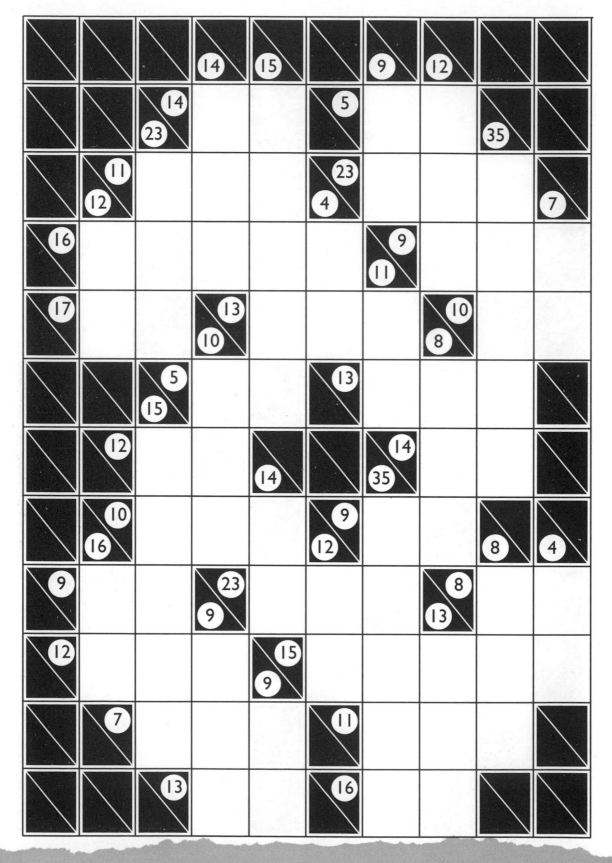

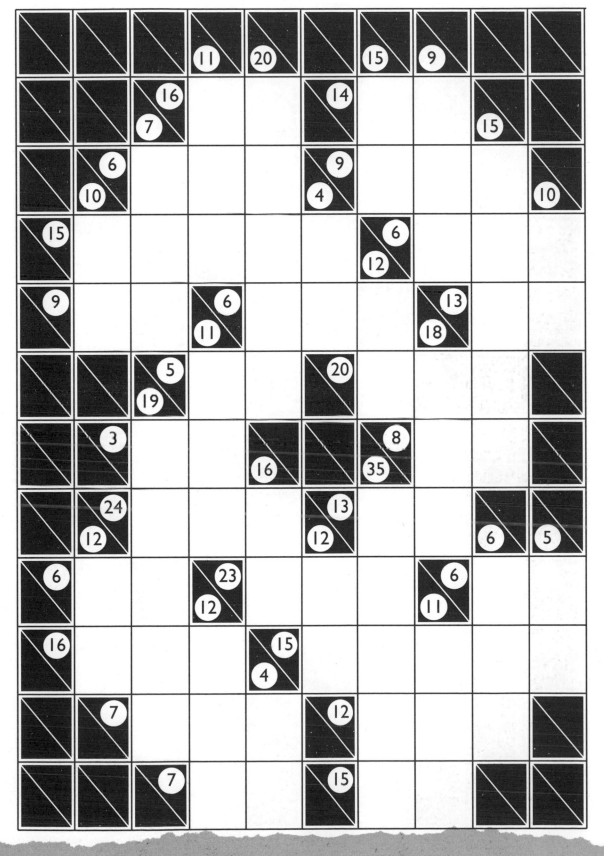

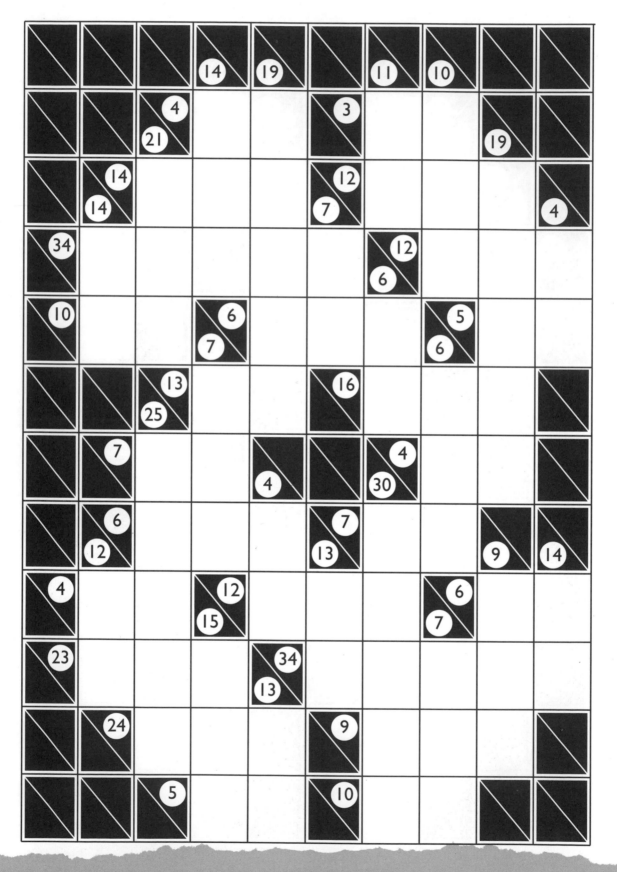

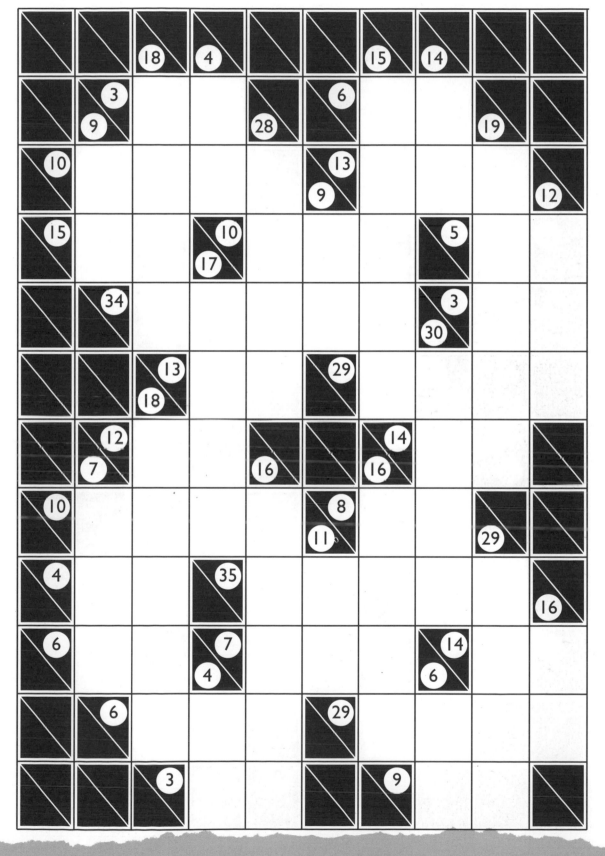

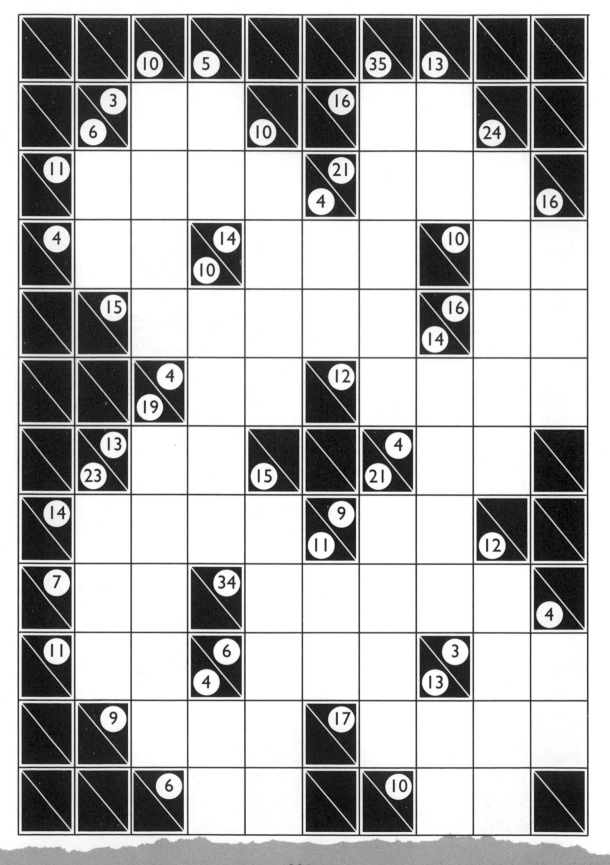

Kakuro for masters 38

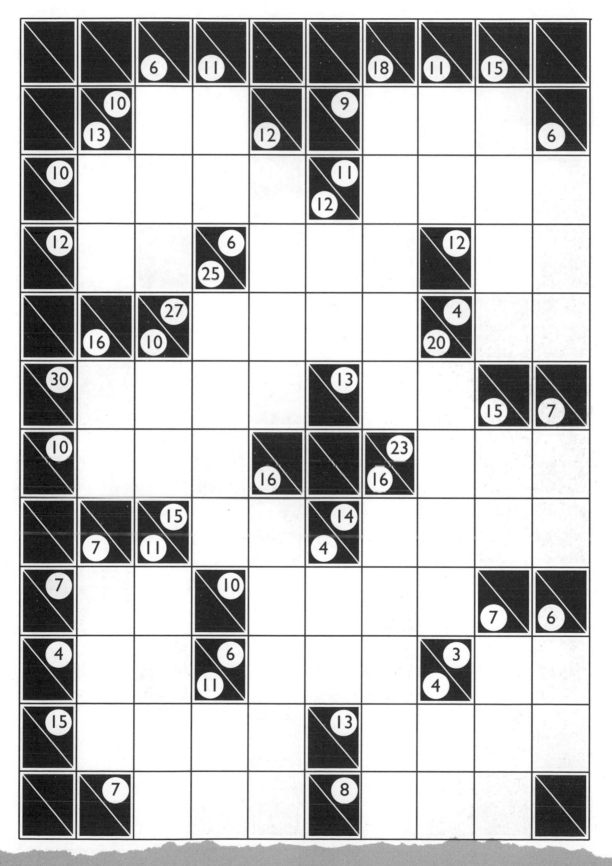

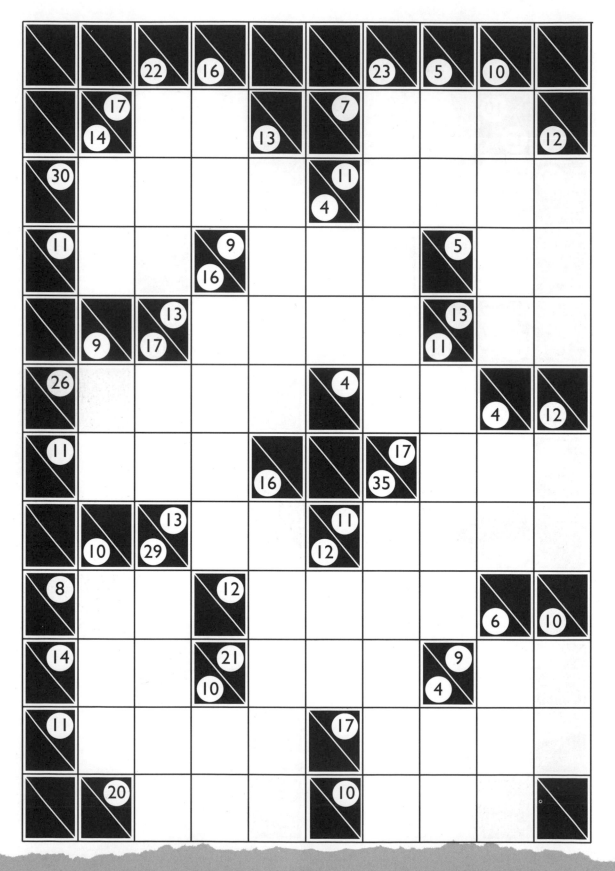

Kakuro for masters 39

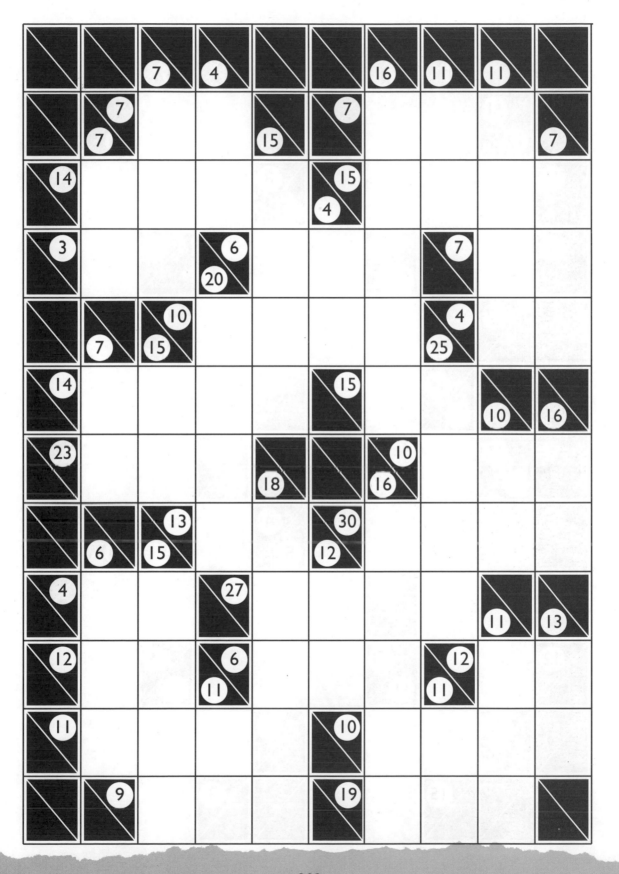

Kakuro for masters 40

Kakuro for masters 41

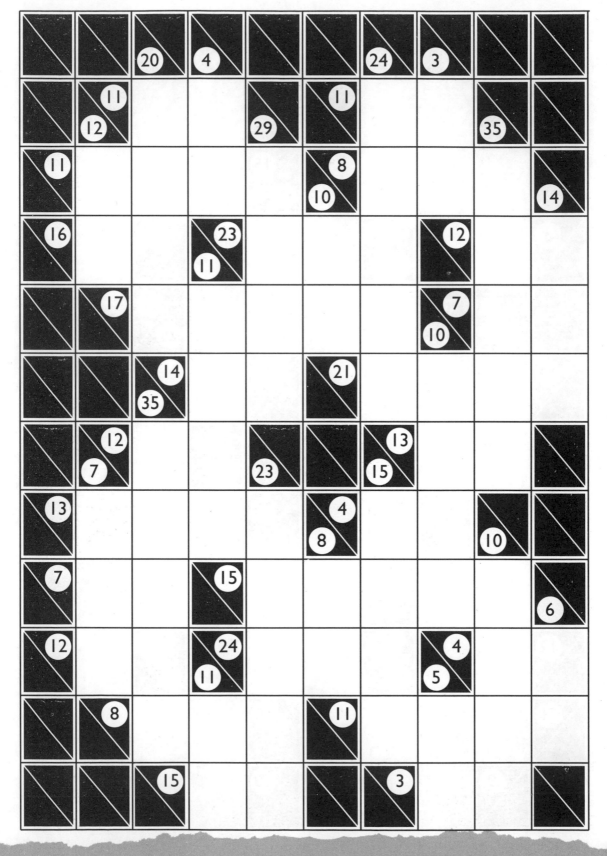

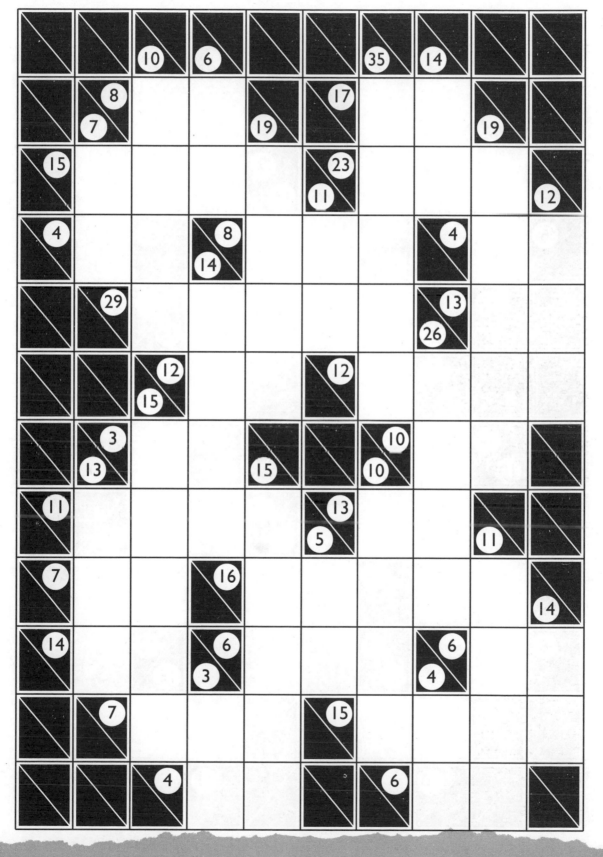

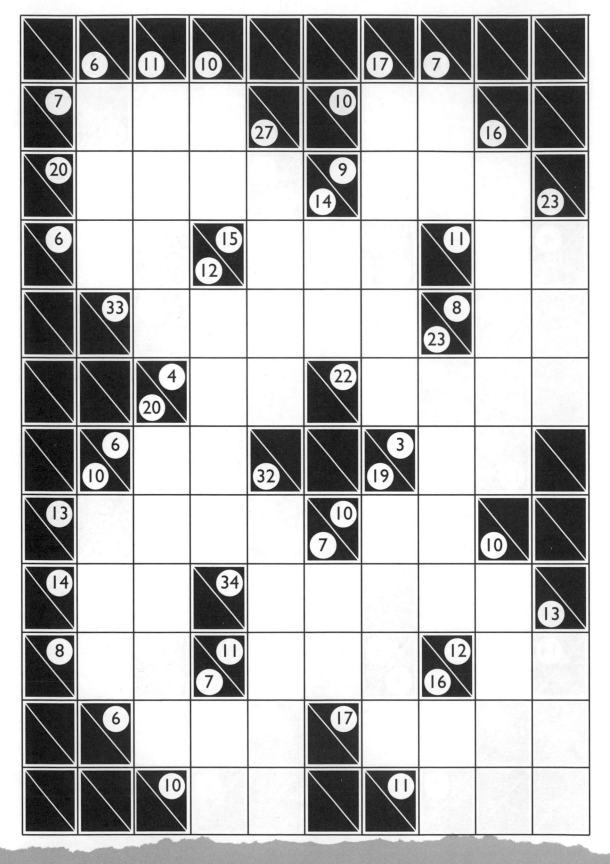

Kakuro for masters 44

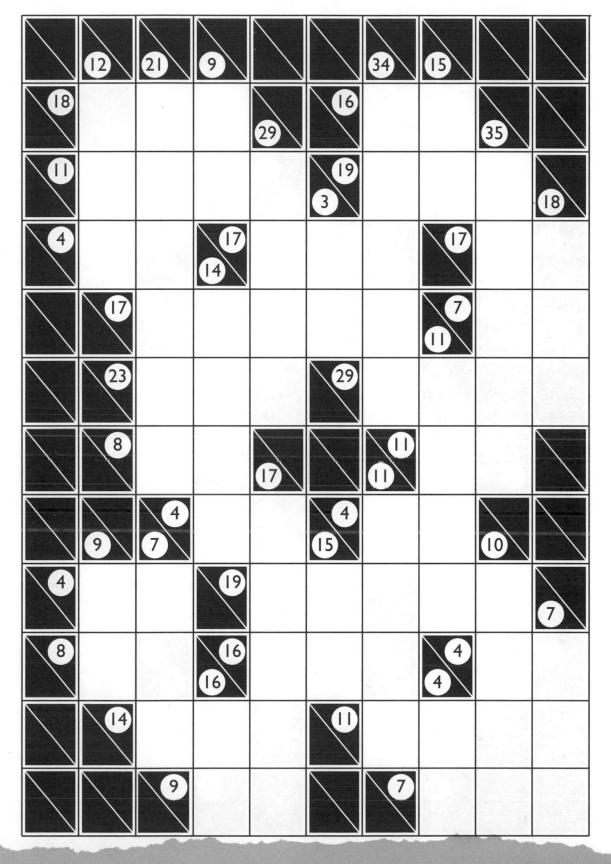

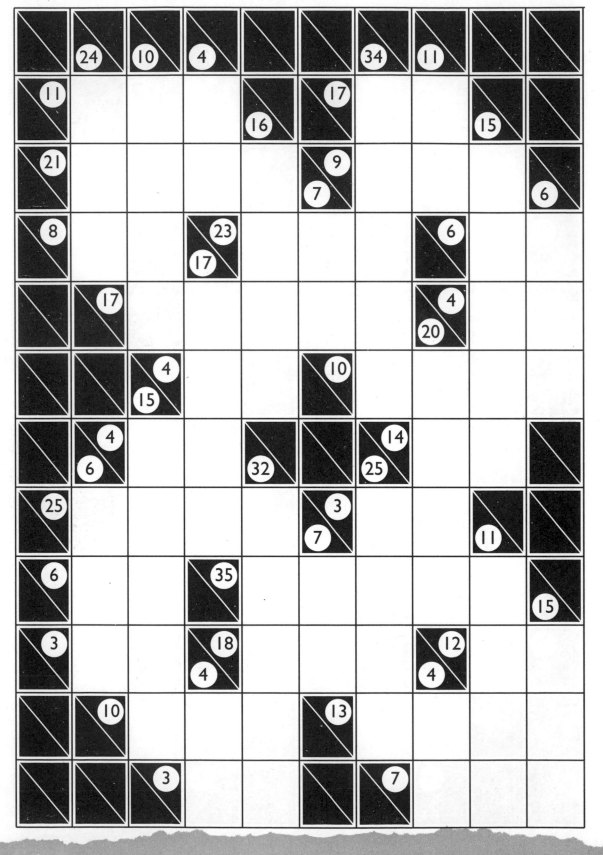

Kakuro for masters 46

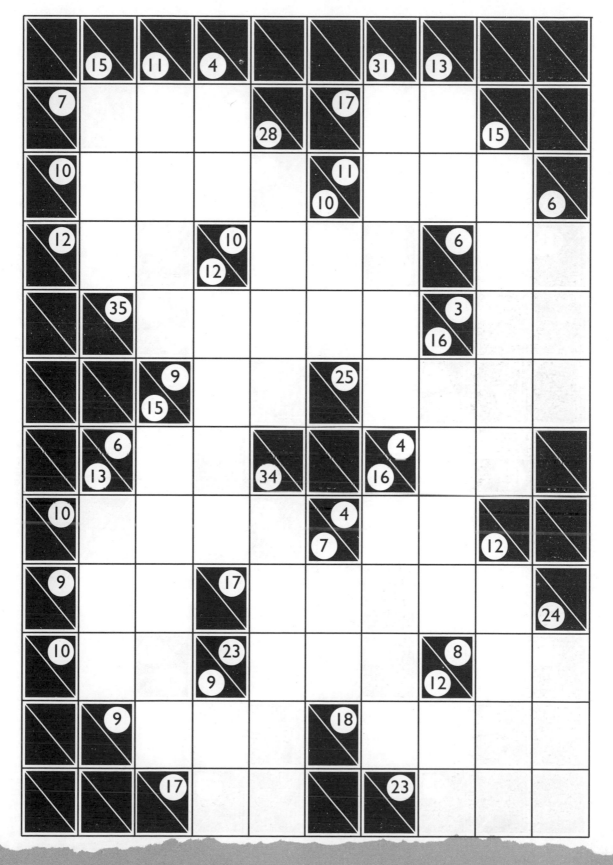

215

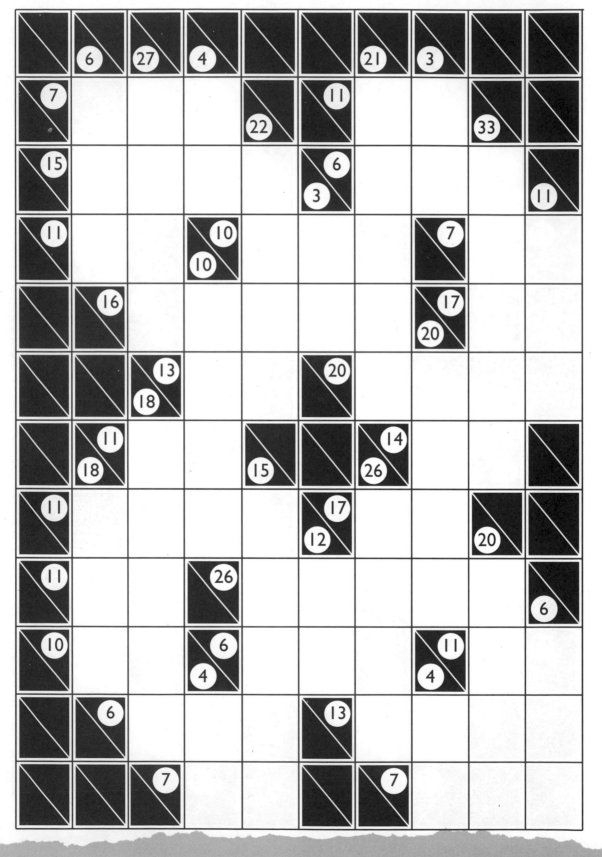

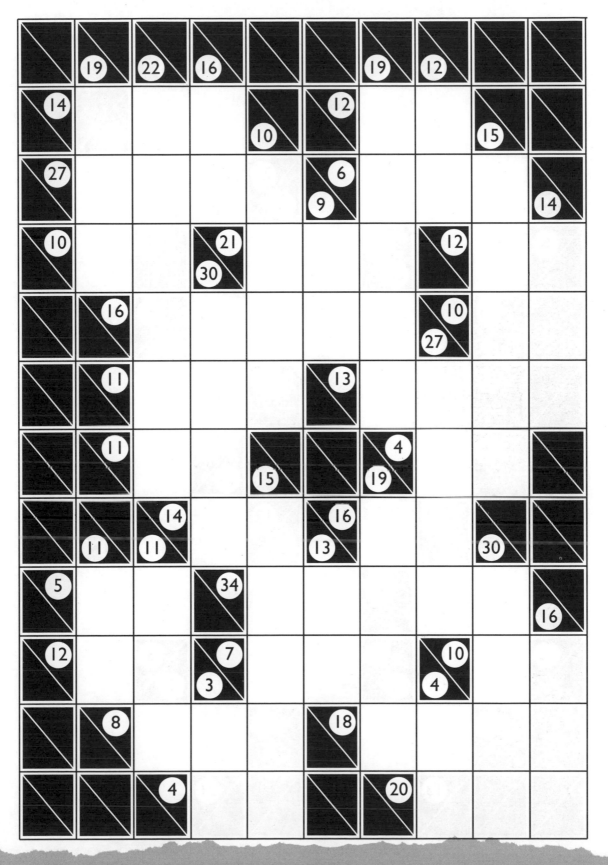

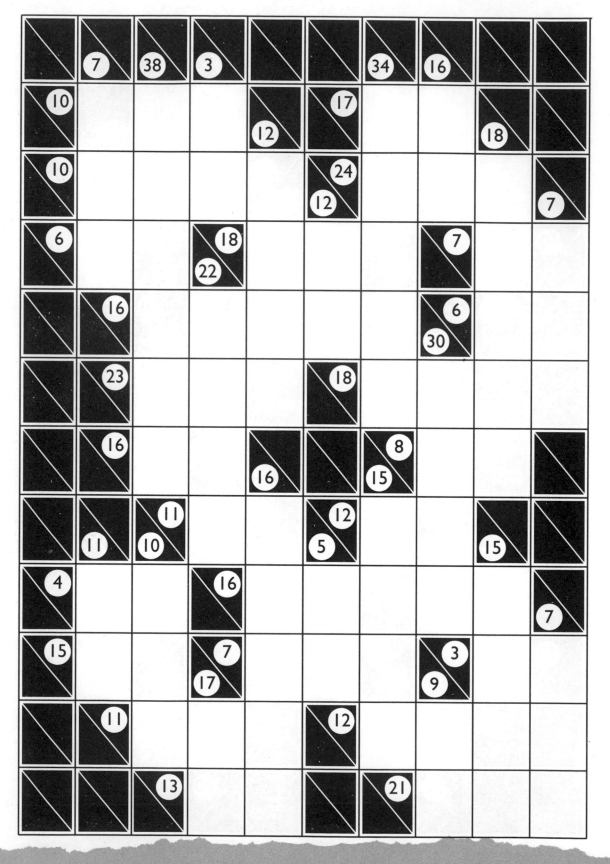

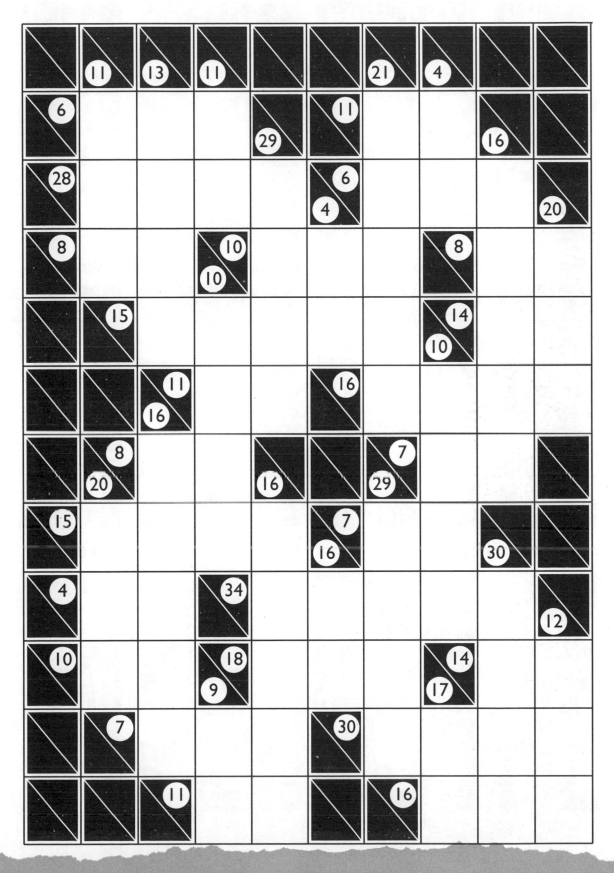

Answers

Kakuro 1

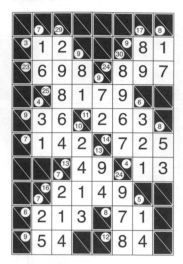

Kakuro 2

Kakuro 3

Kakuro 4

Kakuro 5

Kakuro 6

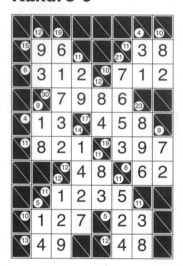

Kakuro 7

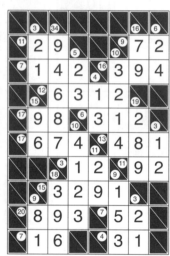

Kakuro 8

Kakuro 9

Kakuro 10

Kakuro 11

Kakuro 12

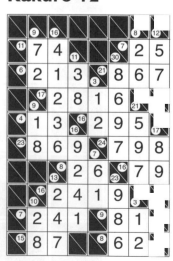

Answers

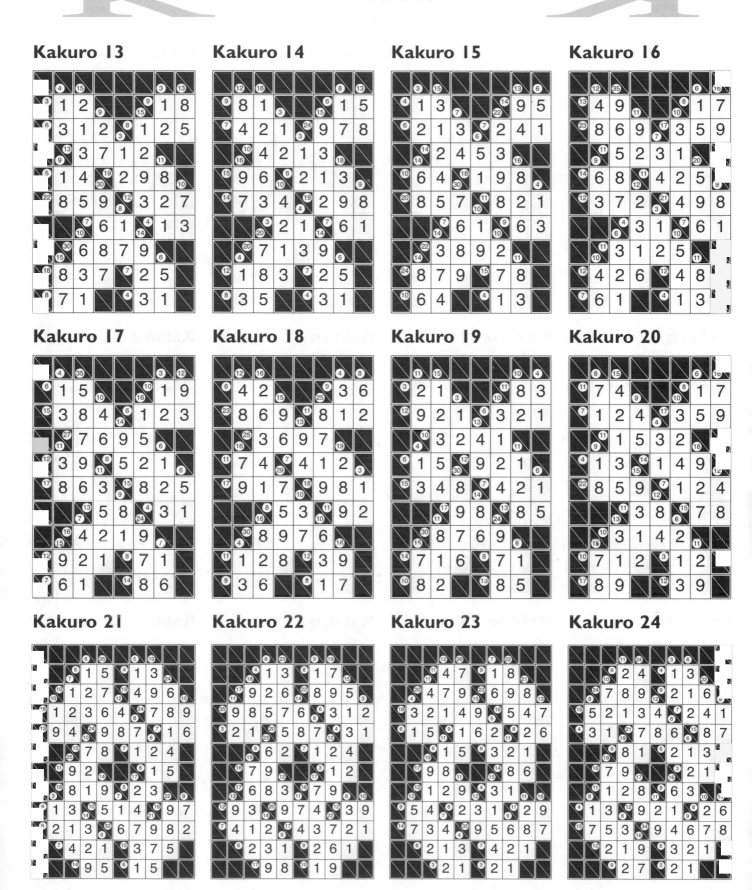

Kakuro 13

Kakuro 14

Kakuro 15

Kakuro 16

Kakuro 17

Kakuro 18

Kakuro 19

Kakuro 20

Kakuro 21

Kakuro 22

Kakuro 23

Kakuro 24

Answers

Kakuro 25
Kakuro 26
Kakuro 27
Kakuro 28
Kakuro 29
Kakuro 30
Kakuro 31
Kakuro 32
Kakuro 33
Kakuro 34
Kakuro 35
Kakuro 36

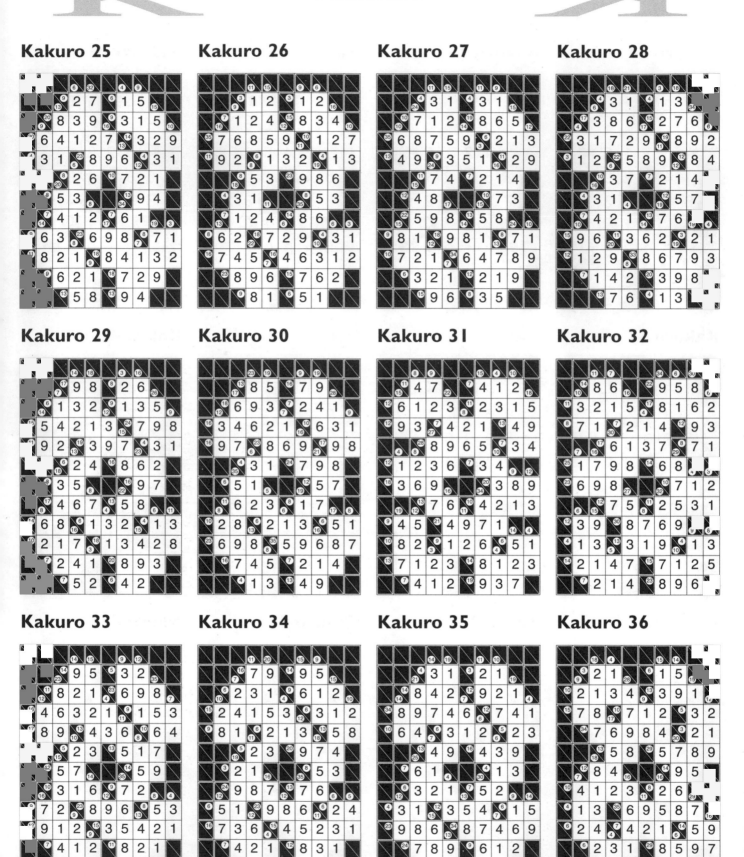

Answers

Kakuro 37

Kakuro 38

Kakuro 39

Kakuro 40

Kakuro 41

Kakuro 42

Kakuro 43

Kakuro 44

Kakuro 45

Kakuro 46

Kakuro 47

Kakuro 48

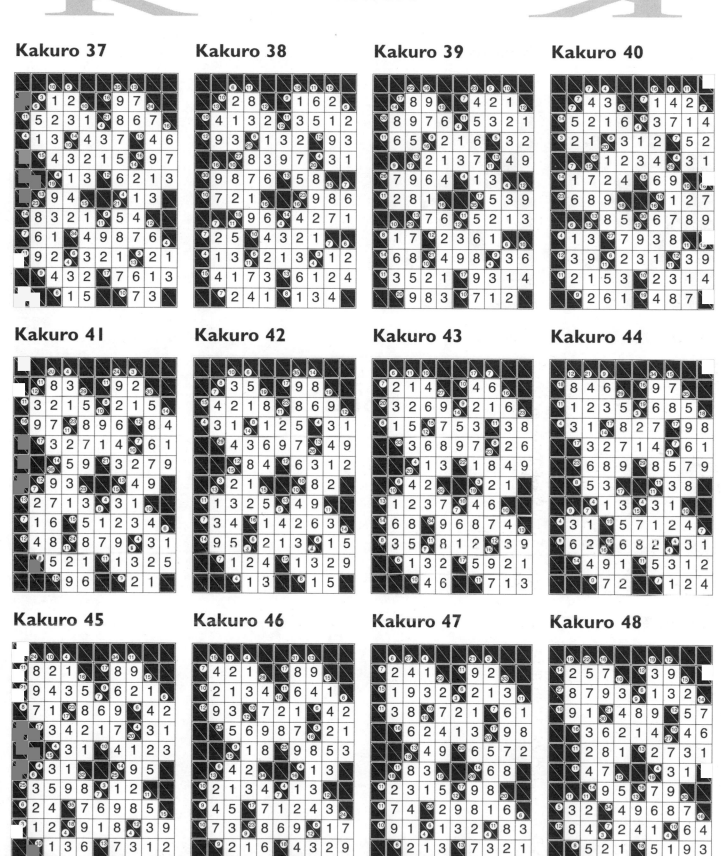

Answers

Kakuro 49

Kakuro 50

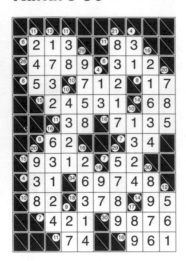

Notes